The Political Economy of the Gulf Sovereign Wealth Funds

Using four Gulf sovereign wealth funds as case studies – Iran, Kuwait, Saudi Arabia and the UAE – this book examines and analyses the history, governance and structure, and investment strategies of the above mentioned funds, in the context of ongoing debates about their transparency.

The book discusses how most Gulf sovereign wealth funds were established under colonial rule, and have operated in the global financial system for many decades. With the increase of oil revenues, it goes on to look at how the funds have broadened their asset classes and their institutional development. Debate over the transparency of sovereign wealth funds has highlighted various global practices. Recently, organizational measures have been introduced for calculating possible risks from the non-commercial investment incentives of funds, whose politically driven investment strategies are viewed as potentially a major threat to the national security of their host countries.

Highlighting a number of incidents that triggered the transparency debate, the book scrutinises the reaction of some of the Gulf sovereign wealth funds to these recent regulatory codes and strategies. It is a useful contribution to development, political economy and Middle East studies.

Sara Bazoobandi is visiting fellow at the Middle East Institute of the National University of Singapore.

Routledge Studies in Middle Eastern Economies

This series provides up to date overviews and analyses of the region's economies. The approaches taken are not confined to a particular approach and include analysis of growth and future development, individual country studies, oil, multinational enterprises, government policy, financial markets and the region's role in the world economy.

The Political Economy of the Gulf Sovereign Wealth Funds

A case study of Iran, Kuwait, Saudi Arabia and the United Arab Emirates

Sara Bazoobandi

Routledge
Taylor & Francis Group

LONDON AND NEW YORK

First published 2013 by Routledge

2 Park Square, Milton Park, Abingdon, Oxon OX14 4RN
711 Third Avenue, New York, NY 10017, USA

Routledge is an imprint of the Taylor & Francis Group, an informa business

First issued in paperback 2017

British Library Cataloguing in Publication Data
A catalogue record for this book is available from the British Library

Library of Congress Cataloging in Publication Data
Bazoobandi, Sara.
Political economy of the Gulf sovereign wealth funds: a case study of Iran,
Kuwait, Saudi Arabia and the UAE / Sara Bazoobandi.
    p. cm. – (Routledge studies in Middle Eastern economies)
  Includes bibliographical references and index.
  1. Sovereign wealth funds–Persian Gulf Region. 2. Monetary policy–
Persian Gulf Region. 3. Persian Gulf Region–Economic policy. I. Title.
HJ3841.P35B39 2012
332.67′2520953–dc23   2012019906

ISBN: 978-0-415-52222-9 (hbk)
ISBN: 978-1-138-10866-0 (pbk)

Typeset in Times New Roman
by HWA Text and Data Management, London

Contents

Figures

Tables

Foreword

The global economic order is currently undergoing a massive transformation. This is usually conveyed in terms of the rapid growth of the Chinese economy, over a thirty-year period, and the shift of industrial production from Europe and America to China. To the extent that wider dimensions are considered, they usually figure as side issues, dwarfed by the huge impact of China's manufacturing pre-eminence and the financial implications that this carries.

Yet the phenomenon is much wider and deeper than anything related to China alone, or anything deriving from China's experience and development. The transformation is also fuelled by, and represented in, the rapid industrial and services development of many other Asian economies. The rapid growth of the Indian economy has been particularly important in this respect, due to the size of the Indian population and the consequent impact that the country's rapid economic growth can have on the rest of the world. Other Asian countries with large populations, such as Bangladesh and Indonesia, are also growing rapidly and establishing strong industrial infrastructures. The Asian country with the fastest rate of economic growth predicted for 2012 is not China but Mongolia. Outside Asia, the rapid development of a number of Latin American countries, with Brazil carrying the greatest economic weight and impact, also plays a part in the economic transformation. The massive potential of the African continent, furthermore, now figures in projections of ongoing global economic transformation. The economic tribulations currently faced by Europe and America stand in stark contrast to these developments, although they may well impinge on the more optimistic future projections of the latter.

This is the global context in which the rapid rise in prominence of sovereign wealth funds (SWFs), most of which are controlled by institutions outside the established (largely Western and Organisation of Economic Co-operation and Development) centres of financial expertise and activity, such significance. They constitute a key part of the wider transformation. While some SWFs are based in East and Southeast Asia, the fastest growing in the middle-to-end of the last decade were those based in oil-producing countries, reflecting the revenue impact of higher oil prices. The well-endowed SWFs of the Gulf were central to this phenomenon.

Sara Bazoobandi's work on the SWFs of the Gulf, therefore, covers a critical element in the global economic transformation that is currently taking place.

The Gulf is itself part of Asia, and therefore in some respects Gulf developments forms part of the 'West to Asia' shift. The financial strength of the Gulf SWFs adds a further dimension to the variety of ways in which Asian countries are gaining a new and far-reaching influence in the global economy. In other respects, however, the Gulf is itself reflective of the changing economic balance between the West and East/Southeast/South Asia. Starting from a position where almost all of their assets were invested in the Western world, the Gulf SWFs have in recent years been redirecting some of their attention to other Asian countries. This complements what is happening in the trading relationships of the states concerned, with other Asian countries rapidly assuming leading positions as trading partners of Gulf states. Although Western countries still constitute the major target to which Gulf SWF investment is directed, there is nonetheless a developing trend to seek opportunities elsewhere. The most profitable and secure investments are no longer necessarily in the Western world.

Sara Bazoobandi documents carefully the development of this particular element of global economic transformation: the character of the institutions involved, and the manner in which their operating procedures differ from those of Western financial institutions. She also addresses the question of whether the Gulf SWFs pose a threat to Western economies and polities, by virtue of their huge resources and the apparent opaque and secretive nature of their procedures. It is the latter dimension that has created considerable adverse publicity for the SWFs in the Western world. Rather suddenly, in 2007, they came to be regarded as problematic. With the sharp rise in oil prices that had occurred over the previous five years, the realization spread that Gulf SWFs were now able to exert significant influence on international financial markets.

Up to 2005, even the name 'sovereign wealth fund' had not even been invented, although most of the institutions had been there for some time – benefiting from a relatively low profile. Early in 2007, however, journalistic and specialist writing took up concerns as to whether these institutions would be able to buy up large parts of the Western economic infrastructure and what the political as well as the economic results of this might be. The financial crisis of 2008 made clear the paradox inherent in much of the Western commentary on this subject. On the one hand falls in stock market share prices created a substantially expanded opportunity for the SWFs to buy into and perhaps buy out some of the largest Western companies and corporations. Cause for alarm certainly seemed to exist. On the other hand, the Western economies now needed – much more than ever – the investment and financial support that the SWFs were able to provide.

Western attitudes towards the SWFs of the Gulf have been marked by paradox in other ways as well. On the one hand, there is the insistence that the SWFs should be more transparent and be organizationally autonomous of the governing regimes in the Gulf. The institutional processes by which decisions are made, the rationale of their investment strategies, and a reasonable amount of information about the areas of economic activity where investment has been undertaken, should all be accessible. Furthermore, decisions must be shown to be taken on the basis of economic considerations alone, rather than swayed by political considerations (although this does not always apply to similar decision making in the Western world). No doubt there is a need for greater transparency, and Sara Bazoobandi shows that some progress has been made in these directions.

On the other hand, however, Western commentators have not always recognized that the lack of transparency of Gulf SWFs has sometimes proved beneficial to them in the past, and that greater transparency may not be to the advantage of the Western economies. Up to the present, the Gulf SWFs have operated in a realm where local populations have had no significant role in influencing decision making. It is clear from comment in Gulf newspapers that there are concerns felt by some Gulf citizens about the investment patterns of Gulf SWFs. Questions are raised as to why more money can not be invested in the home countries of the SWFs and whether is it right to invest so much in countries whose governments have in the past frozen the investments and funds of Arab countries whose policies and actions have run counter to their interests. The likelihood, then, is that greater transparency may increase the pressure on SWFs to adapt their investment strategies further – diverting some of the investment that has previously gone to the Western world to investments in the home country and to non-Western countries.

There are, therefore, many complexities and difficulties surrounding SWFs, and Sara Bazoobandi's book comes at a timely moment to guide us through the issues concerned. It does not seek to provide solutions to the problems but shows where the problems lie and how significant they may or may not be. Her lucid explanation is just what is needed. Enough time has now passed since the SWFs shot to prominence for a serious assessment to be made of the positive and negative aspects of their role in the global economy.

Tim Niblock
Institute of Arab and Islamic Studies
University of Exeter

Preface

The opportunity to write this book presented me with an exciting challenge. The topic of sovereign wealth funds was in the headlines and the growth of the assets of the funds was an intensifying topic of debate when I started this project at the Institute of Arab and Islamic Studies of Exeter University. At the time, there was not much of scholarly work on the topic and finding information about some of these organizations was a key challenge. My understanding of sovereign wealth funds developed as the international debate was gradually working its way through some of unknown aspects of the activities of these institutions.

The topic fascinated me in the sense that coming from an oil rich country, I grew up with a public debate around the issue of managing the oil wealth. After I visited two of the Arab Gulf countries for the first time, UAE in 2001and Saudi Arabia in 2002, I could not help but comparing Iranian economy with our neighbouring oil rich states of the Gulf. Soon I found myself puzzled with the question, 'What is the best way for hydrocarbon rich countries to manage the income generated from natural resources?' I started the journey of seeking answer to this question in 2008, in a beautiful town in the south-east of England. But soon it took me to many exciting places around the world where I met some of the most amazing people of my life, who then became the greatest friends of mine. I thank all of these friends, most of whom remained unnamed, for their time, friendship and support.

I also extend my gratitude to Professor Tim Niblock, who guided the research on which the initial draft of this book was based; my mother, Dr. Soudabeh Chegini, who without her presence I would have been a different person and, without her support, this research would have never been possible; and my stepfather, Dr. Mohammad Reza Jamali, who has been the greatest support for our family and never left my mother alone since I flew to London nearly one decade ago. This book also owes much to its editor, Joe Whiting at Routledge, and the great copy-editing team there.

A number of individuals should be thanked by name: I am particularly beholden to my beloved friend Dr. Christian Luber for his patience and generous support with the initial draft of this book. I am also much indebted to my friend Rafiq Ajani for his time and kind support; Sharifa Hashem for being my encouraging friend and sister; Abdulaziz Al-Sager and his groundbreaking Gulf Research Centre who accommodated me during my field research.

Notes on transliteration

This book uses the form of transliteration specified by The Library of Congress in ALA-LC Romanization Table for the Persian Language but without diactriticals. The transliteration table can be found online at http://www.loc.gov/catdir/cpso/ romanization/persian.pdf. The transliteration system has not been applied to proper names: the generally accepted spelling used in global media is also used throughout the book.

1 Introduction and definition of sovereign wealth funds

Introduction

The term sovereign wealth fund (SWF), referring to a state-owned investment fund composed of financial assets including properties, stocks and bonds, was coined in 2005 by Andrew Rozanov, a financial analyst from the City of London. SWFs have recently raised attention in the global financial system, as they have highlighted the increasing financial power of governments in comparison with private financial institutions within the international economic structure.

This controversy was further triggered by the size of the assets under management (AUM) of these funds. In May of 2007, Morgan Stanley published a report on the estimated size of SWFs and predicted that the AUM of the funds would grow from the estimated 2007 figure of US$2.5 trillion to double that size before 2010, and reach around $12 trillion by 2015 (Jen, 2007).

The Morgan Stanley forecast was proven to be less plausible in the aftermath of the global financial crisis of 2008. Like many other investment institutions, the portfolio of investments of the SWFs was affected by the financial crisis. Most of these funds recorded significant losses in the value of their assets. Deutsche Bank predicted that by 2019 total assets under SWF's management are likely to amount to US$7 trillion, which was more than twice the volume of those assets in 2010 (Kern, 2010). A study by International Financial Services London (IFSL) in 2010 reported that the SWFs were about 2.5 times bigger than hedge funds and their assets stood about US$1.2 trillion above the AUM of private equity funds (see Figure 1.1). Despite the impact of the global financial crisis, the SWFs are expected to gain more power in international financial markets, and their portfolio of assets is predicted to grow more in the decades to come.

Definition

The SWFs are not the only type of government-owned investment institution. There has been a debate amongst financial analysts, as well as academics, on the definition of the SWFs. Here some of the definitions provided by various sources will be reviewed.

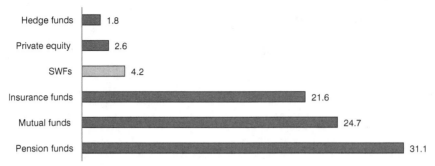

Figure 1.1 Total AUM of global investment funds ($ trillion)
Source: TheCityUK, (2011)

In 2005, Andrew Rozanov defined the SWF funds as:

> ...by-products of national budget surpluses, accumulated over years due to favourable macroeconomic, trade and fiscal positions, coupled with long term budget planning and spending restraint. Usually these funds are set up with one or more of the following objectives: insulate the budget and economy from excess volatility in revenues, help monetary authorities sterilise unwanted liquidity, build up savings for future generations, or use the money for economic and social development.

In 2008, the International Working Group of SWFs, established by the International Monetary Fund (IMF) in cooperation with the fund's managers to review the operation of the funds and propose a voluntary code for best practice of the SWFs, defined the SWFs to be the

> ... special purpose investment funds or arrangements that are owned by the general government. Created by the general government for macroeconomic purposes, SWFs hold, manage, or administer assets to achieve financial objectives, and employ a set of investment strategies that include investing in foreign financial assets. SWFs have diverse legal, institutional, and governance structures. They are a heterogeneous group, comprising fiscal stabilization funds, savings funds, reserve investment corporations, development funds, and pension reserve funds without explicit pension liabilities.

The Sovereign Wealth Fund Institute, a research institute monitoring the SWFs, defines these funds as:

> ... (state-owned investment funds) or entity that is commonly established from balance of payments surpluses, official foreign currency operations, the proceeds of privatizations, fiscal surpluses, and/or receipts resulting from commodity exports. The definition of sovereign wealth funds exclude, among other things, foreign currency reserve assets held by monetary authorities for

the traditional balance of payments or monetary policy purposes, state-owned enterprises (SOEs) in the traditional sense, government-employee pension funds, or assets managed for the benefit of individuals. Some funds also invest indirectly in domestic state-owned enterprises. In addition, they tend to prefer returns over liquidity, thus they have a higher risk tolerance than traditional foreign exchange reserves.

(http://www.swfinstitute.org/fund/what-is-a-swf/)

This study defines the SWFs as institutional investors, which have some (or in some cases all) of the characteristics that are listed below:

1   Owned and financed by their respective governments.
2   Often, but not always, managed by separate organizations than the central banks.
3   Financed from the government surplus revenue (after planned government spending and/or off-budget expenditures are paid from the government commodity or non-commodity export incomes, the surplus is deposited in the SWF's account).
4   Aim to protect the national economy from income volatility.
5   Sterilize the national monetary system from surplus liquidity to control inflationary effects of surplus liquidity.
6   Accumulate assets for future generations.
7   Diversify the government incomes from oil sector.
8   Use the surplus incomes to transfer new technologies and expertise to support economic and social development.
9   Often, but not always, holding highly diversified portfolio of investments in income generating assets spread across the world.

As noted above, the source of assets of the SWFs is the surplus revenue of their sponsoring government. The major difference between the commodity and non-commodity SWFs is the source of their assets. While the commodity-rich governments finance the SWFs from their surplus commodity export income, the non-commodity SWFs are financed from the surplus of non-commodity export income. The main focus of this study is to review the commodity-based SWFs. In order to provide a better understanding for commodity-based funds, few key characteristics of the commodity-based SWFs are reviewed below.

Commodity-based SWFs have a higher risk appetite in comparison with those that are sponsored by surplus non-commodity export income. Given the global demand for commodities, particularly hydrocarbon resources, the oil exporting countries are fairly certain that their natural reserves can generate significant revenue for the foreseeable future. The non-commodity funds rely on surplus income from the export of goods, which may not necessarily have an increasing global demand even in the short to medium term. Therefore, the continuous inflow of oil export revenue driven by global energy demand has made the oil exporting countries less concerned about the investment risks they take when investing their petrodollars.

In addition, the governance and management of most of the commodity-based funds are highly influenced by the ruling power of their sponsoring governments. Finally, the commodity-based funds tend to have long investment horizons. Again, this is as a result of the reliance of their sponsoring sovereigns on commodity export income to finance the SWFs. It is widely assumed that the source of generating surplus revenue in oil-rich countries is more sustainable than in countries with high non-commodity export revenue. Therefore, increasing oil prices and high global demand for energy allows the governments of oil producing countries to apply longer investment strategies for their SWFs.

Differentiating SWFs from other types of government-owned assets

As noted above, one of the core elements of the debate over the SWFs was the definition of these funds. To draw a distinction between SWFs and other types of government assets (i.e. foreign exchange reserve funds and public pension funds), a brief review of all the three types of state-owned assets is provided below.

Foreign exchange reserves

Foreign exchange reserves are public investment funds, which are financed by the government from fiscal surpluses for economic stabilization purposes, held and managed by central banks (Mitchell et al., 2008). The main purposes of these funds are to maintain currency value, inflation and overall national financial stability at the time of possible economic uncertainties. Traditionally countries with sizeable natural resources (where a major share of the government budget is financed by commodity income) establish such funds in order to secure their national economy against the volatility of commodity markets as well as to protect the national currency against devaluation.

There are various reasons for holding foreign exchange reserves. Since the Asian financial crisis of the late 90s, in order to maintain their domestic monetary stability, most of the emerging economies have implemented a combination of policies, which include large holdings of foreign exchange reserves as well as a mixed exchange rate (Rauh, 2007). The latter has been as a result of the fixed exchange rate regime of nearly all the economies originating the major international financial crises since 1994 (Mexico in 1994, South Asia in 1997, Russia and Brazil in 1998, Argentina and Turkey in 2000). The experience of those economies has proven that without fixed exchange rates there would have not been as severe economic outcomes in the aftermath of the crisis as was the case in the presence of fixed exchange rate policies. China is a perfect example for the application of such a policy combination, by slowly allowing more financial integration and perhaps, in the coming future, more exchange rate flexibility, whilst accumulating massive foreign reserves (Jin et al., 2005). Commodity exporting economies have also had, more or less, the same pattern in place. Most of the oil-rich countries have foreign exchange saving policies in order to maintain their economic growth at the time of oil shocks. The foreign exchange reserves of those countries are primarily held in liquid assets such as short-term securities and foreign bank deposits, which can be easily transferred to their country of origin at the time of a financial crisis.

The size of these assets varies in each case. There are various ways to calculate a minimum required asset holding in the foreign exchange reserves in order to adequately insure against possible shocks (US Treasury Department, 2005). The most common view is for each country to save sufficient foreign reserves to cover three months worth of the country's import revenue (Johnson-Calari and Rietveld, 2008). The key dissimilarity between the foreign exchange reserves and SWFs does indeed come from the purpose of holding of these assets. In other words, foreign exchange reserves are not held as a nation's wealth; instead, they are sources of liquidity, which are often kept by the government outside their contry of origin to be transferred over a short period to protect the domestic economy from potential financial shocks should the government need to do so.[1] China, Japan, Taiwan and Russia hold the biggest reserves of the kind (Hua, 2007).

Public pension funds

Public pension funds are government-owned funds, which are kept to alleviate the effects of demographic disequilibrium on the balance of the social security system. Over the last fifty years, many countries in the world have experienced sliding fertility rates and growing life expectancies. In Asia alone , the number of people over 65 will be over 500 million by 2050 (Bloom et al., 2006). This is mainly as a result of Japan's low fertility rates and small share of immigration and China's one child policy during the past twenty years, which has remarkably reduced birth rates in the country (Mitchell et al., 2008). Public pension funds, therefore, are state-owned investment institutions, which are created specifically to control the negative impacts of such demographic disequilibrium.

These funds are traditionally created either through an explicit fund being allocated by the government into a separate state-owned account, or as a result of excess contributions from the people of a particular age group in the government saving scheme during a demographic transition (Mitchell and Hsin, 1994). In contrast with foreign exchange reserves, pension funds are not constrained by a need for immediate liquidity. One can argue that even though the pension funds have certain liabilities, that is, to serve the interest of the pensioners, they count as national wealth. Therefore, due to their long-term liabilities, pension funds usually invest in their domestic currencies with long-term investment horizons.

Pension funds are often financed by individual pension contributions, rather than other methods of states fund collections such as taxes, privatization proceeds or surplus export revenue. Therefore, in practice current and/or future retirees are somehow considered the owners of the accumulated wealth in pension funds rather than the state. The Japanese public pension fund, with over 900 billion US\$, is the world's biggest pension fund. The California Public Employees' Retirement System and Korea's National Pension fund are other examples of public pension funds (Bloom et al., 2006).

SWFs

Another type of government-owned institutional investment is SWF. The SWFs can be held to serve different purposes including: balance of payment stabilization caused by a government's export income fluctuation (somewhat similiar to foreign exchange reserves), saving for future generations, and transfer of technology and know-how for the development and diversification of the domestic economy from commodity export income (in the case of commodity-rich countries). SWFs are usually funded from surplus government income and often held outside their country of origin. In order to protect the sovereign wealth, in most cases, SWFs are managed separately from other types of public investment funds. As SWFs do not hold specific short- to medium-term liabilities, unlike pension funds and government's foreign exchange reserves, they often invest in assets with relatively higher investment risks and have longer investment horizons than other types of government funds.

As noted, separate government bodies often manage the SWFs; however, the sovereign wealth management institutions function in cooperation with other government financial institutions in order to serve the government's monetary and financial purposes (Kern, 2008; see Figure 1.2). Table 1.1 summarizes the fundamental differences between the three types of government funds.

Commodity-based SWFs

Based on the source of assets, the SWFs fall into two categories: commodity-based and non-commodity funds. While commodity-based funds are funded by excess revenue from the export of natural resources, non-commodity SWFs are usually funded by governments' surplus income from the export of non-commodities. Both types of SWFs are established to serve similar monetary purposes as discussed above: fiscal stabilization, intergeneration saving and balance of payment sterilization. The different source of funding of commodity-based and non-commodity SWFs creates a number of other dissimilarities between the two groups:

- The commodity-based SWFs (CSWFs) are financed by hydrocarbon exports, therefore constitute net financial savings. In contrast, the non-commodity SWFs are by-products of controlled exchange rate policies and financed from excess monetary reserves.
- The growth of assets of CSWFs is directly related to the price of oil; while the increase of assets of non-commodity SWFs is directly linked with the increase of local currency debt (Rozanov, 2009).
- AUM of non-commodity SWFs do not represent net national savings. CSWFs, on the other hand, do represent net government savings.
- Non-commodity SWFs invest a significant share of their portfolios in commodities while the CSWFs do not, although the CSWFs of the Gulf countries have shown interest in investment in commodities other than oil and gas and included agribusiness investments in their portfolio.

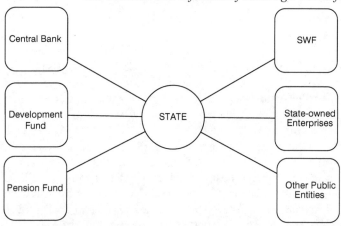

Figure 1.2 State-operated financial institutions
Source: Steffen Kern (2008)

Table 1.1 Summary of government funds

Fund	Wealth/Liquidity	Investment philosophy
Foreign Exchange Reserves	Liquidity	Safety / fast transfer when needed / accessibility
Pension Funds	Wealth	Safety / serve the interest of pensioners / long-term investment
SWFs	Wealth	High risk-adjusted return / serve the interest of the sovereign (strategic investment) / inter-generation saving investment / long-term investment horizon

CSWFs are often recognized as a crucial element in the governments' defence mechanisms against the risk of unpredicted commodity price decline. In theory, the governments of commodity-rich countries have the following options in order to self-insure their economies against volatile prices: diversification of export structure and accumulation of financial assets. Diversification of export structure can be achieved through the development of non-commodity producing sectors of the economy. This requires human capital, investment and technology. The experience of the oil-rich Arab states of the Gulf shows that accumulation of assets has evidently become the favoured solution by most of the oil exporting governments.

Another purpose of CSWFs is intergeneration saving. These institutions are primarily the government's effort to save the prosperity of natural resources for future generations. Since reducing the production and keeping the crude resources in the ground might not be a useful method of saving the wealth for the next generation, simply because they might lose their value over the time, creation of the CSWF as a mediator to transform the natural assets to other types of assets for future generations is a method for preserving the nation's wealth for future generations.

The sponsoring governments often use the CSWFs as a defence tool, which serves more than one purpose. For example a CSWF can be used to protect the domestic economy against the oil price fluctuation for the current generation, and preserve the nation's wealth for future generations. Today, there are ten CSWFs around the globe with stabilization as their central policy; the rest have the combined objectives of savings and stabilization (Das, A., 2008). (See also Table 1.1.) Stabilization SWFs are very similar to traditional foreign exchange reserves due to their similar liabilities: therefore it is not a coincidence that they are often managed by central banks (such as the Saudi Arabia CSWF).

The investment pattern and saving requirement of CSWFs has never been the subject of public disclosure. However, due to a lack of a specified balance sheet liability they are, by and large, known to apply longer investment horizons in comparison with other government investment institutions. Regardless of the source of their funding, most of the SWFs hold a long-term, globally diversified portfolio of assets with a high risk appetite in exchange for higher expected returns. The governance and structure and the relationship between the funds and other government bodies are also not quite clear in most cases. However, due to high control of the governments in these organizations, they are most likely to inherit their main characteristics from the governments of their countries of origin.

Collective significance

The debate over SWFs has been intense. There have been two views in the debate on the role of SWFs in the global economy. One view is that they are cash rich investment vehicles that are able to bring their capital surplus into the global financial system and help stabilize the international economy: they contributed to the bailing out of the Wall Street banks in the beginning of the financial crisis of 2008. The opposing view underlines their role in endangering the balance in the global economy. Traditionally, the Western-developed economies have provided the major share of the financial resources of the global economy. This trend has started to change over the last few decades. The capital scarce economies of the developing countries have become major liquidity providers of the global economy in the light of their increasing trade surplus revenue. Therefore while some view these funds as one of the anticipated outcomes of financial globalization in which more developing economies are merged to the global financial system, there has been a growing concern over the destabilising role of the SWFs in the world economic order (Beck and Fidora, 2008).

The debate over the SWFs originated from the significant size of the AUM of these funds. Although some institutions, such as the Kuwait Investment Authority, have been operating actively in international financial markets for more than five decades, they have recently attracted attention amongst the business leaders and scholars. As noted above, they have recorded a massive growth recently and some have shown a higher risk appetite in their investment regime than they used

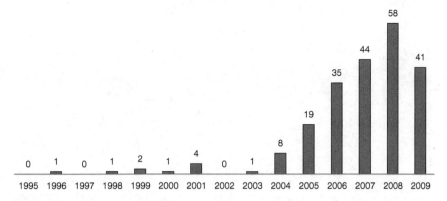

Figure 1.3 Annual investments by SWFs ($ billions)
Source: Stefen Kern (2010)

to. In addition, since 2005, some of these funds have invested in assets which have often been seen as strategic moves of their sposoring governments by the host sovereign. Such growth and investment strategies have put them in a rather controversial position as their financial power is increasing dramatically.

As a result of the growth of their assets, SWFs have become extremely active institutional investors over less than one decade. Western financial institutions, which previously provided services to the SWFs as clients for a number of decades, have noticed that the relative asset size of these funds to financial firms in the West have increased dramatically since 2003. As Figure 1.3 shows, the total annual volume of completed investment transactions by SWFs increased from US$8 billion in 2004, to US$58 billion in 2008. In other words, the SWFs have been particularly active in accumulating various types of assets across the world since 2004. Such an active asset accumulation track record has highlighted the significant role of the SWFs in the global economy.

Another aspect of significance in the analysis of the SWFs (in addition to the growth of the AUM of the SWFs globally) is the concentration of wealth in a handful of these funds. In 2010, there were about fifty SWFs operating in the world (according to the list provided by SWF Institute at the time at which this study was conducted). Only five of these funds, as shown in Table 1.2, hold more than US$1.3 trillion, which is about one third of the total SWF assets globally. Inevitably, the concentration of wealth in a small number of SWFs has highlighted the significant financial power of the sponsoring governments of the respective funds.

Hydrocarbon producing countries own a significant share of the assets held by SWFs. TheCityUK, a financial research institution, estimated the total assets of SWFs in 2011 to stand around US$4.2trillion. In 2010, over a half of the oil exporters' foreign investment assets were held by governments and wealthy individuals (TheCityUK, 2011). One can therefore argue that such a concentration of assets would potentially make these funds capable of influencing the global financial system. It is worth noting that, except for Iran's SWF, all case studies in this book are chosen from the five largest SWFs of the world.

Table 1.2 Five largest commodity SWFs of the world

Country	Fund name	Year of inception	Sources	Objectives	Assets (US$ billion)
UAE	Abu Dhabi Investment Authority	1976	Oil revenue	Saving	627
Norway	Government Pension Fund-Global	1990	Oil revenue	Saving and stabilization	593
Saudi Arabia	Saudi Arabian Monetary Agency	1952	Oil revenue	Saving and stabilization	533
Kuwait	General Reserve Fund/Future Generation Fund	1953/1976	Oil revenue	Saving and stabilization	296
Russia*	National Welfare Fund	2008	Oil revenue	Saving and stabilization	150

* This includes the oil stabilization fund of Russia.

Source: Sovereign Wealth Fund Institute (2011).

The governments of the Arab Gulf states own the three largest commodity SWFs of the world. Given that the rise of crude oil prices will boost the size of the assets owned by these countries, the total assets held in the CSWFs of the Gulf Cooperation Council (GCC) member states is likely to stand significantly above those of their non-commodity counterparts in other regions. If one takes the size of the population in the GCC states into account, the concentration of SWFs assets in the Gulf region would have a further implication. Most of the GCC countries, except Saudi Arabia, have a rather small population. The total population of each country is barely more than a couple of million; therefore the growth of the Gulf funds will increase the concentration of capital amongst a significantly small percentage of the world's population.

Another factor, which makes the study of Gulf SWFs rather significant, is the political system of the sponsoring governments of those funds. The political system of all the Arab states of the Gulf has been formed through the traditional tribal structures of their societies and there have been very little signs of reform, democratization and transparency. Now if one adds a key element of the activities of SWFs of the Gulf into the picture, which is to invest the sovereign wealth in the Western developed economies, one may well see a great challenge imposed by these institutions on the global financial system, particularly in respect to Gulf–West investment relations. As the assets held by these funds have increased over the last decade, the flow of investment by these institutions to the Western world has also increased. Given the long-standing transparency issue of the sponsoring government of these funds, there has been a huge debate amongst the Western policy makers over the potential strategic threats imposed by these funds to their host countries in the West, empirical evidence of which will be provided later in this book. Therefore the growing size and active investment regime of the investment institutions sponsored by the GCC states has further emphasised the significance of these organizations in the global financial world.

As the world economic condition has drastically changed over the last decade, the emerging markets have introduced new investment opportunities to the SWFs. These opportunities have become profitable alternatives to those in the Western economies. Due to the expected high investment returns in emerging economies, the investment operations of the Gulf's SWFs in those markets have significantly expanded over the past decade. Therefore, a new cycle for the flow of capital has been created in which the developing economies with natural resources are providing the capital for investments in the developing economies with emerging markets. In this cycle, the Western economies, which have historically provided the capital for investment in the developing world, have been evidently excluded. Therefore the role of SWFs in shifting the global financial cycles has highlighted the significance of these institutions for the future of the international economy.

In order to add to the scholarly debate over SWFs, this book is specifically focusing on the sovereign wealth management policies of the Gulf region (including three GCC member states and Iran). The available literature on the topic tends to generalize the various types of SWFs as a large group of institutional investors, regardless of factors such as the source of their funding, the geographic location of their sponsoring countries and the maturity of the organization. For that reason one of the major motives of this research is to narrow down the scope of studying the SWFs to this particular geographic region. The Gulf countries have been the most strategically important part of the world for the supply of global energy and some of the countries of the region have recently became key players in the global financial system. Therefore, understanding the role of these organizations within the political system, history, structure and governance of the Gulf SWFs is going to be of high value.

Studying the SWFs: history, investment and governance

This study focuses on the SWFs of the four oil-rich states of the Gulf: Kuwait, Saudi Arabia, United Arab Emirates (UAE) and Iran. Moreover, in order to provide a perfect model for transparency of SWFs, the Government Pension Fund – Global of Norway, which is the largest and the most transparent CSWF in the world outside the Gulf region, will be reviewed in this book. The study approaches the topic through an orderly comparison of the key aspects of these funds including: the history of establishment, asset size, investment strategy, governance and structure. In addition, one of the key issues regarding the SWFs reviewed in this book is the issue of transparency. The various events that led for the call for transparency of SWFs by the Western economies, the different measures that are taken by various Western governments in order to monitor the activities of the SWFs in their economies, and the reaction of the SWFs to the transparency debate are the core aspects of this issue that are examined in this book.

The study examines the results of the application of two different models for management of surplus oil income by the governments based on the economic development theories for natural resource rich countries. One theory argues that in order to achieve a higher economic development, the oil-rich states should keep their surplus commodity income outside their domestic economy and transfer their wealth to various income generating types of assets. The rationale for this theory is to maintain the security of the sovereign's wealth by keeping the wealth outside the national economy as well as to generate a stream of income for the future generations who may not be able to have access to oil windfall.

The second theory offers a model in which a significant share of the surplus commodity export revenue is invested in the domestic economy to support the country's non-oil production units in various sectors. In other words, the government supports the national non-oil industry, both in the public and the private sector, to enable it to develop and eventually compete globally. In this model, the government aims to protect the domestic economy from volatile oil markets by diversifying the country's income from oil exports and ultimately to generate a stream of income for the future generation who may not have access to oil royalties.

While some countries of the Gulf such as Kuwait and the UAE applied the first model in the management of their sovereign wealth, others such as Iran and, to a lesser extent, Saudi Arabia have chosen the second model. Various economic, social and political factors have contributed in formation of the sovereign wealth management policies of the Gulf countries, namely: size of population, the development of the domestic non-oil sector, the size of the domestic economy and the political relations with the developed economies. For example, being under heavy political and financial sanctions, Iran has been a unique case for practicing management of the national oil revenue. Therefore, Iran was brought in as a case study in this project in order to provide a different example for SWF management in the region and to highlight the importance of the above-mentioned factors in shaping the SWF management policies.

Information gathering

The information was collected through documentary search of published data sets, review of existing literature, a field trip to the UAE, fieldwork in the City of London and Oxford, and phone and email interviews with bankers and scholars in the USA. The focus of the field trip in the UAE was data collection from the following local authorities and the private sector financial investment institutions: Abu Dhabi Investment Authority (ADIA), Mubadala Investment Company, Invest AD, National Bank of Abu Dhabi, Abu Dhabi Investment Council, Istithmar World, Carlyle Group, EFG-Hermes and Barclays. In addition, columnists from leading local newspapers, *The National* and *Gulf News*, in Dubai and Abu Dhabi and analysts from the Gulf Research Centre were interviewed.

The fieldwork in London was conducted to collect data from the following banks: Bank of America Merrill Lynch, State Street, Morgan Stanley, Nomura and Barclays Capital, as well as research centres including: Eurasia Group and RGE Monitor. A meeting was held with Dr. Yusef Al-Awadi, the former head of Kuwait Investment Office in London to collect information on Kuwait SWF. This is mainly as a result of the difficuly in getting a visa to Kuwait as an Iranian national. The fieldwork in Oxford included attending a number of meetings and interviews with experts of the field from Oxford Analytica and Oxford University.

A series of phone, email and in-person interviews were also conducted to collect information from various experts on the topic from a number of organizations in the USA including: the IMF, George Washington University, Georgetown University and Peterson Institute for International Economics.

About twenty-five one-to-one interviews were conducted. This does not include informal conversations with experts and individuals who worked on various aspects of SWFs. Most of the contacts were made to arrange the interviews in advance and the interview questions were compiled before the meetings. The questions were centred on three main themes: the investment strategy of the GCC SWFs, the issue of transparency and the size of assets held by these funds. Nevertheless, the extent to which each of these three themes was covered varied based on the background of the interviewees and their level of openness in speaking about the organizations.

The interviewees were from five groups: SWF's current and former portfolio managers, SWF's communications departments, bank portfolio managers, scholars, consultancies and multinational organizations. The interviews generally lasted a minimum of one hour and were mostly conducted at the offices of the interviewees or in coffee shops, with the obvious exception of those conducted over the phone or via email.

The interviewing experience led to some interesting observations. Firstly, persistent follow-ups were crucial in setting up interviews; follow-up phone calls were essential when dealing with the local organizations in the UAE. Secondly, arranging the meetings in advance, and sending the interview questions and consent forms by email helped in establishing trust and accelerated the process of making an appointment for interviews. Thirdly, for an Iranian national researcher, travelling around the GCC countries was quite a challenging task.

Almost all the individuals from the financial sector tended to be overly secretive in answering questions about the topic. The portfolio managers who were employed by the SWFs were more cautious than those who were employed by banks in making comments about these organizations. Both groups, however, were reluctant to give consent to be referred to by their name in the project's written output. In contrast, academic researchers and private consultants were willing to openly comment on the topic and to be mentioned by name.

Finally, due to the difficulties of collecting information on the government institutions in Iran, the field research for Chapter 6 was carried out remotely. Five phone interviews with private sector business owners in Iran and two interviews with Iranian journalists in the City of London were conducted. In order to safeguard the privacy of the interviewees the information about the individuals has been kept confidential. Other sources of information for Chapter 6 were Iranian government-owned news agencies, as well as some Western news agencies including British Broadcasting Corporation (BBC) Persian service, *The Guardian*, *The Financial Times* and *Reuters*. The studies by the Majlis Research Centre (MRC) have also been an important source of information for the chapter. MRC is a research institution that plays a supporting role for the Iranian parliament (Islamic Consultative Assembly or Majlis). The centre has a leading role in the decision making and legislative procedures of the parliament. All the reports and studies of the MRC are available through the official website of the centre. The language in which the interviews were conducted and the literature used to gather the information for this chapter (including press releases by the Iranian news agencies, and the MRC reports and studies) was Farsi.

The MRC was established in 1993 in order to assist the parliament and representatives to ratify the drafts and bills. For about two decades the MRC have been actively conducting research on various topics and it has published more than 10,000 research papers and other publications. According to the Functions Act of MRC, the purpose of establishing this centre is to provide continuous expertise and research services to the parliament. The MRC governing elements include: the board of trustees including the (Majlis) speaker, the chairman and members of the board of parliament committees, the head of the MRC, and the research council. The research council consists of a head, five individual specialists and academic figures from parliament representatives that are elected by the board of trustees as well as five researchers with higher education (at least associate professor) that are elected on the recommendation of the head and who receive the approval of the board of trustees (http://www.majlis.ir/mhtml/index. php?newlang=english).

The structure of the book: chapters and themes

Following this introduction, the remainder of the book consists of eight chapters. Chapter 2 aims to highlight the important characteristics of the Gulf CSWFs. It discusses the main goals of the commodity-based funds of the Gulf. The chapter also evaluates the impact of the recent global financial crisis on the investment strategy of the Gulf CSWFs.

Chapters 3–6 trace the institutional development and structure of the Gulf SWFs by examining three main aspects: history of establishment, governance structure and management, and investment strategy. Although there has been an information vacuum available in some of these aspects, the objective of these chapters is to bring out the dynamics shaping events, highlighting the interconnection between different factors, and the role of key individuals in the formation of the events as well as the structure of the organizations. The following elements are discussed throughout these chapters:

1   History of establishment: this element provides a chronological review of formation of sovereign wealth management policies and the respective organizations in each country. Each chapter provides an analysis of how the early years of operation of these institutions has formed the current strategy and structure of the organization.
2   Governance structure and management: the objective of this element is to provide an understanding of the role of the political elite on governance of the sovereign wealth investment institutions in each country. In this respect the examples of failed management experience and financial scandals related to each of the organizations are also reviewed.
3   Investment strategy: each of the CSWFs that are reviewed in this book has applied an investment strategy of their own. In some cases the strategies have changed and/or developed over the time. Such changes/developments are studied in this book.

Chapter 3 reviews the oldest CSWF of the Gulf: the Kuwait Investment Authority. The British government played an important role in the formation of the Kuwait Investment Board and the transition of power from the board to the Kuwait Investment Office, which for some years was the country's SWF. The British government has also played a significant role in the application of an investment strategy in the early years of the operation of the Kuwait SWF. This chapter elaborates those historical links between the two countries and the way in which they formed the structure of the Kuwaiti sovereign wealth investment institution. This chapter also elaborates the governance, structure and investment strategy of the Kuwait Investment Authority, which is currently the sole sovereign wealth management organization in the country. In this context, the political crises of Kuwait in the aftermath of the Iraqi invasion are reviewed to demonstrate a unique case for the role of SWFs in the stabilization of their country of origin.

Chapter 4 examines the history, structure and investment strategy of the Saudi Arabian Monetary Agency. Although the Saudi Arabian Monetary Agency is the central bank of Saudi Arabia, historically, it has also been in charge of the management of the country's sovereign wealth. The political and economic links between Saudi Arabia and the USA, which date back to the early years of establishment of the country, have had a significant impact on the formation of the overall structure and strategy of the Saudi Arabian Monetary Agency's management of the country's sovereign wealth. The emergence of the Saudi Arabian Monetary Agency's assets has been influenced by various regional events. The size of the Saudi population and the nature of the economic environment in Saudi Arabia have had a significant impact on the institutional development and investment strategy of the Saudi Arabian Monetary Agency's foreign assets and this is examined in this chapter.

Chapter 5 covers the various sovereign wealth investment institutions of Abu Dhabi and Dubai. The chapter reviews the three elements of these investment institutions as discussed above (history, governance, and investment strategy). In this chapter, a greater emphasis is put on reviewing the commodity-based SWFs of Abu Dhabi due to the significant size of their assets and the important role of Abu Dhabi in the federal system of the UAE. Dubai state-owned institutional investors are reviewed in order to provide a full picture of the Emirati economy. Given that foreign borrowing has formed a major share of funding in Dubai government investment institutions, the global financial crisis of 2008 has made a different impact on these organizations from those sponsored by the government of Abu Dhabi that are solely financed by surplus oil income.

Chapter 6 reviews Iran's sovereign wealth management experience. The chapter reviews various aspects of the Iran Foreign Exchange Saving Account (IFESA). The Iranian experience of managing the country's sovereign wealth differs significantly from that of the Arab countries in the Gulf region. The issue of sovereign wealth management has been a matter of controversy amongst the Iranian political elite since 2005. Since then, the government has been heavily criticized for its oil revenue management policies. This chapter examines the shift in the government sovereign wealth management policies since the establishment of the IFESA.

Chapter 7 explores the Norwegian SWF. The aim of this chapter is to compare the experience of the Gulf SWFs with that of Norway. Norway has had the most transparent commodity-based fund in the world. Studying the Norwegian experience can provide a road map for a so-called 'perfect model' for the institutional development of its counterparts in the Gulf region. This chapter's objective is, therefore, to highlight the areas in which the experience of the Gulf SWFs lags behind the successful experience of the Government Pension Fund – Global of Norway.

Chapter 8 focuses on the debate over the transparency of SWFs. This chapter aims to elaborate further on the lack of transparency of the Gulf commodity-based funds. The formation of International Working Group of Sovereign Wealth Funds and creation of the voluntary code of conduct for the practice of SWFs (the Santiago Principles) show how some of the challenges faced by the SWFs can be tackled. This chapter reviews the response of the Gulf funds to the debate over transparency in the context of the Santiago Principles.

Chapter 9 concludes the study. The chapter aims to answer the question, 'Do the SWFs of the Gulf operate transparently enough to satisfy the expectations of the Western host sovereign nations?' If not, 'What are the reasons?' Moreover, the chapter looks at how the global financial crisis has changed the transparency debate, and evaluates the success of the international initiatives discussed in Chapter 8 in regulating the investments of the SWFs.

Note

1 Personal communication with Andrew Rozanov, London, 9 January 2010.

2 The Gulf's commodity-based sovereign wealth funds

Introduction

The governments of the Gulf have established various investment organizations to manage their sovereign wealth. Some of these organizations were established as early as the 1950s to serve the interest of their sponsoring sovereign nations through the following:

1 To provide an opportunity to raise the rate of return on the government's foreign exchange investments.
2 To insulate the government budget and the domestic economy against volatile commodity prices.
3 To convert finite natural resources into a diversified portfolio of assets for future generations (Cohen, 2009).

An important shared characteristic of these funds is lack of transparency of information amongst almost all the Gulf CSWFs. The Gulf CSWFs are ranked as some of the most secretive state-owned investment institutions of the world (Truman, 2008a). Various research organizations have created indices to measure the level of transparency of these funds. The latest index published by the Sovereign Wealth Fund Institute in March 2012 ranks the transparency index (maximum 10 and minimum 1) of the Gulf CSWFs: Iran (1), Saudi Arabian Monetary Agency (4), Abu Dhabi Investment Authority (5) and Kuwait Investment Authority (6) (SWF Institute, 2012).

Size and growth of the assets of the Gulf CSWFs

As the most hydrocarbon-rich region in the world, the Gulf countries managed to accumulate a significant amount of capital from oil export revenues. The sponsoring governments of these funds have been reluctant to reveal information on the size of assets held in their sovereign wealth accounts. All available data on the size of these funds is based on speculative work. During the field research, a number of interviews were conducted with some of the globally known analysts in the field who have done estimates and calculations on the size of assets held by these funds. The findings of those interviews show that the speculative works use similar calculation methods based on the price of oil.

Morgan Stanley conducted one of the early studies in estimating SWF assets in May 2007, when the company published its report 'How Big Could SWFs be by 2015?' The report estimated SWFs held about US$2.5 trillion in their account (Jen, 2007). The study did not divide the assets of commodity-based funds and the other SWFs. However, if one assumes that roughly 50 per cent of the total AUM of global SWFs is managed by the CSWFs, given that the assets held by Russian and Norwegian CSWFs were included in Morgan Stanley estimated figure, between 30 and 40 per cent of the world SWFs assets (between US$75 billion and US$1 trillion) were controlled by the Gulf CSWFs in 2007.

In early 2009, a study by Deutsche Bank demonstrated that SWFs' total assets were as high as US$3 trillion (including the commodity-based funds and the others). Based on that estimate, the AUM of the SWFs stood US$1.5 trillion above the total assets managed by hedge funds worldwide and accounted for about 3 per cent of the total assets of the global banking sector (Kern, 2009). CSWFs controlled 46 per cent of the total SWFs' assets, which is about US$1.65 trillion (Kern, 2008).

Two quarters after the Deutsche Bank report in 2008, McKinsey reported that the petrodollar accounted for US$5 trillion in foreign financial assets. McKinsey's estimate included the six GCC states, as well as other oil producers in the Middle East and North Africa, Norway, Russia, Venezuela and Indonesia. The report was not limited to the SWFs: the assets held by central banks have also been included in the study (Roxburgh et al., 2009). Given the high oil production of the Gulf countries, if one assumes 40 per cent of the total petrodollars calculated by McKinsey were owned by the CSWFs of the Gulf region, the AUM of these funds would be about US$2 trillion.

In the same year (2008), Jean Francois Seznec of Georgetown University, and a former banker, came up with a different number for the total AUM of the Gulf funds. Seznec suggested that the evaporation of the wealth in the GCC countries (the government budget expenditure in the public sector, ruling family allowances and defence expenditure) is as high as 71 per cent of the total revenue in some GCC countries such as the UAE and Saudi Arabia (Seznec, 2008). Consequently, he argued the total assets held by the CSWFs sponsored by those countries are considerably less than previous estimates. As noted above most of the estimates of the size of the AUM of these funds are based on the price of oil and the crude productions over a specific period of time, in most cases with an additional 20–25 per cent of investment returns on existing assets from the previous period. Therefore, the volatility of the global oil price and the financial markets has led to various results in the calculation of the size of assets owned by these funds. In some cases, the gap between different estimates is huge, particularly between 2007 and 2008, when the oil prices reached a historic record high.

Some analysts have counted various channels for evaporation of wealth between its production point, when the wet crude is sold, and its savings point, when the cash is deposited into the SWF account. Various calculation methods have estimated different numbers for the total AUM of these funds, but have reached the same conclusion: the wealth has increased, so have the oil prices. The price of crude oil rose from US$23 per barrel in 2002 to over US$145 per barrel in July 2008. This has had a knock-on effect on the accumulation of wealth by the oil producing countries.

By 2009, five out of the eight largest SWFs of the world were commodity funds holding around 43 per cent of the total SWFs' assets, three of which are owned by Gulf countries. According to an estimate by Deutsche Bank in 2009, the sovereign wealth assets of Saudi Arabia, Abu Dhabi and Kuwait were nearly US$ 1.2 trillion (Kern, 2009). A study conducted by the TheCityUK, a research organization in London, estimated in April 2011 that Middle Eastern SWFs owned 36 per cent of the total assets held by SWFs, equivalent to US$1,504bn (The CityUK, 2011). Table 2.1 summarises estimated assets held by largest SWFs of the world between 2002 and 2012.

The impact of the financial crisis on the GCC funds

The AUM of the Gulf region CSWFs have grown significantly between 2005 and 2008. This was a result of two factors: record prices of oil and investment earnings. Both factors of growth of the Gulf CSWFs were negatively affected during the global financial crisis 2008. Fluctuations of oil prices have had a sharp and direct impact on the size of the assets of these funds. An estimate by Brad Setser and Rachel Ziemba in 2009 suggests that if the price of oil was US$50 a barrel on average, the Arab Gulf countries would need to spend the total investment returns of their SWFs as well as their surplus oil export income to maintain the 2008 import level. However, at US$75 a barrel they would have been able to add roughly US$140 billion to the foreign assets of their central banks and SWFs. Therefore, the GCC economies would need to transfer a substantial amount of their foreign reserves at any price below US$75 per barrel (Setser and Ziemba, 2009). The price of oil never dropped below US$50 a barrel, which would have led to the first scenario; however, the portfolio of the GCC funds was estimated to have shrunk. Such a decline in the assets of these funds was as a result of the drop in oil prices and the loss made on the value of the investments held by these funds.

The second factor of growth of assets of these funds is the portfolio investment returns. The Arab Gulf SWFs, like other institutional investors, struggled with issues such as revenue erosion and decline of portfolio book values as a result of the crisis. Various sources reported that the funds have emerged strongly from the crisis, despite the significant losses, which they made during 2008. Steffen Kern of Deutsche Bank, for example, reported that the large SWFs (including commodity and non-commodity funds) had grown from US$3 trillion in early 2009 to US$3.7 trillion by the end of the same year (Kern, 2010).

Another impact of the crisis on the Gulf SWFs was the need to provide financial support in their country of origin. Supporting the domestic economy at the time of potential financial difficulties has been one of the mandates of most of the Gulf region CSWFs. The economic hardship of 2008 prompted the

Table 2.1 Estimated assets held by largest SWFs of the world 2002–2012 (US$ billions).

	2002	2003	2004	2005	2006	2007	2008	2009	2010	2011	2012f
ADIA	140	188	232	276	380	456	340	430	477	479	540
KIA	73	98	123	152	215	262	228	275	312	333	382
SAMA non-reserve + pensions	22	38	66	129	200	335	475	444	485	578	690
GPFG	87	126	168	206	285	371	323	454	520	551	650
Kazakhstan Stabilization Fund	2	4	5	8	15	20	27	24	31	44	56
LIA		0	0	20	30	40	55	50	65	55	50
Chile Stabilization		0	0	0	2	14	20	11	13	17	21
GIC	98	128	156	173	225	245	166	215	244	243	276
Temasek			30	35	50	75	55	85	97	108	130
KIC						20	25	30	36	50	50
CIC							75	100	135	140	200
Russian Sovereign Funds	44	73	121	176	295	157	225	152	114	112	120

Source: Ziemba, Rachel. 'Updated Estimates of Sovereign Wealth Under Management.' Unpublished report by Roubini Global Economics, March 2012.

Gulf SWFs to provide capital to bail out the domestic financial institutions. The exact amount of capital, which was transferred by the sponsoring governments from these funds to the domestic economies, is not clear. There have been news releases, which occasionally covered some of the transactions. For example, in October 2008, the government of Kuwait gave the approval to the KIA to increase investments in the Kuwaiti stock market to shore up the declining local bourse (Laessing, 2009). In the same month, the KIA was speculated to have transferred US$15 billion from its investments abroad to inject liquidity in the local markets (Reuters, 2008d).

The transfer of foreign assets to the local economies was not only a supporting mechanism for the local businesses, but also a response to the public anxiety about the management of the national assets by the government. The severe global financial meltdown has created a public debate in the region about the impact of the global financial crisis on the investment portfolio of these funds. Such debate led to some public pressure by the media on the governments to change the investment strategy of the funds. The situation in Kuwait was perhaps the most intense amongst the neighbouring countries. As a result, Bader al-Saad, the chairman of the KIA, appeared on al-Arabiya TV channel to explain that the KIA was not in the business of bailing out falling Western banks; instead the disasters in the US economy and some European countries created enormous investment opportunities for the KIA and the authority at some point would be investing again in those institutions (Khalaf, 2008).

All in all, there are various estimates for the total losses made by the Gulf SWFs. The findings of this study, based on various interviews with London-based bankers and consultants, show a total loss between 25 and 30 per cent by the funds as a result of the crisis. The underlying factor leading to a high loss is a combination of the following three factors: oil price decline, investment losses and the withdrawal of funds to support the economies in their countries of origin.

Investment strategy of the Gulf SWFs

Similar to the size of the assets held by the Gulf SWFs, the asset allocation strategy of these funds has also remained unclear due to the lack of information. Given the heavy consolidation of SWFs' assets in Western markets (see Figure 2.1) made the funds particularly venerable to the latest global financial crisis, the investment strategy of these funds have gone through some changes after 2008. A comparison between various aspects of the investment strategy of the Gulf SWFs before and after the crisis is reviewed below.

Despite the visible impact of the global financial crisis on the Gulf CSWFs, some of the investment characteristics of these funds have remained unchanged. The main unchanged attribute of these fund is their investment horizons. As noted, the SWFs do not have particular short-term liabilities. As a result of this the GCC commodity-based funds have a much longer investment horizon than most of the public and private institutional investors. In other words, the Gulf SWFs can afford to be patient investors in the volatile markets, simply

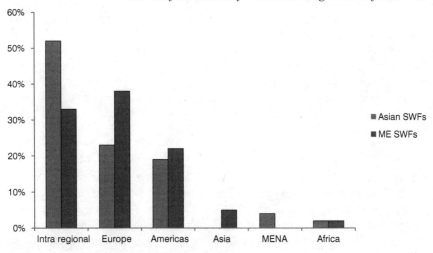

Figure 2.1 Geographic investment targets of SWFs
Source: Kern 2010

because they do not have clearly defined liabilities, as opposed to other types of investment institutions such as hedge funds and pension funds. There has been a debate on the positive or negative effects of the investment horizon of these funds on the markets. On the one hand, the long investment horizon of these funds can minimize the risk of destabilizing the markets created by a potential rapid shift in their investments. On the other hand, the absence of balance sheet liabilities gives these funds the freedom to be able to afford to turn their backs on the markets when they are most needed. In the context of the 2008 financial crisis, the Gulf SWFs have remained long-term investors and this trend is not likely to change in the near future.

Another aspect of the investment patterns of these funds that has remained unchanged after the crisis is their potential for having politically driven investments goals. There has been an intense debate over the non-commercial investment incentives of the SWFs. The debate was formed based on the lack transparency of the operation of these funds. The core of the argument originated from US policy makers who strongly argued for the USA's right for demanding higher transparency by foreign investors, including those of the Gulf SWFs. Such a demand was introduced as a defence mechanism to protect the US domestic economy against the potential threat of the non-commercial investment strategy of these funds. However, as far as the investment strategy of the GCC funds is concerned, none of the Gulf sovereign investors has been proven to have non-commercial investment motives before or after the financial crisis.

As noted above, the market power and the potential signalling impact of these funds are undoubtedly huge; nonetheless, there has not been any solid evidence found to support the Western transparency argument. A London-based investment banker explained the role of these funds as: '…certainly strong enough to influence the global balance of economic and, to some extent, political power should they decide to – providing they maintain ownership in strategic sectors. However, they have not done anything yet which gives a signal for such intention.'[1]

Most of the analysts who have been interviewed during the field research for this project strongly believe that the costs of any non-commercial leverage would be enormous for the sponsoring governments of these funds; therefore, they are unlikely to take advantage of their strategic influence in their host economies before or after the financial crisis.

The Gulf SWFs' investments in high-profile assets

One of the key attributes of the GCC sovereign wealth investment strategy before the crisis was the increase of their interest in prestigious and iconic acquisitions. The Chrysler Building and Ferrari deals by Abu Dhabi SWFs are good examples of the kind. The interviewees of this study had expressed different views on the reasons for the high interest of these funds in high profile investments prior to the crisis. One argument is that even though most of the Gulf sovereign investment institutes have been actively operating in the global financial system for many decades, with the significant growth of their assets, a key strategy for them was to advertise their brand name and bring their financial power to the attention of the Western world by such investments.

Another point of view argues that the main motive for the rising number of acquisitions of iconic assets by these funds prior to the financial crisis was a significant lack of understanding of the markets and financial expertise. The following quote from one of the interviewees in the City of London is an example of such an interpretation of the Arab Gulf SWF's investment strategy in regards to these investments:

> Before the crisis they [the Gulf SWFs] were suffering from a huge lack of expertise and appropriate professional investment strategy. Even the older funds and the most sophisticated ones, made many mistakes in taking unnecessary risks and irrational investment decisions. That is why they have made enormous losses.[2]

In addition to promoting their national reputation, funds have also acted as facilitators for transferring expertise to their sponsoring countries. The investments of Gulf SWFs in the banking sector coinciding with the booming financial sector in the region is a good example of the facilitating role of these funds in the transfer of expertise to particular sectors of their domestic economies. Another example of such a strategy is Abu Dhabi SWF investment in General Electric, which includes arrangements for General Electric renewable energy technology to be transferred to Masdar City, a project by one of Abu Dhabi's SWFs, the Mubadala Development Company (Bansal, 2008). Another iconic investment by the Gulf funds is a US$2.7 billion transaction to Daimler, which was completed in March, 2009. This investment gave Aabar Investments, an affiliated investment company of Mubadala, a 9.1 per cent stake in Daimler and involves a joint venture for electric automobiles and a training centre in Abu Dhabi for its engineers (Lowe, 2009).

All in all, a combination of various factors has led the Gulf SWFs to engage in some iconic investments, which have not been merely for profit making. The interest of these funds in investing in high profile assets has reportedly declined since the crisis. Such a decline has been partially as a result of the losses, which the funds made in some of their investments across the sectors.

Growth of the GCC funds in emerging markets post-crisis

For many decades the Gulf governments have been investing their surplus petrodollars in various asset classes in the developed economies, particularly in the USA. Between early 2007 and the peak of the financial crisis in the third quarter of 2008, investments in the collapsing financial institutions of the US and Europe became a recurring pattern for investments of the Gulf SWFs. The investment flows of these funds during this period were evidently biased towards American financial institutions to support Wall Street's collapsing banks. As a result of the lower economic growth in Western markets, however, those investments have started to decline since 2008. Consequently, between 2008 and 2010, the Gulf SWFs had shown more interest in investments in intra-regional and European investments than those in the USA (see Table 2.2). The eurozone crisis of 2011 is, however, expected to change this pattern.

In contrast to the decline in investment in the Western markets, higher expected returns have become a key incentive for the Gulf governments to invest in emerging markets. A banker from the City of London who was interviewed for this study commented in this issue: 'Today, when an investment bank approaches the Arab SWFs to offer them financial products in Europe or the US, they are not shy to refuse to buy them; instead, they express huge interest in the Asian markets.'[3]

Table 2.2 Estimated 2008 gains and losses of selected SWFs ($ bn)

	Value (est.) Dec. 2007	Value (est.) Dec. 2008	Capital gains/ losses	New inflows	Gains/ losses(share of Dec 2007 portfolio)
ADIA	453	328	−183	59	−40%
KIA	262	228	−94	57	−36%
SAMA+ assets under management of other government institutions	358	501	−46	162	−12%
Norwegian Government Pension Fund-Global	371	325	−111	64	−30%

Source: Brad Setser and Rachel Ziemba (2008).

This shift of investment interest from the Western markets to the emerging economies is not limited to Asia. According to a financial product provider from a well-established London-based bank:

> ...most of the emerging markets which are growing faster than the US or EU economies are now popular in the Gulf. Latin America is becoming increasingly attractive to the Arab investors. For example: Brazil has become an investment destination for Abu Dhabi after the senior managers of Abu Dhabi Investment Authority paid a visit to the country.[4]

In addition to the lower investment return of the Western markets, the Gulf governments have become under pressure from the West to clarify their investment motives. This pressure has also had a negative impact on the investments of the Gulf funds in those markets. In May 2010, the governor of the UAE central bank, Sultan Bin Nasser Al Suwaidi, warned the Western governments of a future response to the pressure that they have put on the Gulf government-owned investment institutions to clarify their commercial investment goals:

> Another reason that makes me think that SWFs from our region might change the flow of their direct investments is that once we see the proposed regulations re sovereign wealth funds in the industrialized advanced economies start being implemented, more questions will be asked and more forms will become necessary to fill and more disclosure and transparency will be demanded. This behaviour will signal that there is no strong need for foreign capital in the West, and that the political mood has changed. Therefore, we might see gradual tightening of the scrutiny on capital flows from SWF countries at one stage, especially funds that are destined for direct investment in certain companies. Faced with all this nonsense, SWFs will certainly come to the conclusion that it is time to change strategy. This could make SWFs avoid direct investment in certain companies, or even avoid direct investment in all companies, and become more of passive investment vehicles in the West. As SWFs have large sums to invest, this might make them a direct part of their investments to existing or newly created companies in the region. This situation, if it happens soon, will lead to creating a new regional development cycle.
>
> (Arabian Business, 2010b)

The Gulf SWFs' investment risk appetite

Due to market uncertainties since the 2008 crisis, the Gulf SWFs have become more cautious in their investments across the sectors in order to avoid engaging in loss making activities. The findings of this study show that they have put various protection measures in place against risky investments. An example of such measures is to share the risk of their investments with another investment institution. A banker from London who was interviewed for this project pointed out that there has been a rising interest amongst the Gulf SWFs for co-investment with other investment institutions as a cautious measure to avoid future losses. He explained:

> Now their [GCC CSWFs] bottom line for entering in any new deal is alignment of interest in the form of co-investment. After the crisis they have had a different strategy in dealing with the banks and the external asset management companies who approach them to offer various financial products than what they did before.[5]

The Gulf SWFs (with the exception of SAMA) have had a fairly diversified portfolio of assets, which include a wide range of higher-risk/higher-return financial instruments, such as corporate bonds and equities.[6] As noted above, SAMA has been an exception to such a strategy and remained faithful to investments in US Treasury bonds. While other Gulf SWFs invest over 50 per cent of their assets in equities and alternative investments, SAMA holds 80 per cent of its portfolio in US Treasury bonds (Setser and Ziemba, 2009). Due to such a conservative investment strategy SAMA has neither generated as much investment return as the other GCC funds over the previous decade, nor it has lost as much on the value of its assets after the financial crisis of 2008 as did the other Gulf funds (see Table 2.2).

The Gulf SWFs' passive investments

The Gulf SWFs often hold passive or indirect investments in the Western companies in which they hold major stakes. Most of these funds heavily rely on using external asset management companies rather than managing their assets directly. Moreover, in most cases their investments are held below the voting right threshold. Therefore, they tend to be silent investors who do not take part in the management of the companies in which they invest. This is mainly due to the following reasons:

- To prove their investment goals are purely commercial and that they are not strategically seeking to intervene in the management of the Western companies.
- To avoid management responsibility in the companies in which they invest: having seats on corporate boards would bring them additional responsibility in the management affairs of the respective businesses.
- To avoid public announcement of their acquisitions by keeping their share below a certain threshold.

Since the financial crisis of 2008, there has been some pressure by the recipient companies on the GCC sovereign investors to take part in the management of the companies in which they are stakeholders. The rationale here is that given the SWFs are fairly powerful investors, whether or not the funds' investments pass the voting right threshold, in practice they will always be able to influence key decisions of those companies unofficially. Therefore, the recipient companies argue that it would be in the best interests of other shareholders, as well as the company, if the funds practice their voting rights and take responsibility for their decisions. Such practice will help keep all the company operations/activities on record and ensure they are handled in a more transparent manner.[7]

Gulf SWFs' investment interest in the financial sector

In the aftermath of the financial crisis, the Gulf SWFs invested heavily in American banks. Abu Dhabi's acquisition of 4.9 per cent of Citigroup' shares, Kuwait's 5.7 per cent purchase of shares in Merrill Lynch, and Qatar's substantial 8.9 per cent shares in Barclays and 20.4 per cent acquisition of the London Stock Exchange are the best examples of this kind. The main driving factors for such investments were the following:

- Availability of funds: the Gulf funds had sufficient funding, which provided them with substantial buying power.
- Attractiveness of the financial sector: until 2008, the financial sector had been an attractive investment target, with high expected share price growth and dividend payments. This encouraged Gulf investors to engage in such investments hoping for the same growth shortly after the crisis.
- Low share prices: the financial turmoil has caused a share price decline in most banks and other financial resources since mid-2007. At the peak of the crisis, the market value of most major banks has fallen to between 60 and 20 per cent.
- Strategic opportunities: the GCC investors saw holding shares of well-reputed financial institutions offering strategic benefits over time, providing the basis for closer business links with their domestic banking and industrial sectors.
- Reputational benefits: the engagement in the American and European financial sectors has had a perceivable reputation gain for the Gulf SWFs. They have experienced a more welcoming reception in the USA and Europe as their investment was seen to rescue the collapsing banks. Their investment was no longer a threat to the national security of the Western countries, instead they were seen as playing a supporting role, which was appreciated by Western policy makers and the wider public (Kern, 2008).

A number of factors including the huge losses made in the Western financial institutions and the change of priorities of the GCC funds towards their domestic economies contributed in decline the of interest in the Western financial sector (see Figure 2.2).

De-dollarization of the Gulf SWFs' portfolio of investments

The GCC SWFs have started a gradual diversification from the US dollar. For the past few decades, the Gulf surplus oil income has been mainly invested in dollars.

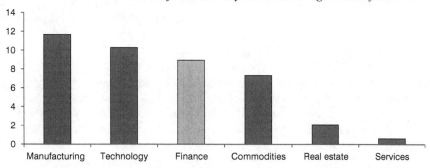

Figure 2.2 Share of completed investment transactions by SWF in 2009 ($ million)
Source: Kern 2010

Arab investors have started to diversify their portfolio of investment towards other currencies, particularly since 2008. The financial crisis of 2008 has raised uncertainties about the future of the US dollar which highlighted the importance of substituting the dollar with other currencies for the GCC sovereign wealth investors. Saudi Arabia, however, has been an exception, holding the main share of the country's SWF assets in US dollars. A study by the IMF in 2008 estimated the investments of the SWFs to be so closely linked with the dollar to the extent to which a shift in the currency of investments of these funds could cause a dollar depreciation of between 6 and 10 per cent in the short run and 2 to 4 per cent over the long term (Barkley, 2009).

In addition to the financial crisis and its impact on the diversification strategy of Arab SWFs from investments in the dollar, there is another view on the shift of Gulf shying away from the dollar, which is based on the political relationship between the Arab Gulf governments and the American administration. Such a shift is arguably one of the outcomes of American foreign policy in the Middle East, particularly after September 2001. The findings of the field research interviews of this study, however, suggest that even though the political climate in America has turned against the Arab nations since 2001, the American credit crunch has been the main trigger for such a shift of currency in investments by the funds. Therefore, while one cannot ignore the role of US foreign and domestic policy towards the Gulf countries in forming the investment strategy of the region's SWFs, the de-dollarization strategy of these funds has been evidently a risk diversification mechanism by the sponsoring sovereigns to protect the value of their assets after the financial crisis.

The decreasing value of the dollar in the money markets was a key reason for the GCC decline of interest in holding their financial resources in dollars. As a result of that, a new debate has emerged over the introduction of a possible multiple currency system to replace the weakening US dollar. So far, capital producing countries have shown strong support for stabilizing the dollar partly in order to maintain the value of their own currencies. This support, however, is anticipated to decline (Luciani, 2010). China and Russia have already proposed an alternative international reserve currency as a replacement for the dollar with a currency basket in the form of the Special Drawing Rights of the IMF. The Russian proposal calls for gold to be a part of this currency basket.

All in all, a combination of factors has affected the world's perception of the dollar. The Gulf SWFs have shown an interest in investments in currencies other than US dollars, more than any other time since they were established. The global economy, however, faces serious challenges in finding a substitute for the dollar, therefore finding a quick solution to de-dollarization of the Gulf sovereign wealth portfolio of investments remains a challenge and drastic changes are unlikely to take place in the foreseeable future (Woertz, 2010).

The Gulf SWFs: changing the game in the world economy

The substantial growth of assets and the integration of the Gulf SWFs into the global financial system have made these investment institutions extremely important players in the world economy. One view on these funds has been a rather positive one in which the funds are capable of bringing their capital surpluses into the global financial system and to further stabilize the global economy. This view has become stronger particularly after 2008 when the funds' contribution in buying distressed Western financial assets was seen as their attempt to support stabilization of the global financial system. The opposing view, however, emphasizes the role of these funds in endangering the world economic balance. Given the pace of sizable wealth accumulation by the Gulf SWFs, these funds play a significant role in shifting the balance of financial power globally. Financial resources have traditionally flowed out from the developed economies in the West. Therefore, a change in the direction of capital outflow from the Western economies to developing countries is seen as a major shift in global financial power.

As discussed above, the growth of economic power in the Gulf region undermines the neoclassic economic theories in which the developed economies are the core of the global financial network that provide the periphery with financial resources. Between December 2001 and September 2009, global reserves almost quadrupled, from US$2.1 trillion to US$7.9 trillion. A large share of the increase is concentrated in the developing world, which accounted for more than 81 per cent of global reserve accumulation during this period, and their reserves approached US$4.9 trillion in September 2009 (Griffith-Jones and Ocampo, 2010). The Gulf economies have been a large part of the global surplus capital accumulation, mainly due to the rapid rise of commodity prices. In 2009, 87 per cent of foreign direct investment (FDI) outflow of the West Asia region had been generated by the GCC economies (UNCTAD, 2010).

In addition to the change of direction in flow of capital, there has been a further concern over the growing financial power of the Gulf SWFs, which is related to their potential non-commercial investment interests. There has been an intense debate over the potential strategic leverage of financial power by the Gulf governments for political reasons. Given the ownership of the SWFs belongs to the sponsoring sovereign nation, and with the growing size of the assets of these funds, their Western host economies have expressed their anxiety over the element of risk for the potential non-commercial motivation of these funds, which may well replace their pure wealth maximization investment strategy.

The debate over the possibility of strategic use of market power by investment institutions leading to market instability is not new. A perfect example of such strategic investments was in the early 1990s, when a number of hedge funds took strategic positions in foreign exchange instruments in coordinated speculative attacks on the British pound and other currencies participating in the European exchange rate system. The GCC funds have been under international scrutiny, despite the fact that they have never been proven to take part in investments in which they exercise their financial power for political purposes.

Another impact of the growing financial power of the GCC funds on the global economic system is the increasing role of the public sector (i.e. the sponsoring government). The shift of wealth ownership from the private to the government sector highlights the inevitable changes that the global financial system is facing. Going back to the neoclassical economic theories the fundamental element of the market economic models of the West is the strength of the private sector, which allows free competition in the market. With the rise of the SWFs, the state-owned investment institutions that are sponsored by the government of the GCC, have become strong players in the global financial markets. Therefore, an increase in the financial holdings of these funds will lead to an increase in the public sector's financial power, which is in conflict with the free market economic model.

Conclusion

The Gulf CSWFs have had various impacts on the global financial system. The major effects of the operation of these funds in the global economy are as follows:

1   Historically, the flow of capital in the global financial system has been from the developed economies with massive capital surplus to the developing economies, which suffered from capital shortage. The Gulf SWFs have changed this trend and become some of the world's largest net suppliers of financial resources.
2   In today's global financial system, the Gulf CSWFs are strong competitors to the institutional investors from developed economies. Given that the assets of these funds are owned by their sponsoring governments, their financial power in the international economy undermines the neo-liberal economic theory in which the private sector is the main economic axis of market economies. With the current oil price fuelled by the global energy consumption, this new system is likely to continue for the foreseeable future.
3   For many decades, the surplus oil income of the Gulf was invested in dollar-denominated assets. This trend has started to change. Further moves towards a new currency or perhaps a basket of currencies are expected in a relatively slow manner. Such a move towards an alternative currency for the Gulf sovereign wealth investments will have a significant negative impact on the dollar value.

4   Gulf SWFs have not been proven to hold any non-commercial investment goal, so far. In the contrary, the sponsoring governments of the funds have repeatedly expressed their intentions for responsible investments to support global financial stability. The debate over the potential destabilizing role of these funds on the national security of the recipient economies will, however, remain a matter of controversy amongst the Western policy makers. Such controversy is likely to increase the risk of protectionist economic policies in the Western countries leading to a disruption of the free flow of capital globally.

Notes

1   Author's interview with an investment banker, London, 18 December 2009.
2   Author's interview with an investment banker, London, 2 February 2009.
3   Author's interview with an investment banker, London, 27 January 2010.
4   Ibid.
5   Author's interview with an investment banker, London, 18 December 2009.
6   Interview with Andrew Rozanov, London, January 2010.
7   Interview with Andrew Rozanov, London, 10 April 2009.

3 Kuwait's sovereign wealth fund

Natural resources and all revenues therefrom are the property of the State.
It shall ensure their preservation and proper exploitation, due regard being
given to the requirements of State Security and the national economy.
(Article 21, Kuwaiti Constitution)

The national economy shall be based on social justice. It is founded on fair
cooperation between public and private activities. Its aim shall be economic
development, increase of productivity, improvement of the standard of living
and achievement of prosperity for citizens, all within the limits of law.
(Article 20, Kuwaiti Constitution)

Introduction

The KIA is the sole sovereign wealth manager for the state of Kuwait. It was
established in 1982, upon the ratification of Law No. 47 by the National Assembly.
The KIA is currently the parent organization of the Kuwait Investment Office in
London, which was initially established as the Kuwait Investment Board. The
latter was founded before the country's independence in 1953. The KIA invests in
various asset classes in international markets.

The government of Kuwait was the first in the world to establish a CSWF. One
can highlight the main purposes for the establishment of the country's SWF into:
protecting the country's oil dominant economy against the risk of potential oil
shocks, economic diversification, intergeneration saving and wealth preservation,
and maintenance of the country's economic and political stability at the time of
unpredictable events and crises.

Like other Gulf countries, Kuwait's economy is highly reliant on oil incomes.
Oil revenues form the major share of Kuwait's total export earnings and act
as the main agent for the growth in the country's economy (see Figure 3.1).
Moreover, the country's manufacturing sector is dominated by petroleum
downstream industries such as refineries and petrochemical production lines
(Economist Intelligence Unit, 2010). Such heavy reliance on the oil sector
makes the economy extremely fragile in the face of oil price fluctuations. It is
therefore not surprising that saving revenues from the single source of wealth

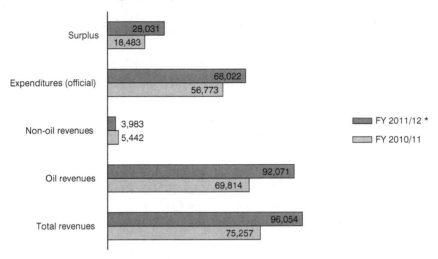

* FY 2011/12 figures are based on estimated oil price of US$105.9 per barrel

Figure 3.1 Kuwait budget forecast 2010–2012 (US$ million)

Source: National Bank of Kuwait (2012)
www.kuwait.nbk.com/InvestmentAndBrokerage/ResearchandReports/$Document/MonthlyBriefs/
en-gb/MainCopy/$UserFiles/KuwaitEconomicBriefJanuary2012.pdf

accumulation has been one of the priorities of the government of Kuwait for more than five decades.

In addition to the stabilization role of the KIA in order to keep economic balance against oil price volatility, diversification from the oil sector has also been a key part of the future economic plans of the government of Kuwait and one of the major aims for establishing a SWF. Kuwait's economy may well be a long way from diversifying from oil, but the fear of running out of oil has motivated the state to take measures for transferring oil revenues into various types of assets across the sector. Therefore, creation of a SWF has been crucial, in order to facilitate the government's investments internationally. Those investments are ultimately aimed at contributing to the country's wealth maximization as well as assisting the government in building economic capacity in other sectors, over time, both domestically and internationally.

Moreover, assets under the management of the KIA have, on some occasions, been mobilized to maintain the country's economic stability and national sovereignty. The two major occasions when the government chose to redirect some of the sovereign wealth assets to the domestic economy were to support the country's stock market after the financial crisis of Souk el Manakh in 1982, and to cover the costs of liberation operations in 1991after the Iraqi invasion, followed by reconstruction costs from the war devastation. The country's SWF spent more than US$80 billion on Kuwait's liberation and subsequent reconstruction efforts. Thus, one key role of the Kuwaiti SWF has been to invest

Table 3.1 Kuwait sovereign wealth enterprises

Name of SWE	Establishment	AUM (US$ million)	Investment focus
National Technology Enterprises Company of Kuwait	2002	311	Transfer new technology in various sectors
St. Martins Property (acquired by KIA in 1974)	1924	3,000	Real estate
Kuwait Real Estate Investment Consortium	1994	88	Real estate
Kuwait China Investment Company	2005	280	Investment in various sectors across Asia

Source: Sovereign Wealth Fund Institute (2010)

the country's oil income in order to create an alternative source of income at the time of crisis.

There are two main government funds under the management of the KIA: the General Reserve Fund (GRF) and the Future Generations Fund (FGF). The KIA may also manage any other funds entrusted to it by the minister of finance. The major share of the wealth is allocated in the GRF and FGF. No assets can be withdrawn from the funds unless sanctioned by law.

The GRF is the main treasury for the government and receives all revenues (including all oil revenues) from which all state budgetary expenditures are paid. Furthermore, the GRF holds all government possessions, including Kuwait's participation in public enterprises such as the Kuwait Fund for Arab Economic Development and Kuwait Petroleum Corporation, and the country's participation in multilateral and international organizations such as the World Bank, the IMF and the Arab Fund.

The FGF was created in 1976 through the transfer of 50 per cent of the AUM of the GRF at that time. Since then 10 per cent of all state revenues are transferred to the FGF every year and the entire fund's investment income is also reinvested. The FGF is composed of investments outside Kuwait in various asset classes. Some of the assets of the FGF account are invested by the KIA in sovereign wealth enterprises (SWE) and are directly under the KIA's control. Table 3.1 shows a summary of the main Kuwaiti SWEs.

The AUM of the authority are owned by the state of Kuwait; the KIA is only an asset manager and does not own any of its entrusted assets. The authority's mission, as stated in 2008 by the managing director of the KIA, Bader Al Sa'ad, is:

...to achieve a long term investment return on the financial reserves entrusted by the State of Kuwait to the Kuwait Investment Authority by providing an alternative to oil reserves, which would enable Kuwait's future generations to face the uncertainties ahead with greater confidence.

(Al Sa'ad, 2009)

Al-Sa'ad defined the KIA's objectives in his keynote speech at the First Luxembourg Foreign Trade Conference on 9 April 2008 as:

1   KIA aims to achieve a rate of return on its investment that, on a three-year rolling average, exceeds composite benchmark by designing and maintaining an uncorrelated asset allocation, consistent with the return and risk objectives that are mandated.
2   KIA will endeavour to be a world-class investment management organization committed to continuous improvement in the way it conducts business.
3   KIA is committed to the excellence of the private sector in Kuwait while ensuring that it does not compete with or substitute it in any field.

Law No. 47, based on which the authority was established, put a legal restriction on any form of disclosure of information about KIA operations. According to Articles 8 and 9 of this law:

> The Authority shall have the body of personnel, in which the employees are appointed in accordance with the regulations adopted by the Board of Directors, but without prejudice to the provisions of Articles 5 and 38 of Decree Law No. 15 of 1979 Concerning Civil Service. The members of the Board of Directors, the employees of the Authority or any of those participating in any form in its activities, may not disclose data or information about their work or the position of the invested assets, without a written permission from the Chairman of the Board of Directors, and this prohibition remains in force even after cessation of the relation of the person with the business of the Authority [Article 8]. Without prejudice to any heavier punishment whoever divulges any of the secrets of the work of the Authority or data or information of which he became aware, by virtue of his work at the Authority, shall be punished with imprisonment for a period not exceeding three years [Article 9].
>
> (KIA, no date c)

There was no official announcement of the total assets, which are held by the KIA until July 2007, when the authority revealed that its total holdings amounted to US$213 billion: US$174 billion in the FGF and US$39 billion in the GRF. In June 2008 Thomson Reuters reported a 14.4 per cent rise in the assets of the KIA, bringing its AUM to US$264 billion (Reuters, 2008c). Apart from the announcement made in the 2007 by the KIA, most of the estimates of the KIA's total AUM have been based on speculation and guesswork. The latest figures by the SWF Institute estimate the KIA's total AUM to be about US$296 billion (SWF Institute, 2011a).

All in all, the KIA has developed into a sophisticated investor, which holds highly diversified risks across asset classes, industries and geographic zones. The role of the KIA in the domestic economic development of Kuwait has been significant. At various times it has utilized its resources to support the national

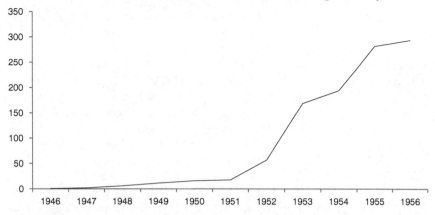

Figure 3.2 Kuwait government oil revenues ($ million) 1946–1956
Source: M.W. Khouja and P.G. Sadler (1979)

market. In this chapter the historical development of Kuwait's SWF is reviewed. Firstly, the initial phases of the creation of the fund before the independence of Kuwait and early post-independence years, between the 1950s and 1970s, then, secondly, there will be an in-depth review of the more recent structure and investment strategy of the KIA.

History of Kuwait's SWF, 1950s–1990s

The Kuwait Investment Board (KIB) was Kuwait's first attempt to establish a fund for saving oil income. The British government initially established the board in 1953. It consisted of five British bankers, chaired by the director of the Middle East Department at the Bank of England. The first oil shipment was exported from Kuwait in 1946, less than a decade prior to the establishment of the KIB. Thereafter, the emergence of Kuwait's modern economy started to become closely linked with oil income. The KIB was established in order to minimize the risks associated with the country's reliance on a single non-renewable resource, as well as to efficiently manage the country's growing sovereign wealth.

As Figure 3.2 shows, Kuwaiti oil production increased rapidly during the first decade of the country's oil export. The significant growth of income inflow between 1947, US$0.76 million, and 1953, US$169 million, was the main factor for the establishment of the KIB. Due to the heavy reliance of the Kuwaiti economy on oil export income, growth of the government oil revenues was the engine behind the expansion of the national economy. Imports expanded swiftly to reach a per capita level of over US$280 by 1952, beetween 1952 and 1960, the value of total imports more than quadrupled and reached as high as US$780 million in 1960 (Khouja and Sadler, 1979: 25–36). All in all, a systematic approach, initially started with the KIB, was needed to manage the increasing surplus oil income. A financial body was required to create and maintain a saving system for the country's revenue, and to safeguard Kuwait's economy against external factors.

The currency of early oil payments to the government was British sterling and London has historically been the heart of most operations of Kuwait's SWF. In the years immediately after the Second World War, the Kuwait Oil Company (KOC) was the sole local company controlling the extraction and export of the country's crude oil. In addition, the KOC had two foreign partners: Gulf Oil and British Petroleum (BP). Both companies paid their contributions to the government of Kuwait through an account in London. BP paid directly in sterling; Gulf Oil paid in dollars, which were then converted into sterling. The oil prices in all Kuwaiti contracts were fixed in sterling and the incomes were paid quarterly into the British Bank of the Middle East in London. These payments were the main revenue of the state budget and the funds in London were transferred to the account of the government at the local branch of the British Bank of the Middle East in Kuwait. The government normally limited its expenditure to the budgeted receipts and usually calculated to leave a small surplus, transferred annually to a reserve account, also held in London (Khouja and Sadler, 1979: 68–85).

The currency of Kuwait's oil deals was influenced by the British government, which sought to maintain the value of sterling. Moreover, Kuwait's trade relationships were strongly oriented toward Britain. In 1958, Kuwait's imports from Britain, which consisted mainly of consumer goods, were valued at £57 million. The cost of the aggregate imports to the country was equal to about half of Kuwait's oil revenue at the time (Shamma, 1959). The close political, financial and trade links between Kuwait and Britain have played a major role in shaping the direction of the flow of surplus government incomes. In order to encourage the Kuwaiti government's investment in Britain, in the 1940s, an agreement was made between the two countries, which exempted all the investments of the state of Kuwait from British taxation. Finally, as Kuwait maintained strong political links with Britain under the Protectorate Agreement, holding the sovereign reserves in sterling and the handling of the accounts in London made good sense.

By the mid-1950s, a potential shift from sterling by the oil-rich states of the Gulf had become a great concern for the British government. It was clear to the British government that if the existing governments, or possible new hostile regimes, decided to diversify the currency in which they held their national wealth, sterling would suffer severely. By 1959 it was estimated that the total assets of the Gulf oil exporters were equivalent to over a quarter of Britain's gold and foreign exchange holdings (Ford, 1959). Any movement by the state of Kuwait to reduce the country's holding in sterling, therefore, would be likely to affect confidence in sterling as an international currency. The anxiety was calmed in 1960 when Sheikh Jabir, president of the finance department of Kuwait at the time, reassured the British authorities that the government of Kuwait had no intention of changing its basic policy of investing the government's surplus income in London (Richmond, 1960).

After independence in 1961, the Kuwaiti authorities tried to become more economically independent of Britain. On the one hand they had promised the

British authorities that they would continue backing sterling, but on the other hand their aspiration and desire for more independence in managing their country's assets was evident. In 1961, a separate investment committee was established in the Kuwait Department of Finance, aiming to break the sole responsibility of the KIB for the management of Kuwait's surplus capital.

In 1962, the Kuwait Fund for Arab Economic Development (KFAED) was founded by the state of Kuwait. The KFAED would allow Kuwaiti authorities to put some of the country's surplus income into an account other than that of the British-run KIB, which would be managed independently. By doing so, the Kuwaitis were asserting their freedom to control the country's assets. At this stage Britain was prepared to accept the new developments so long as Kuwait's accounts balances held in London did not drop below its previous level (Foreign Office, 1961). The British Foreign Office supported Kuwait's proposal for adding a Kuwaiti member to the KIB; however, the chairman of the KIB at the time, H.T. Kemp, rejected this proposal. In protest against this decision, 40 per cent of the holdings by the government of Kuwait in sterling, which was held to support the value of Kuwaiti dinar (KD), was withdrawn from the assets of the KIB by the Kuwaiti authorities (Bank of England, 1961).

Finally, in 1965 the efforts of the Kuwaiti government to create an independent wealth management system succeeded. The Kuwait Investment Office (KIO) was established in London with a total of eleven Kuwaiti staff to replace the KIB, two decades after the first export of oil in 1947. The main aim of this decision was to give more management and decision-making power to the Kuwaiti authorities. Since 1947, the Kuwaiti government's surplus income had been held in London-based banks and in sterling. Therefore, the choice of location for the office was influenced by the historical links between Kuwait and London.

In 1967 there was a major devaluation of sterling, by 16 per cent, which had a big effect on Kuwait's foreign assets. This immediately motivated the government of Kuwait to reconsider the relationship with London and re-evaluate its foreign portfolio investment policy. It was clear that sterling would not remain a major reserve currency for much longer and negotiations were carried out with the British authorities to make sure that they would pay compensation on Kuwaiti investments anytime that the value of sterling fell below US$2.40 to the pound (Khouja and Sadler, 1979: 190–208).

In the 1970s, Kuwait's oil revenue, as well as the foreign assets' investment income was growing dramatically. As Table 3.2 demonstrates, investment income between 1971 and 1977 was growing by about 60 per cent per year. The significant increase in the investment income of the late 1970s highlighted the importance of the investment strategy to the Kuwaiti government. It was clear at the time that the actual receipt of investment income was bound to become a significant factor in Kuwait's economy even if receipts from oil remained unchanged. This motivated the government to expand its investment horizon across various asset classes and currencies. The most favourable destination in which to redirect the Kuwaiti sovereign wealth in the 1970s was New York. This inevitably shrank the sterling holdings in London.

Table 3.2 Growth of Kuwait's government income during the 1970s (million KD)

	1971	1972	1973	1974	1975	1976	1977
Oil receipts	527.9	548.5	1084.6	2369.3	2289.0	2615.0	2587.0
Investment income	108.7	125.5	141.4	202.6	334.0	441.0	429.9

Source: M.W. Khouja and P.G. Sadler (1979)

In the light of the fast and striking growth of Kuwait's sovereign assets in the 1970s a stronger emphasis was placed on the country's wealth preservation policy for future generations. To serve this purpose the FGF was established in August 1976. The mandate of the FGF was to merely save a percentage of the country's assets for future generations. The fund was set up to hold assets with long investment horizons to secure investment income in the future. The FGF received KD 850 million and its management was given to the KIO. The fund allocated to the FGF was 50 per cent of the assets under management of the GRF at that time. It was also to receive 10 per cent of the state oil revenue annually plus all profits earned on GRF holdings

The FGF is obliged to reinvest all of its investment profits every year. Such a choice of investment strategy has contributed to the growth of the AUM of the fund. All the assets of the FGF are kept outside the country and none of its assets can be withdrawn from the fund unless sanctioned by law. Transfer of assets to the FGF is independent of the budget or oil market. Each fiscal year, 10 per cent of the country's oil export income at any given price, as well as all the investment returns of that year, must be transferred to the FGF's account. The government investment policy for the FGF played a key role in boosting the fund's asset accumulation. By the early 1980s, Kuwait's foreign investments were generating more income for the country than the direct sale of oil.

The second oil price shock following the Iranian revolution caused dramatic growth in Kuwait's financial reserves. The total foreign reserves of the country were estimated to have quadrupled between 1979 and 1982 (Economist Intelligence Unit, 2001). With the increasing amount of oil revenue and investment return, a larger and more sophisticated management body was required. This led to the establishment of the KIA in 1982. The KIO, which had been a major player in the management of Kuwaiti sovereign assets since the establishment the country's first SWF and had enjoyed extensive prestige and autonomy because of its age and track record, was brought under the overarching responsibility and direction of the KIA.

In accordance with Law 47 of 1982 the KIA was established as an independent legal entity that operated under the umbrella of the Kuwaiti Ministry of Finance. On behalf of the state of Kuwait, the KIA was given responsibility to develop and manage full operations of the GRF and FGF. The main purpose of the establishment of the KIA was to improve the quality of investment operations and decisions. Over time, it also took over the ministry of finance's role in managing and developing the financial reserves. The KIA remained the parent organization of the KIO. It issued various guidelines for the KIO activities as an investment manager, including an instruction to ensure that employees of the KIO are rotated occasionally with Kuwait-based personnel.

The KIA has been successful in the management of Kuwaiti sovereign assets to the extent that in 1987 Kuwait's foreign investments produced US$6.3 billion, compared to US$5.4 billion from oil. In 1990, the total AUM of the Kuwait SWF was estimated at over US$100 billion, two thirds of which was believed to be held in FGF (El-Erian, 1997).

The impact of the Iraqi invasion on Kuwait's sovereign reserves

The role of Kuwait's SWF during the invasion of the country and the years following liberation was significant. Being the main Kuwaiti financial institution abroad, the KIO played a key role in managing the country's foreign assets during the invasion, including providing funds for exiled Kuwaitis, funding the foreign military operation for liberation, and most importantly funding the reconstruction projects subsequent to liberation. The rise of Kuwait's national assets before the invasion, as well as the post-invasion exhaustion of the reserves, is reviewed in the following paragraphs.

The total revenue of the government fluctuated significantly between the early 1980s and the early 1990s. The oil price declined in 1986–1987, which drastically decreased government revenues. As a result of such a decrease in the revenue, the government started to pursue rather conservative fiscal policies, which constrained budgetary expenditure in order to assist the KIA to continue the accumulation of sovereign assets. Reflecting the country's large foreign assets, investment income amounted to 86 per cent of oil export receipts in the year prior to the Iraqi invasion (1989). In the same year, Kuwait experienced a significant budget surplus of about 30 per cent of GDP that was double the annual average of the previous three years (El-Erian, 1997). The Iraqi invasion in August 1990, however, changed this trend and made a significant depleting impact on the government's revenue and the country's foreign assets.

In the aftermath of the invasion the regular budgetary activities were stopped due to the interruption of oil sales. The invasion and subsequent occupation of Kuwait caused serious destruction of physical assets and of administrative and social services, as well as the temporary exile of a large part of the population. It imposed widespread physical damage and led to large budgetary and balance of payments deficits, domestic financial market disturbance, disrupted foreign trade, and paralysis of the labour market. Over 60 per cent of the existing oil wells were set on fire. Estimates of the total damage to oil facilities were in excess of US$10 billion (Hussein, 1995: 27).

In addition to disruption of the oil export income as a result of the invasion, which had a negative impact on the country's sovereign wealth holdings, the country's assets were depleted by the cost of the liberation operation and reconstruction. Factors which have affected the Kuwaiti foreign assets in the aftermath of the invasion include:

- Sharp fall in oil output and export.
- An erosion of investment income due to the significant drawdown in foreign assets.
- Large payments associated with the Desert Shield and Desert Storm operations.
- The costs of restoring the country's infrastructure after liberation.
- Higher government payments for wages, salaries and transfers.

The economy underwent a considerable fall in investment income – from 27 per cent of GDP in 1989–1990 to less than 8 per cent of GDP in 1994–1995 – as a result of the drawdown of the sovereign foreign assets in the aftermath of the occupation. Total revenue fell by 66 per cent in 1990–1991, while expenditure rose by 126 per cent. More than 80 per cent of the total expenses during 1990–1991 were large official transfers abroad for payments to foreign governments for the Desert Shield and Desert Storm operations. Kuwait contributed US$21.6 billion to the military operations for liberation, then (by the end of 1994) signed arms purchase agreements worth US$5–6 billion (al-Ebraheem, 1996). Moreover, the country's income from oil exports was interrupted during the occupation and the year following, because of the devastation of oil production capacity as a result of 742 of the 1080 Kuwaiti oil wells being set on fire by the Iraqis (Economist Intelligence Unit, 1998). A deficit of about 120 per cent of GDP was recorded, which was financed by drawing on official foreign assets (Fennell, 1997).

All oil well fires had to be extinguished and all existing wellheads had to be either repaired or re-drilled. In 1994, the refinery capacity returned to the levels achieved prior to the occupation. By 1995, oil production capacity was above pre-invasion levels and exports reached 2 million barrels a day. The regaining of the oil export level was reflected in surpluses on the external current account and GDP growth, which allowed the authorities to start repaying a bank syndicated loan of US$5.5 billion, contracted after liberation (Economist Intelligence Unit, 1998).

The cost of the seven months of Iraqi occupation and expulsion came to US$49 billion. With reconstruction, total costs came to US$66.7 billion by the end of the fiscal year 1994–1995. A quarter of this amount represents the cost of debt forgiveness policy to support the Kuwaiti citizens. The post-liberation spending left Kuwait with just 40 per cent of its pre-invasion foreign reserves. Kuwait's foreign reserves fell from their US$100 billion pre-invasion estimated level to US$46.7 billion. In addition, US$5 billion was lost in a series of investments in Spain (al-Ebraheem, 1996). By 1997, strong performance in world equity markets was estimated to have boosted the FGF and the GRF to around US$50 billion (Fasano, 2000). There is no reliable reference to clarify whether the transactions that were made to cover the reconstruction costs were from the GRF or FGF. However, due to the considerable share of the FGF in the total SWF's assets (two thirds), the author expects that despite the general restrictions for withdrawals from the FGF, under the circumstances, transactions were made from both accounts.

Governance and structure of the KIA

The KIA is governed by a board of directors, which is chaired by the minister of finance, and other seats are allocated to the energy minister, the governor of the central bank, the undersecretary of the ministry of finance, and five members from the private sector. The members of the board are appointed for an extendable four-year period through the council of ministers by an *amiri* decree. The board of directors is responsible for the affairs of KIA and has all the powers necessary for attaining its objectives, which are mainly dealing with issues such as the formulation of the general policy of the authority and supervision of its accomplishments, preparation and follow-up of investment programmes, adoption and administration of financial and managerial policies necessary to the authority, transactions of assets and investments, and approval of the KIA's draft budget, along with the annual account reports, before submission to the relevant authorities (KIA, no date a).

The chairman of the board is officially responsible for communications between the KIA and the government. He submits the annual draft budget of the authority to the council of ministers together with a detailed report on the activities and the position of the invested assets. In addition to this, the chairman of the board is responsible for delivering frequent reports evaluating the authority's performance, in accordance with the government policies for the long-term development of Kuwait. Since the KIA was established, the chairman of the executive committee has been frequently appointed from the members of the royal family (see Table 3.3).

The board of directors forms an executive committee comprising five members. All the members of the executive committee are members of the board and at least

Table 3.3 Chairmen of KIA (1982–2008)

Name	Year
Abdullatif Yousif al-Hamad	1982
Sheikh Ali Al-Khalifa Al- Athbi Al-Sabah	1983
Jassem Mohammad Al-Khorafi	1985
Sheikh Ali Al-Khalifa Al-Athbi Al-Sabah	1990
Nasser Abdullah Al-Roudhan	1991
Sheikh Dr. Ali Salem Al-Ali Al-Sabah	1998
Sheikh Dr. Ahmed Abdulla Al-Ahmed Al-Sabah	1999
Dr. Yousif Hamad Al-Ibrahim	2000
Sheikh Dr. Mohammed Sabah Al-Salem Al-Sabah	2003
Mahmoud Abdul-Khaliq Al-Nouri	2003
Bader Meshari Al-Humaidhi	2005
Mustafa Jassim Al-Shimali	2007

Source: www.kia.gov.kw

Table 3.4 Managing Directors of KIA, 1982–2008

Name	Year
Dr. Fahad Mohammad Al-Rashed	1982
Abdulla Ahmad Al-Qabandi	1991
Ali Abdulrahman Al-Rashid Al-Bader	1993
Abdulmohsen Yousif Al-Hunif	1999
Saleh Mubarak Al-Falah	2000
Bader Mohammad Al-Sa'ad	2003

Source: www.kia.gov.kw

three of them are private sector appointees. The board then appoints a chairman for the executive committee from one of the private sector representatives. The chairman of the executive committee is also the managing director of the KIA. The managing director is responsible for the management of the day-to-day affairs at the KIA. Table 3.4 shows all the serving managing directors of the KIA since the authority was established

As of February 2012, only one of the members of the board is from the royal family, and he is also the minister of energy. The government of Kuwait has reduced the involvement of the ruling family in managing the country's SWF since the 1990s, particularly following the financial scandal of Torras after the liberalization of the Kuwait. The scandal of the 1990s (covered below) has highlighted importance of having a distinct line between the national wealth and individual assets held by the members of the ruling family to the Kuwaiti legislative system. Moreover, the scandal underlined the need for a well-defined auditing procedure in the KIA to oversee the operation of the country's sovereign wealth fund. This chapter will review in depth the financial scandal of the KIO in the 1990s.

The Torras scandal: a case study in managerial weakness

Starting in the mid-1980s, Kuwait invested almost US$5 billion in Spain. The KIO bought a high number of Spanish industrial companies over a short period of time. At their peak, Kuwait's Spanish firms, ranging from chemicals to food to real estate, had assets worth US$7 billion (Cohen, 1993). By 1992, Kuwait's empire in Spain was ruined and either heavily in debt or insolvent. The news raised an enormous level of anger amongst the Kuwaiti public. The debate over the incident consequently led into some actions to minimize the role of ruling family in the management of Kuwait's sovereign wealth assets.

The controversy of the missing money hurt the credibility of the state of Kuwait while the country was already suffering severe economic problems as a result of the Iraqi invasion of 1990, which had significantly exhausted the sovereign wealth assets. The public fury was provoked further by newspaper reports. The fraud was referred to as 'the worst exploitation and mismanagement of public funds and a betrayal of national trust' (Ibrahim, 1993).

The major share of the investments was concentrated in one conglomerate; Grupo Torras. Javier de la Rosa, a famous Catalan financier, built the KIO's Spanish empire and served as vice-chairman of Torras. De la Rosa, who entered the financial industry at a very young age, served in various positions including as the director general of Banco Garriga Nogues, which had had lost more than US$1 billion in 1985 (Pollak, 1993). Although de la Rosa left the bank before this, there were still rumours that he had some links with the fraud. After the collapse of Torras, referring to the financial fraud of Banco Garriga Nogues, de la Rosa's appointment by the KIO was criticized heavily by the public.

De la Rosa was at the heart of the KIO's operations in Spain. Using KIO money, he quickly penetrated in prime real estate and old industrial companies in various fields, such as chemicals, food processing and paper. All the companies in which the KIO had invested were then put together under the umbrella of Grupo Torras. When de la Rosa was leaving Torras, his personal wealth was reportedly significantly more than when he joined the company, including 80 per cent of a private holding company, Quail Espana, and 25 per cent stake in one of the country's first three private TV networks, Tele 5 (Marcom, 1991).

Del la Rosa worked with the KIO for about six years. His close association with the KIO began in 1984, when he handled a highly profitable deal, buying a small Catalan paper mill called Inpacsa, for the KIO. From then on, the KIO's policy in Spain changed from being a cautious and secretive investor to an aggressive empire builder. De la Rosa advised Kuwaiti authorities based on the idea that the growing Spanish economy was about to boom and the KIO managers welcomed his prediction. Shortly after the first KIO deal in Spain, Grupo Torras was formed out of a troubled Catalan company, Torras Hostench. In seven years, the KIO grew into Spain's largest industrial investor. De la Rosa told *The Independent* that he took 3 or 4 per cent commission on anything the KIO acquired (Webster, 1993). Torras was Spain's largest industrial conglomerate in 1990. It is estimated that the group's value was at least US$2 billion (KIO, 77 per cent; de la Rosa and associates, 23 per cent) (Marcom, 1991).

To avoid being identified as an investor, the KIO bought shares in Spanish companies indirectly through offshore accounts, sold them to Torras and banked the profit once the prices of the shares had increased. Torras became the eventual owner of the shares at rather high prices, which it borrowed money from various banks to pay. The strategy was planned to keep Torras at a low profit level, to pay lower taxes, while the KIO benefited from the share deals. This strategy, however, pushed Torras deeply into debt and made the company extremely vulnerable to any downturn in the market. From about 1989, investors started to lose trust in Torras.

By 1992, the KIO faced the need to inject cash in its Spanish holding companies every month, at a rate of US$ 200 million a year, with no income, as it was used only to pay the interest on bank loans and the expenses of running the companies. At the time the company owed more than US$1.8 billion to Spanish banks, US$200 million to Credit Suisse and US$200 million to Bank of America. The Grupo Torras was under suspicion. The government of Spain demanded explanations and the investigation began. The crown prince and prime minister of Kuwait, Saad Abdallah al-Sabah, announced that KPMG, an auditing firm in charge of auditing some of the funds under the management of the KIA, started to investigate the KIO's Spanish investments. Losses for 1991 were reported to be around US$513 million. After further investigation, the figures reached US$2 billion (Webster, 1993). The KIO repaid the debts, and 25,000 jobs were lost in as a result of the collapse of Torras (Ibrahim, 1993).

There were different views on the Torras scandal. As far as the Spanish government was concerned, a lack of sufficient supervision and control by the government of Kuwait before the invasion, as well as the total collapse of the state upon invasion, which led many Kuwaiti officials to believe that Kuwait might never be independent again, were the main catalysts of the failure of Kuwait's investments in Spain. It was even rumoured that about US$2 billion of the US$5 billion loss in Spain was transferred to some Kuwaiti exiled royal family members during the invasion (Murphy, 1993). A Spanish official from the finance ministry was quoted by the *New York Times* in 1993:

> The extraordinary thing in all this, is the absence of controls; a dozen Kuwaitis were managing over US$ 70 billion in London with virtually no control. In the end, the people of Kuwait were robbed. In Spain, their money was used chiefly to produce commissions and profits for a few insiders.
>
> (Cohen, 1993)

Kuwaiti officials blamed mismanagement, poor financial advice and weak government regulation in Spain, and insisted Kuwait was a victim. The KIO's former managers said they were the victims of bad economic conditions in Spain, which coincided with the impact of the Gulf War. Regardless of the effect of the investments in Spain, KIO's assets were heavily affected by the costs of war. During the invasion, the KIO's holdings became Kuwait's national treasury-in-exile, responsible for both financing the exiled government and paying the costs of international support for liberation after the war.

De la Rosa's claim, however, was different from those of the Spanish and Kuwaiti governments. He alleged that he was a victim of the political power struggle of the Kuwaiti officials. He believed that the Kuwaiti opposition had become stronger as a result of the parliamentary election in 1992 and that they were determined to attack the Kuwaiti royal family by blaming Sheikh Fahad and Sheikh Ali Khalifa, two first cousins of the emir, for the KIO scandal. He repeatedly insisted that his personal profit was earned legitimately and that he had acted according to the instructions from the KIO and had done nothing illegal. In an interview with *The Independent* in 1993 he said:

> I am aware of the transfer of about US$ 300 million that was made from the *Torras* in order to make political payments to gain support for the war effort, but again, I was merely acting on instructions from London [KIO].
>
> (Webster, 1993)

Three attempts were made by lawyers hired by Kuwaiti officials to bring criminal charges against de la Rosa. A Barcelona judge rejected all the suits and one appeal was made.

As a result of the scandal, the political and social environment in Kuwait was intense; Kuwait was devastated after the invasion, and the country was in need of money to finance the reconstruction projects. In order to limit the public controversy, the government banned local newspapers from daily coverage of the scandal (Cohen, 1993). Ali Rashid Al-Bader took over from Sheik Fahad as chairman of the KIO in February 1992.

The new management began a serious attempt to track the Spanish investments (Murphy, 1993). Three former officials of the fund were investigated in relation to the scandal. Kuwait's finance minister at the time of the investigation, Nasser Al-Rodhan, issued instructions to seize properties of all three suspects of the case:

1   Sheikh Fahad, a cousin of the emir who was chairman of the KIO from July 1984 until 8 April 1992. He worked in the ministry of finance until 1964 when he joined the KIO as an administrative manager. Sheikh Fahad served in various positions at the KIO and his first management position was in 1967 when he became the general manager of the KIO.

2   Fouad Jaffar, deputy chairman and general manager of the KIO from 1 July 1984 to 21 April 1990. During the Iraqi invasion of Kuwait, which began on 4 August 1990, Jaffar returned to the offices of the KIO to assist on a voluntary part-time basis, which he described to the Royal Court of Justice in London as an advisory rather than an executive role.

3   Sheikh Khaled, a younger member of the Al-Sabah family and a London University graduate. Upon his graduation he devoted himself full-time to training and then working with the KIO. In 1983, Sheikh Khaled was an analyst at the KIO for the Japanese department. In 1987 he was promoted to assistant general manager, reporting to Jaffar. In December 1989 he became deputy general manager (Royal Courts of Justice, 2000).

Finally, Ali Al-Khalifa Al-Sabah, who served as Kuwait's oil minister before the invasion, and was the finance minister during the occupation, was another government official and royal family member whose reputation was damaged by the scandal. Ali Al-Khalifa and his team had been running the KIO for more than twenty years before the crisis happened in Spain. Until then, the KIO was a self-governed organization dedicated to generating revenue without being held back by the bureaucratic restrictions of other government-owned Kuwaiti investment institutions. Upon the liberation, he was forced to leave the government in 1991.

The debate over the collapse of the Grupo Torras was intense. The KIO issued a writ in the Spanish high court against Sheikh Fahad, Fouad Jaffar, de la Rosa and four other Spaniards working for the company for producing losses of over US$870 million, falsifying commercial and public documents, fraud, price manipulation and tax evasion. Moreover, a Kuwaiti parliamentary commission called for legal action against all KIO employees in Britain in the same year

(Murphy, 1993). Kuwait's parliament demanded details about the investment scandals and salaries, which were paid to a number of public officials, and which became the first and most serious investigation involving the ruling family. The assembly passed an investment law in 1993, which required immediate reporting of all public investments, and the companies in which the government had more than a 25 per cent interest to the parliament. It also imposed penalties of up to life imprisonment for anyone who misused public money in Kuwait (Cohen, 1993).

London's Commercial Court found Sheikh Fahad guilty of participating in a conspiracy to spirit funds out of the KIO's Spanish subsidiary, and the Sheikh was found liable for damages of almost US$500 million. Sheikh Fahad allegedly said: 'This case is about international politics [not the best interests of Kuwait]. I am proud of what I did and the part I played in the liberation of Kuwait' (*The Independent*, 1999). In his defence Sheikh Fahad's told the court that the money in question was given to countries and leaders, including Serbia's Slobodan Milosevic, in exchange for their support of Kuwait after Iraq's invasion.

Fouad Jaffar, the former managing director of the KIO in London, was also found guilty of dishonestly receiving money. He did not appeal against the decision (*The Independent*, 1999). The fraud was not limited to Kuwait's investments in Spain: in Paris, French authorities closed the Kuwaiti French Bank in order to conduct an investigation on the missing assets of the bank. Moreover, an investment fund in Switzerland, which managed Kuwait's government assets, was reported for fraud. Adnan Abdelqader Al-Mussalem, an economist from a local financial newsletter, told The *New York Times* in 1993: 'The losses, fraud and misappropriation of funds are much bigger than Spain. There has been a massive abuse of public money in the past' (Ibrahim, 1993).

The history of the organization during the years prior to the scandal, shows that despite some government's effort to increase the control over management of Kuwait SWF, the senior management in the office in London has resisted to provide the government with access to transparent information on the KIO affairs. In 1986, the KIO's executive committee, led by the emir's financial adviser, Khalid Su'ud, had flown to London in an attempt to increase the government's control on the KIO. The in-house managers of the KIO in London, however, have refused to provide them with information by shutting down access to their offices and computers so that the executives would have limited access to the trading information. At the time, two royal family members, Fahd Al-Mohammed Al-Sabah and Ali Al-Khalifa, held major management control of the KIO while the only government figure more senior to them was the emir. The emir had, reportedly, never exercised his supremacy because of the sensitivity of his relationships with Sheikh Fahad and Ali Al-Khalifa. Relations between the emir's side of the royal family and Khalifa's side were already tense due to a dispute going back two generations, when Khalifa's grandfather was killed in a purge by the emir's grandfather (Marcom, 1991).

In the late 1980s, the return on the KIA investments was equal to or even higher than the total oil revenue. The experience of the KIO in Spain had become a turning point in the history of the Kuwait's sovereign wealth management.

Kuwait's SWF made the biggest loss of its history in investments made through Groupo Torras. In the aftermath of the liberation, Kuwait's SWF's assets were at a historically low level due to a combination of factors. Various transactions were made from the AUM of the KIA in order to cover the government expenditure after the liberation. In addition to the huge losses of the KIO, and the costs of the military operation of the war, the government had to spend a share of the foreign assets on bailing out banks, writing off the utility bills of Kuwaiti consumers, and distributing cash to Kuwaiti citizens as compensation for their losses during the invasion.

In addition to the investigation of the individuals who were involved in the operation of the KIO and Torras at the time of the crisis, the government applied a series of organizational restructures. The finance committee of the parliament was made responsible for defining the accountability and tasks carried by those who were appointed to run the KIO after the crisis. Until the crisis, the KIO was not controlled by the national audit office, nor by the ministry of finance. The Kuwaiti legislature, therefore, set up a monitoring system to oversee the management of public funds, which until then had been highly controlled by Al-Sabah and the business allies of the ruling family. As noted above, prior to the crisis, decision making at the KIO was monopolized by a few individuals from the ruling family. This trend has, however, gradually changed. Since the early 1990s, the involvement of the ruling family members in the management of Kuwait's SWF has been gradually declining. From 2003, none of the chairmen or managing directors of the KIA has been appointed from the royal family. The procedures and operation strategies of the KIA have become subject to tighter restrictions than before. The dispute within the ruling elite, if not solved fully, is less likely to have a direct effect on the KIA's operations, as a result of reduced direct engagement by members of the royal family at executive levels. Instead, the parliament has assumed a much bigger part in forming the overall strategy of Kuwait's SWF. Since early 1990s, it has taken a rather proactive role in supervising the KIA; at the same time the KIA is expected to 'police itself' (Monk, 2010).

The lack of sufficient supervision measures to control the Kuwaiti SWF operation, coupled with loose regulation in the Spanish financial system led to an unsuccessful experience in early 1990s, from which it took some years for the KIA to recover. The organizational structure, monitoring procedures, technical competence, risk management expertise and decision-making processes of the KIA have developed over the years of operation, and will minimize the possibility of future misconduct to such a scale. The KIA has recovered from the experience. Since 2008, the authority has achieved the highest transparency index amongst its counterparts in the GCC countries. However, the engagement of the parliament in sovereign wealth management has created lengthy and bureaucratic decision-making procedures for the government's financial affairs, which often lessen the efficiency of those decisions. Time-consuming decision making caused by potential disputes between parliament and the KIA management is likely to arise following the 2012 parliamentary election when the opposition took over two-thirds of the seats in the parliament.

Investment strategy of the KIA

According to the KIA's official website, safety, income appreciation and capital protection have been the three main pillars of the Kuwaiti sovereign wealth investment strategy since the early years of the establishment of the country's SWF. The KIA investment strategy has developed over more than five decades of operation. The authority has, directly or indirectly (via investment agents), invested the country's sovereign wealth in various asset classes and different sectors across the globe.

Geographic allocation of assets

From the early 1950s until the mid-1970s the KIO assets were concentrated solely in the UK. After that the KIO entered the US markets for the first time. The first investments of the KIA were in the top seventy-five most reliable companies on the New York Stock Exchange. While the KIO was managing its investments directly in London, in the USA the investments were handled via agents. Soon after KIO entered US markets, it became one of the major shareholders in all the seventy-five companies. By the late 1970s, the KIO holdings in those companies were high enough such that if it remained restricted to the same group of companies every year, it would have had a significant effect on their market prices. In other words, such a position in a limited number of companies would inevitably make the KIO's investment safety extremely vulnerable against any potential unfavourable move in the performance of those companies. Therefore, a new strategy was needed (Khouja and Sadler, 1979: 190–208, 162–189).

As a result, the KIO started to create new portfolios, and expand its existing ones, in other countries. Equity portfolios outside America and Britain (Germany, Switzerland, France, Belgium, The Netherlands and Japan) were created and handled by local banks. As well as penetration into new markets geographically, the KIO started to expand its investments in the American equity market to companies other than the list of the top seventy-five companies on the New York Stock Exchange and into more speculative investments. By entering such investments the holdings of the government of Kuwait in top companies were kept under the ownership thresholds, which would allow the KIO to maintain the confidentiality of its investments.

Before the late 1980s, a considerable share of the authority's assets was invested in developed Western economies. The investments had been mainly in medium- or long-term ventures and scattered across forty-five different countries, a high number of which were in the Organisation for Economic Co-operation and Development (OECD) – mainly the UK, the USA, France and Germany. Towards the end of the 1980s, the KIA started for the first time to engage in direct investments in emerging markets in countries such as Brazil and Taiwan (Economist Intelligence Unit, 2001). In 1985, it was reported that the lion's share of the GRF assets were invested locally (60 per cent), and the remaining 40 per cent apportioned as follows: 31 per cent in Arab countries, 5 per cent in other foreign countries and 4 per cent with international financial organizations such as the IMF. In the same year, however, the authority was reported to be applying a different strategy for the management of the FGF. The major share of the assets (75 per cent) were invested in non-Arab foreign countries, 23 per cent was invested locally and the rest in Arab countries (Economist Intelligence Unit, 2001).

Over time, due to the global financial climate, the KIA has paid more attention to investment in the emerging markets, in particular the ones in Asia. It has contributed to the establishment of several companies, primarily to develop Kuwait's investments in Asia. Kuwait China Investment Company (KCIC) is one of the major investment organizations of this kind, and was established in 2005. In addition, an announcement was made in summer 2008 that the KIA is considering allocating up to US$50 billion, or 20 per cent of its assets, in Japan. This plan was introduced as part of the authority's efforts to rebalance its portfolio (Behrendt, 2008). Another main investment project of the KIA in Asia was signing more than US$27 billion of investment agreements with nine Asian countries, including Brunei and the Philippines, in August 2008. The agreements mainly included investments in the oil and health sectors. The Kuwaiti Finance Minister, Mustafa Shamali, commented on KIA–Asian economies agreements in the local newspapers in Kuwait stating: 'The value of the accords and economic and commercial protocols are more than US$ 27 billion, with US$ 3 billion to US$ 4 billion of investments and possible commercial partnerships with each country.' He also noted that Kuwait would 'cooperate with South Korea, Thailand and the Philippines, in the health sector' (Reuters, 2008e).

By 1974, Kuwait's sovereign wealth investment strategy, which was previously heavily concentrated on long-term investment, took a different direction: roughly 60 per cent in equities, industry and real estate, and 40 per cent in bonds and first class medium- and long-term securities of over seven year's maturity. The investments in equities were used as a cover against inflation, while the bonds and securities were to provide a turnover of liquid capital. Moreover, new sectors in various geographic locations were added to the investment universe of the KIO. In 1974, for the first time, and through the Kuwait Investment Company (KIC), Kuwait entered the real estate market. The early purchases were Kiawah Island, a major holiday resort on the east coast of America, and St Martins Properties in London, a group with wide interests, but at that time in urgent need of liquidity.

Building trust by patient money

Although the investment strategy of the Kuwait SWF has changed throughout five decades of operation, one aspect of it has remained unchanged: Kuwait's government has remained a patient and quiet shareholder in its holdings around the world. In other words, Kuwait's SWF has, on a number of occasions, acted as a long-term investor and avoided moving its assets from sector to sector, or company to company, even if those holdings were not commercially profitable at the time. The experience of the Kuwaiti government's holdings in Daimler (a major German car production company) and the British iconic oil company, BP, are two great examples for this aspect of the country's sovereign wealth management. The Kuwaiti government has been a shareholder in Daimler since 1969. The company acquired an American car making company, Chrysler, in 1998. The transatlantic merger of the two businesses was not successful and, in 2007, Daimler-Chrysler confirmed a deal to sell its loss-making American unit, Chrysler, to a US private equity firm called Cerberus (Landler and Maynard, 2007). After Chrysler was sold off, there were valid reasons for KIA to divest from Chrysler. A divestment of the Kuwaiti government's holding in Chrysler would have had a strong negative signalling effect on the already suffering American car production industry. The KIA decided instead to keep its stake patiently to avoid imposing further volatility on the US car market.

Further evidence of the patience of the Kuwaiti government in its investments is the KIA holding in BP. In 1986, the government of Kuwait (through KIO) set out to acquire almost 21.6 per cent of BP's shares, which was more than 7 per cent of the country's overseas investments at the time (Crystal, 1992). The deal prompted fear in London, as it put the Kuwaiti government in a position to be capable of exercising its power as a major shareholder in BP. Three years later, the British Monopolies and Mergers Commission ordered Kuwait to sell more than half of its holdings in the company. In January 1989, BP announced it would buy 11.7 per cent of its shares back from Kuwait reducing Kuwait's share to 9.9 per cent (Crystal, 1992). In 1997, the KIA again built up to nearly a 22 per cent holding in BP, after the sale of a tranche of the company's shares by the British government on the 'Black Monday' stock market collapse. The KIA purchased the BP shares when few other investors were willing to put their money at a high risk of loss by BP. Less than a year later, as the dust settled in the British stock market, the holding of the KIA in BP was reviewed by Britain's competition authorities. The authorities ordered the government of Kuwait to reduce its stake to less than 10 per cent within 12 months (Macalister, 2010). Kuwait's SWF holdings in BP have fluctuated significantly over time and depended on the demand in the company for cash injection. The government of Kuwait has patiently responded to this demand and decreased its holding in the company as the British government has required.

As noted above, over more than five decades of Kuwait's SWF's operation, the country has allocated its resources in a way in which the government's holdings globally have caused minimum threat to the stability of the host markets. The examples of the KIA investments in Chrysler and BP show that the Kuwaiti government has been willing to patiently enter and stay in the markets when its resources were needed and exit the markets when the host sovereign nations required – even at times when the moves were not fully profitable for the Kuwaiti SWF.

Inward looking investments

Since the global financial crisis of 2008, the Kuwaiti government, like many other countries affected by the crisis, faced high demand for liquidity in the domestic economy. As a result, in November 2008, the KIA reportedly withdrew about

US$3.66 billion from abroad to invest at home, particularly in the local bourse as it was severely hit by the global financial crisis (Reuter, 2008b). The transfer of assets of the Kuwaiti SWF from overseas, in order to support the local economic activities, has been repeated since the peak of the global financial crisis. In 2011, the KIA announced its plans to increase its investments domestically. Kuwait has long had the most conservative fiscal policies amongst the GCC states. However, in the aftermath of the global financial crisis the government has increased its spending on social transfers and infrastructure in order to support domestic consumption, which, in one way or another, will reduce the new flows into the KIA.

In March 2011, the KIA reportedly decided to allocate US$3.6 billion of its assets to the domestic property markets. Such move was not unprecedented, as the KIA already had domestic holdings, which were boosted by the government's policy for support of the domestic economy after 2008 financial crisis. There has been a new factor, however, contributing to the formation of the government's asset management strategy, which is the potential for social unrest in Kuwait as a result of economic difficulties. Therefore, transfer of assets to the domestic economy is one of several measures taken by the government of Kuwait to stabilize the economic outlook of the country, mainly in order to minimize the risk of an uprising of a similar scale to the other Arab countries in the face of the Arab Spring (Roubini Global Economics, 2011).

Conclusion

Kuwait is the only GCC country to have a clear saving policy for its CSWF. According to the country's constitution, 10 per cent of the country's oil income at any given price of oil for each fiscal year, as well as the investment returns, must be transferred every year to the FGF's account.

The KIA has been the sole institution in charge of management of the Kuwait's SWF (both the FGF and the GRF). It has diversified the country's sovereign wealth assets across the markets in various asset classes and geographic locations. The investment strategy of the fund is designed to include various asset classes including real estate, equities and fixed income in the portfolio of investments of the KIA from North America to emerging economies in Asia. The KIA's interest in investing in emerging markets, particularly those in Asia, has been on the rise since 2005.

The governance and management structure of the Kuwait SWF has developed over more than five decades of operation. In comparison with other GCC fundss, KIA has a clearer relation with the political elite and this is due to the country's parliamentary system. The country has applied strong supervisory measures to its sovereign wealth management since the 1990s, in which the parliament plays an important role in monitoring the KIA's activities. Although such a monitoring system has often led to bureaucratic and time-consuming decision-making procedures by the government, it has successfully minimized the risk of financial fraud.

Like other CSWFs of the Gulf, the KIA has been a rather passive investment institution and has intentionally avoided practicing its ownership rights in most of the companies in which it invests. Moreover, the experience of BP and Chrysler has shown that the Kuwait's sovereign wealth management strategy has been to practice patient investment management mainly to build trust and avoid potential political backlash with the host government of the economies in which the country's SWF invests.

Finally, the investments of the Kuwaiti SWF have become more engaged with Kuwait's national economy, since the global financial crisis of 2008, when the demand for government bail outs increased in order to rescue the domestic financial institutions. Moreover, in the light of the Arab awakening starting in 2011, the government has raised its domestic holdings in order to minimize the risk of political and social unrest in Kuwait, which could be triggered by economic difficulties.

4 Saudi Arabia's sovereign wealth funds

Introduction

Saudi Arabia is the Gulf's most well-endowed country, with proven reserves of 264.1 billion barrels of oil as of the end of 2008 (http://www.iea.org). The country has reportedly the second largest government assets in the GCC after Abu Dhabi (although, depending on the source, some analysts estimate that Saudi foreign reserves are bigger than those of Abu Dhabi). As of April 2011, Saudi Arabia is the leading oil producer amongst the Organization of the Petroleum Exporting Countries (OPEC) with an average daily production of over eight million barrels per day (Reuters, 2011b). Given the size of oil reserves and output of Saudi Arabia, and the underdevelopment of non-oil sectors, oil export is the major source of income for the Saudi government. Saudi oil income has progressed gradually since 1962, as a result of oil production increase, while the country's foreign exchange reserves increased significantly between the early 1970s and the early 1980s due to the oil price booms and increasing investment returns. For many decades, the government has been applying various sets of policies in order to save a share of the country's oil income.

The size of the Saudi Arabia government's income been closely linked with global oil markets. Table 4.1 presents the main indicators of the Saudi economy. As is shown in the table, Saudi Arabia's average oil exports between 2006 and 2010 were US$208.3 billion. In 2008, however, the country's crude exports reached US$281 billion, which was the highest level from the previous five years. This is due to the record oil prices in 2008. In 2009, there was a sharp decline in the oil markets, which led to a significant decline in oil revenues, and reflected the shock of the global financial crisis, which shrunk the oil markets. The export income has started gradually to catch up in 2010.

Unlike other GCC countries where a separate government entity is in charge of the government sovereign wealth management, in Saudi Arabia the central bank acts as the country's SWF, too. The Saudi Arabian Monetary Agency (SAMA), which was established in 1952, has been the main government body for the management of Saudi sovereign wealth. As the central bank of Saudi Arabia, in addition to management of the country's SWF, the SAMA has various responsibilities including:

Table 4.1 Saudi Arabia's main economic indicators (2006–2011)

	2006	2007	2008	2009	2010	Average (2006–2011)	2011 (est.)
GDP (US $ bn)	356.6	384.9	476.3	375.8	451	408.9	486.5
Private consumption (US $ bn)	94.8	112.4	132.5	143.3	156.8	128.0	173.0
Government consumption (US $ bn)	83.1	85.9	92.0	92.9	103.4	91.5	114.3
Gross fixed investment (US $ bn)	66.8	82.6	105.6	98.2	109.3	92.5	122.3
Exports of goods and services (US $ bn)	225.5	249.3	322.9	202	246.1	249.2	261.3
Imports of goods and services (US $ bn)	113.5	145.3	176.7	160.6	170.3	153.3	190.2
Oil production ('000 b/d)	9,222	8,760	9,158	8,196	8,291	8725.4	8,508
Oil exports (US$ bn)	188.9	205.5	281	163.1	203.1	208.3	214.6

Source: EIU (2010)

- Regulating the country's banking system, which includes the supervision of commercial banks, and maintaining the soundness of the financial system.
- Monetary stabilization responsibilities, which includes issuing national currency, acting as a banker to the government, monetary policy making, maintaining the value of the riyal, holding monetary reserves, and assisting the ministry of finance with the annual budgets.

As the SAMA is the central bank of Saudi Arabia and holds other responsibilities, in practice it is not specified as a SWF like its GCC counterparts. This has raised a question amongst the scholars of whether or not the SAMA should be considered as a SWF. In contrast with other GCC oil exporters, where due to the high oil income, the governments have constantly experienced budget surplus, the Saudi government had suffered from a budget deficit for many years. Such a deficit had provided the Saudi government with very little opportunity to accumulate sovereign wealth. That is why some scholars, including Christin Smith Diwan, do not consider the SAMA as a SWF. Diwan argues that '…there can be no sovereign wealth fund without sovereign wealth, and Saudi Arabia spent much of the past decade in a debtor's position'(Diwan, 2009). This book, however, takes a different view on the SAMA.

While Saudi Arabia is the leading oil exporter of the GCC with the highest oil export income in the region, it has the biggest population amongst the Gulf countries leading to the consumption of a large portion of the country's oil revenue by public expenditure. In addition to factors such as the size of the Saudi government expenditure domestically, the cost of the major regional crises (i.e. the Gulf Wars) drained Saudi oil export income during the 1990s and led the Saudi government to accumulate debt. It is a fact that the Saudi government had lagged behind some

Table 4.2 Saudi Arabia SWFs

Name of the entity	Establishment	AUM (US $ billion)	Investment focus
SAMA	1952	532.8	Gold, foreign bank reserves, securities
Sanabil el-Saudi	2008	5.3	Commodities, treasury, real estate, equities, foreign currencies

Source: Sovereign Wealth Fund Institute, and http://www.swfinstitute.org/fund-rankings/, and Taghide http://taighde.com/w/Sanabil_al-Saudia

of its counterparts in the Gulf in wealth accumulation during the 1990s. However, the government has applied a series of debt reduction policies since 2004. As a result, 9 per cent of the government's debt was reduced in 2004, followed by another impressive phase of the Saudi debt reduction in 2005, which decreased an additional 29 per cent of the government debt (Ziemba, 2008). The debt reduction policies of the Saudi government led to significant wealth accumulation by the SAMA by 2011. The IMF estimates that Saudi Arabia's foreign assets increased to US$535 billion by the end of 2011, up from US$441 billion at the end of the 2010 and from US$25 billion in 2000 (IMF, 2011b). Therefore, given the definition of a SWF, provided in Chapter 1, in the absence of a separate organization, the SAMA is indeed considered Saudi Arabia's SWF for to the following reasons:

1   The major source of wealth for the SAMA is commodity export income.
2   The purpose of wealth accumulation by the SAMA is stabilization of the Saudi economy against economic shocks, particularly those imposed by the volatile oil markets.

The Saudi government launched a new government investment organization in 2008, *Sanabil el-Saudi*. There is very little information available about the structure and the purpose of establishing the organization. However, the establishment of such an organization has shown the government's intention for creating a sovereign wealth management institution similar to the ones of the other GCC countries. Table 4.2 shows a summary of Saudi sovereign wealth investment institutions.

The history of the establishment of the SAMA

In 1948 George Eddy, who at the time was working in the Office of International Finance of the US Treasury Department, and Raymond F. Mikesell, from the US State Department, travelled to Saudi Arabia to study a possible currency reform in the country. In 1951, the Saudi government signed a technical assistance agreement with the USA to reform the monetary and fiscal system (Long and Maisel, 2010). Upon this agreement a financial mission, under the management of Arthur Young, was sent to Saudi Arabia to help the government reform the budgetary and administrative system of the ministry of finance. The most important recommendation of Young's mission was the creation of a central bank. Arthur Young convinced King Abdulaziz (the Saudi ruler at the time) that it was crucial for the state to have some monetary and banking regulations and he drew up a plan for what became the SAMA (Young, 1983). SAMA was then established under royal decree No. 30/4/1/1046 issued on 20 April 1952 by King Abdulaziz. On 5 August 1952, George A. Blowers, a US citizen, was appointed as the first governor of SAMA (http://www.sama.gov.sa). The term monetary 'agency' was chosen to avoid using other terminologies such as 'bank' or 'financial institution', which are associated with financial activities like charging or paying interest that are forbidden in Islamic banking. Charging and paying interest were specifically forbidden in the SAMA charter for that reason (Long and Maisel, 2010). Although technically the management of the country's sovereign wealth is one of the activities of SAMA, the government of Saudi Arabia has never officially referred to SAMA as the country's SWF.

The emergence of Saudi Arabia's sovereign assets

The sale of Saudi oil began in 1948. This caused a significant increase in government revenues (see Table 4.3). By 1953, the annual oil revenue was over US$100 million and by the end of the 1950s it stood at US$333.7 million (Niblock, 1982: 75–105). With the accession of Faisal to the throne in 1964 the modern development of Saudi economy began (Birks and Sinclair, 1982: 198–213). When King Faisal assumed the power, he applied more conservative government saving

Table 4.3 Saudi Arabia government revenue (1902–47)

Year	Approximate annual revenue of the government
1902–12	£50,000
1913–25	£100,000
1926–37	£4–5 million
1938–46	£5–6 million
1947–8	£21.5 million

Source: Tim Niblock (1982)

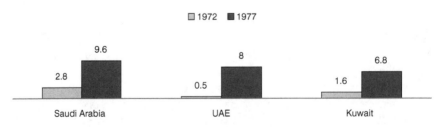

Figure 4.1 GCC selected countries oil revenue (US $billion)
Source: Keith McLachlan and Narsi Ghorban (1978)

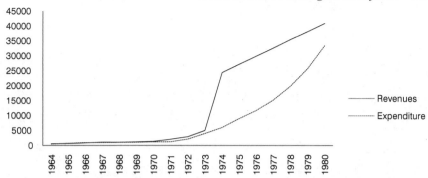

Figure 4.2 Saudi government revenues and expenditures, 1964–1980 (US $ million)
Source: SAMA Annual Report (1982)

policies, leading Saudi Arabia to emerge as a financial giant in the 1970s. In the light of the oil price boom in October 1973 coupled with the high Saudi crude exports the country's oil revenue was boosted to a historically high level (see Figure 4.1).

The fluctuation of oil prices had a direct impact on the Saudi oil revenue. As the price of oil increased from US$3 per barrel in 1972, to US$35 per barrel in 1980, Saudi oil revenue had risen from around US$3 billion in 1972 to US$102 billion in 1980. Due to a non-OPEC production increase coupled with the increase in Iran and Iraq's export in response to their financial demands driven by the cost of war, the global oil prices declined by 61.4 per cent between 1980 and 1986, leading to a sharp decline in Saudi oil revenue from US$113.2 billion in 1981 to US$42.3 billion in 1985 to US$20 billion in 1986 (Foley, 2010: 85–132). The oil price decline of the mid-1980s and high government expenditure led Saudi Arabia into a massive budget deficit financed by foreign borrowing. The government expenditure expanded from just above US$1 billion in 1970 to US$33 billion in 1980 (see Figure 4.2). The growth of government expenditure continued through the 1980s while the oil revenue shrunk as a result of high expenditure and volatile crude export income. The costs of the development plans and the war operation in the early 1990s had pushed Saudi Arabia to the edge of bankruptcy by the late 1990s. The Saudi government borrowed emergency loans to finance its debt.

Saudi Arabia's foreign assets have varied in reflection of the changes in oil revenue. Foreign assets reached US$131.3 billion in 1981, US$137.9 billion in 1982 and US$136.2 billion in 1983. Following these remarkable years, the level of foreign assets declined due to the oil price decrease and the costs of the military operation during the 1991 Gulf War. In 1991, foreign assets fell to US$6.1 billion. Export revenue started to increase gradually between 1995 and 2000. Consequently, the gross foreign assets of the SAMA grew from US$54.5 billion in 1999 to US$62.3 billion in 2000 and US$72.8 billion in 2003 (Economist Intelligence Unit, 2004). The recovery in oil prices helped rebuild the SAMA's net foreign asset position. Table 4.4 shows the SAMA's assets since 2005. As is illustrated in the table, there has been a sharp increase in figures for all the asset classes between 2005 and 2008, which reflects the record oil prices during that

Table 4.4 SAMA's financial position 2005–2010 (US $ million)

Asset type	2005	2006	2007	2008	2009	2010	Average (2005 to 2010)
Currency cover (gold)	89,751	94,319	106,054	121,066	123,127	123,638	109,659
% from total	0.14	0.11	0.09	0.07	0.08	0.08	0.09
Cash in vault	18,262	12,777	23,842	27,053	23,876	22,550	21,393
% from total	0.03	0.01	0.02	0.02	0.02	0.01	0.02
Deposits with banks abroad	113,954	123,346	246,792	379,487	335,673	318,796	253,008
% from total	0.18	0.14	0.21	0.22	0.21	0.20	0.19
Investments in foreign securities	369,973	625,667	790,559	1,154,247	1,071,542	1,126,127	856,353
% from total	0.60	0.71	0.66	0.68	0.68	0.70	0.67
Other assets	27,464	28,215	29,569	28,142	16,435	19,589	24,902
% from total	0.04	0.03	0.02	0.02	0.01	0.01	0.02
Total	619,404	884,324	1,196,816	1,709,995	1,570,653	1,610,700	1,265,315

Source: Saudi Arabian Monetary Agency (2010)

period coupled with government spending cuts. As a result, after a long period of current account deficit, a surplus of US$134 billion was reported in 2008, which was due to an increase of 41.4 per cent in export income for goods and services (36.9 per cent in the oil sector and 16.5 per cent in the non-oil sector) (Behrendt, 2008).

In contrast to the growth of assets in 2005–2008, there was a decline in the SAMA's total assets during 2008–2010, which reflects the impact of the global financial crisis. The SAMA's foreign holdings were estimated to be more than $300 billion in 2008 (Behrendt, 2008). The SAMA's portfolio has been extremely overweight in foreign securities – on average 67 per cent of the total assets during 2008–2010 were invested in securities. This has been one of the main reasons that, after the crisis, the SAMA reported smaller losses on its portfolio in comparison with other GCC sovereign wealth funds, who, it is speculated, have lost about 20–30 per cent of their assets. The IMF reported the SAMA's foreign holdings to stand about US$535 billion in 2011.

Investment strategy of the SAMA

The Saudi sovereign wealth investment strategy has had different characteristics in comparison with other GCC economies. While countries like Kuwait and the UAE have been accumulating sovereign wealth by investing the crude export income surplus in various asset classes outside their economy of origin, for many decades Saudi Arabia's crude export income has been spent to finance significantly high government expenditure. The relationship between the state and the nation in Saudi Arabia has been highly influenced by oil income. The government has used different channels, such as granting contracts for development projects, and public or individual subsidies, to distribute wealth amongst Saudi citizens (Long and Maisel, 2010) to maintain a good relationship between the ruling family and with the public. Moreover, the defence expenditure in Saudi Arabia has been significantly higher than its GCC neighbouring countries. As the International Institute for Strategic Studies (IISS) reported in 2011, Saudi Arabia has the highest defence spending compared to the overall size of the country's economy. The Saudi government spent over 10 per cent of the country's GDP on the defence sector in 2011, up from around 8 per cent in 2005 (International Institute for Strategic Studies, 2011). Finally, the cost of government-sponsored local development projects has contributed to the increase in public expenditure. For example, government expenditure of US$214 billion in 2011 and US$187.2 billion in 2012 has been mainly spent on social programmes, including education and training, and health and social affairs, as well as stimulus measures including the minimum wage rise, social housing and government-brokered credit to individual Saudis (Saudi Arabia Ministry of Finance, 2011). Although the defence budget was not disclosed in the 2012 budget, it will likely form a high percentage of government expenditure.

As noted, the lion's share of Saudi sovereign wealth has been channelled towards the government expenditure for many decades, but this does not provide the full picture of the Saudi sovereign wealth investment strategy. Heavy reliance on oil export incomes as the only source for financing Saudi Arabia's high government expenditure has made the Saudi economy extremely vulnerable to oil price fluctuation. To tackle this, despite high public expenditure, the government has been cautious and set aside some of the petrodollars to protect the economy against oil price shocks. SAMA is the main Saudi government organisation managing the government wealth. The key purpose of SAMA asset accumulation and wealth management strategy has been stabilization of Saudi economy. These assets have been kept in rather conservative investment portfolios to minimize the investment risks. Most are held in low-risk, liquid assets with a low investment return such as bank deposits, certificates of deposit and bonds issued or guaranteed by developed economies.

In addition to the safety and security of the Saudi investments abroad, the political and economic alliance of the country has also played a crucial role in forming the country's sovereign wealth investment strategy. The SAMA's investments abroad have been heavily dollarized. The overweight Saudi investment in dollar is indeed a by-product of the historical economic relationship between Saudi Arabia and the USA. Similar to the investment strategy of the Kuwait government, which was mainly affected by the country's economic links with the UK (particularly during the early years of the establishment of the KIA), the Saudi oil income has been directed towards investment opportunities in the USA as a result of various economic links between the two countries. Strong political alliance with the American administration has led to the formation of various factors creating the SAMA's dollar dominated investment pattern:

- Close cooperation with the USA in oil production: Saudi Aramco (Arabian American Oil Company) has been the major oil producer in Saudi Arabia since the discovery of oil. Such close cooperation in the production of oil has boosted Saudi investments in American markets.
- The currency of oil trade: since the early 1970s, OPEC members have invoiced oil sales in US dollars. This decision was made as part of a proposal put forward by the Saudi government, influenced by Saudi–US economic relations (Spiro, 1999: 2–6).
- Saudi–US agreement for the purchase of US Treasury Bills: the Treasury Secretary of the USA, William Simon, signed a secret agreement with the Saudis to buy US Treasury bills before they are publicly auctioned. This agreement between the two countries was made so that the investment of Saudi wealth could finance the US budget deficit to support the value of the dollar, to keep US interest rates low, and to promote American domestic growth and consumption (Spiro, 1999).
- An investment opportunity to safeguard Saudi sovereign wealth: investment of Saudi oil revenue in US Treasury bills protected Saudi foreign assets from the risks of currency conversion and protected the Saudi government portfolio from investment risks (Momani, 2008). In addition, the US government has guaranteed anonymity of the GCC governments' investment in US Treasury

bonds: the American Treasury refused disclosure of the Gulf countries' holdings of Treasury bills on an individual country basis (Government Accounting Office, 1979). Given the strategic situation of Saudi Arabia, both regionally and domestically, such anonymity has served the best interests of the Saudi government. It has also provided the SAMA with sustainable low return, low risk investment opportunities, which suit the Saudi government's demand for safe accumulation of assets abroad to stabilize the domestic economy.

• American financial experts established the SAMA: similar to the KIA, which was initially set up as the Kuwait Investment Board by the British financial experts, the SAMA was established by American banking specialists. After over five decades, one can still find elements of the long-term impact of American advisors during the early years of the SAMA. It is not surprising that the SAMA's foreign holdings have been directed towards the US economy and to support the dollar, for the same reasons as the KIA's assets were invested in the UK and helped to maintain the value of pound for many years.

Development of the SAMA investment strategy in the 1970s

Until the early 1970s, the Saudi government investment strategy was dominated by safety of assets while maintaining economic and political relations with the USA. Holding deposits with foreign banks has been one of the favoured wealth management policies of the SAMA. Thirty-five banks were chosen by the SAMA amongst the most credible institutions globally to receive the Saudi deposit savings. The detailed list of these banks was not found throughout this study; however, the most probable scenario is that only foreign banks with high credit rating were authorized to receive the SAMA's deposits. In 1974 for the first time the Saudi government debated investment opportunities, which would add one more element to the safety and security of Saudi investments and offer higher rates of return. Higher returns would have been associated with accepting a higher level of investment risk by the SAMA. After the oil boom of the 1970s, with the rapid growth of Saudi government income, the SAMA added higher investment risks into its wealth management strategy, than it did prior to that year. The list of thirty-five banks that were authorized to receive the SAMA deposits was revised in October 1975. As a result more European and Asian banks in countries with higher return on bank savings were added to the list. 17 banks were added to the list, including the Royal Bank of Canada (Canada), Mellon Bank (USA), United California Bank (USA), Skandinaviska Enkilda Banken (Sweden), Bayerische Vereinsbank (Germany), Westdeutsche Landesbank (Germany), Credit Bank of Brussels (Belgium), Hong Kong Shanghai (China), Sumitomo Bank (Japan), Dai Ichi Kangyo Bank (Japan) and Bank Kobe (Japan) (Field, 1976). The Saudi government started to diversify sovereign wealth investments in order to incease the investment returns

In addition to changes in the SAMA's bank deposit holding strategy, the Saudi government entered the equity market for the first time in the 1970s. As global demand for capital in the petroleum industry was increasing, the Saudi government saw an excellent investment opportunity in foreign petroleum companies. Ahmad Zaki Yamani, the Saudi Minister of Petroleum at the time, had played an important role in directing the government's investment policy towards opportunities in foreign oil companies as well as downstream oil operations in importing countries. It is worth noting, like the equity investments of the government of Kuwait, the SAMA's equity holdings have often been kept under the notification thresholds to keep the wealth management strategy of the Saudi government low profile. In 1973, the government established a new committee, headed by the late King Fahad Al-Saud, who was the minister of interior at that time in King Faisal's cabinet, to review the government investment policies and to recommend new investment opportunities (Well, 1974: 23–68). Saudi government investments in equity markets were expanded to other sectors.

SAMA's changed investment pattern during the 1980s and 1990s

The SAMA's investment pattern changed during the 1980s and the key element of change in the Saudi government's investment strategy was in the currency allocation of the SAMA's portfolio. By the mid-1980s, the SAMA's asset currency allocation was 60 per cent in US dollars and 40 per cent Deutsche Marks and yen (Askari, 1990). Diversification of the heavily dollarized portfolio of the SAMA to other currencies was a reaction to the global political environment. The freeze of the Iranian government's foreign assets by the US government in 1980 triggered anxiety amongst the Saudi government policy makers. The Saudi government became concerned about the potential danger of holding an overweight portfolio of assets in the US markets at the time of any political crisis with the American administration. As a result of this the Saudi government reviewed the country's investment approach and gradually reduced Saudi holdings in the USA.[1]

The 1990s was perhaps one of the most difficult decades for the Saudi economy. There has not been any particular change of investment strategy in the SAMA during this period. As was discussed earlier, the Saudi government had to use their financial reserves (accumulated during the oil booms) to finance huge domestic expenditures and the costs of the Gulf War. By mid-1992 official foreign holdings were reported to stand at the minimum level needed for maintaining the Saudi national currency. The government was forced to borrow heavily in the international market. Despite the high demand for capital in the global markets during this period, there was no sign of moving towards high income generating investment by the SAMA, due to lack of resources. The reliance of the government on oil income was higher than in the previous decade. In the 1990s, oil revenues accounted for around 90 per cent of GDP, up from 75 per cent during the 1980s (Krimly, 1999: 256). A large share of the country's foreign holdings as well as crude export inflow of capital were exhausted, and for most of the 1990s the wealth accumulation strategy and the foreign investment strategy was put on hold in Saudi Arabia as a result of massive government expenses.

The SAMA investment strategy in the light of the 2008 financial crisis

Despite the fluctuation in the size of the SAMA's dollar-dominated investments, the Saudi government has maintained favoured dollarized safe investments throughout the history of its operation. In 2008, the SAMA was reported to hold about 85 per cent of Saudi's foreign exchange reserves in dollar-denominated fixed-income securities (England, 2008b). After the financial crisis of 2008, most of the global investment institutions, including the Gulf CSWFs, reportedly shifted their investments from the US markets into European and emerging markets. The SAMA, however, has not made any visible shift in its investment strategy. In an interview with CNN in January 2010 Mohammad Al-Jasser, the governor of the SAMA, explained the rationale for the Saudi government investment's policy:

> The dollar peg has served our interest very well since 1986 and there is no emotional attachment. It's basically self-interest. And that is based on the objective analysis of our balance sheets. One hundred per cent of our exports are denominated in dollars, and this is because of international markets; it is not by our choice, and about 70 per cent of our imports are denominated in dollars. In the past and in the present, and probably for the foreseeable future, the peg to dollar has served our economy very well. But, never say never. If our economy diversifies much greater, then probably there will be reconsideration for this system.
>
> (CNN, 2010)

In the aftermath of 2008 financial crisis, the SAMA's heavily dollarized asset allocation strategy has served its portfolio quite well. As opposed to the other Gulf SWFs, the SAMA has not engaged in investments in risky assets/markets. Therefore, while most of the Gulf funds have made huge losses as a result of the global financial crisis, the SAMA's overweight investments in US Treasury bonds have not made significant losses in value (Setser and Ziemba, 2009).

The SAMA's post-2008 investment strategy

The key investment goal for the SAMA has been to protect the domestic economy against oil price shocks, and this goal has remained unchanged since the 2008 crisis. The SAMA's assets have been kept in a highly liquid and accessible portfolio of investment, although it includes many asset classes that are riskier than a classic central bank portfolio such as equities, corporate bonds and alternative funds (Ziemba, 2010). The SAMA's conservative investment strategy (in comparison with other Gulf SWFs) including high exposure of fixed income and relatively underweight equity investment has also remained unchanged since the 2008 global financial crisis and, despite some equity investments, it has never engaged with direct investments, real estate or exotic financial products (England and Khalaf, 2007).

Based on the definition of the two different types of SWFs, described in previous chapters, the SAMA is a stabilization fund rather than a wealth maximization or intergeneration saving sovereign wealth management organization. Therefore, the key focus of the SAMA in all of its investment activities at all times has been to maintain the initial value of the assets through safe investments in assets with low risk-adjusted return. In 2011, the *Financial Times* reported that the foreign assets of Saudi Arabia's central bank had passed US$500 billion for the first time, which as a per capita measure or as a percentage of GDP was substantially higher than China's. Most of these assets were reportedly invested in US Treasury bills, which has been the best option in terms of size, liquidity and depth (Hall, 2011).

Governance and structure

A board of directors with five members (including a governor and deputy governor) is the main governing body at the SAMA. The governor and deputy governor are appointed by royal decree for terms of four years, which are extendable. The other three members of the board are appointed from the private sector. These members are also appointed by royal decree and are for a period of five years. The minister of finance and the council of ministers advise the king with recommendations for appointments of all the members of the board of directors of the SAMA.

Over the decades of operation, the SAMA has been proven to have a high level of institutional stability at senior management levels (see Table 4.5). All the top management figures at the SAMA have served for long terms of office. Hamad Saud Al-Sayari, a former governor of the SAMA, was the longest serving head of the central bank in the Gulf and stayed in his position for twenty-six years (from 1983 to 2009). Upon Al-Sayari's retirement, the SAMA's deputy governor, Muhammad Al-Jasser, was appointed as governor in February 2009. Although the change of Al-Sayari happened through a government reshuffle by King Abdullah, who changed thirteen government officials, including replacing the head of the religious police and appointing the first-ever woman

Table 4.5 SAMA governors since its establishment

Name	Year
George Bowlers	1952
Ralph Standish	1954
Anwar Ali	1958
Abdulaziz Al-Quraishi	1974
Hamad Al-Sayari	1983
Modammad Al-Jasser	2009
Fahad Al-Mubarak	2011

Source: www.sama.gov.sa

deputy minister of Saudi Arabia, Al-Jasser's appointment was not expected to lead to a drastic change of strategy at the SAMA. Instead it was expected that there would be a smooth transition with the change of governor and the overall strategy of the organization would remain unchanged. Al-Jasser left the SAMA in December 2011, becoming the shortest serving governor of the SAMA since George Bowlers (the first governor of the SAMA who was an American), although he was deputy governor of the SAMA for four years prior to his appointment as governor.

Fahed Al-Mubarak was a chairman and a managing director at Morgan Stanley. There is a long history between Morgan Stanley and JP Morgan, Following the Glass–Steagall Act in US financial regulations, it was not possible for a corporation to have investment banking and commercial businesses under a single holding entity. J.P. Morgan & Co. therefore, chose the commercial banking business over the investment banking business. As a result, in 1935, some of the employees of J.P. Morgan & Co., most notably Henry S. Morgan and Harold Stanley, left J.P. Morgan & Co. and joined some others from another financial institution called Drexel partners to form Morgan Stanley. Being one of the closest financial advisers of SAMA, JP Morgan may well have had an influence in the appointment of Al Mubarak.

History of governance at the SAMA

For the first twenty-two years of its establishment, non-Saudi individuals managed the SAMA due to the lack of sufficient local expertise. During those years, three foreign governors served the SAMA, the first two of which were American and the third was of Pakistani origin. Thereafter, the growing resources of the government were used to build an efficient administration in the SAMA and Saudi managers have run the organization that has became one of the most powerful central banks of the Gulf (Hertog, 2010: 84–136).

The longest serving non-Saudi governor of the SAMA, Anwar Ali, took office from his American predecessor six years after the establishment of the SAMA in 1958. Anwar Ali was hired by the Saudi government in October 1957 to design and implement a programme of fiscal and monetary reform. Prior to his employment in Saudi Arabia, Ali was the director of the Middle East department of the IMF. He graduated from Ismailia University in Lahore in 1934, with an MA in economics. He served as undersecretary in the ministry of finance in India, deputy undersecretary in the ministry of finance in Pakistan and director of the national bank in Pakistan before he took the post with the IMF (Shea, 1969). He stayed as the SAMA governor for sixteen years until he died in November 1974.

Abdulaziz Al-Quraishi replaced Ali and was the first Saudi governor of the SAMA. Al-Quraishi received an MBA from the University of Southern California and began his career for Saudi Railways Organization in Dammam, in 1961. From 1968–1974, he served as president of the civil service bureau in Riyadh. During that time, he also served as minister of state for the council of ministers. From 1974–1983, he was governor of the SAMA.

In 1980, Al-Quraishi was retired by royal decree. For three years the SAMA did not have a governor and Hamad Bin Saud Al-Sayari ran the organization as deputy governor. At the end of the three years, Al-Sayari was appointed by the king as the governor, a post he remained in for the next twenty-six years (http://www.sama.gov.sa). Al-Sayari had an MA (in Economics) from the University of Maryland, USA. Prior to his joining the SAMA he was the director general of the Saudi Industrial Development Fund and had also served as the secretary general of the Public Investment Fund. Al-Sayari led the SAMA during a turbulent yet prosperous time for the Saudi economy. During more than two decades of his career as the governor of the SAMA, Saudi Arabia experienced some of the most critical years in the Gulf's history, the most important of which was the First Gulf War. His position and track record have brought Al-Sayari a great deal of admiration in the global financial community. He was ranked seventeen among fifty of the most influential people in the financial community worldwide by the *Institutional Investor* magazine. *Institutional Investor* described Al-Sayari as 'a rock upon which Saudi Arabia's oil-based economy has been built' (AME Info, 2009).

Most of the governors of the SAMA have served in their posts until the age of retirement. Moreover, since the mid-1970s, when the first Saudi governor of the SAMA took charge of the organization, the governor's office has been assumed by the deputy governor rather than an outsider. Therefore, the transitions have been smooth, as the individuals have often been given the chance to grow within the organization and experience their role at different levels of management.

The SAMA investment policies have remained consistent regardless of the individual governors' personal management strategies. It has followed the perfect model for central banks according to the IMF frameworks, while at the same time it has managed the country's sovereign wealth throughout various time periods in which the Saudi economic policies fluctuated depending on the financial conditions of the country. The SAMA has also become a key organization in serving the best interests of Saudi domestic and international politics. Close technical and training collaboration with leading Western financial institutions has assisted the SAMA to gain a high level of in-house expertise over decades of operation (Al-Dukheil, 2004).

Finally, governance at the SAMA has been kept relatively independent from the ruling family, which is in contrast with other GCC sovereign wealth funds. Members of the Al-Saud family have never been appointed to senior management level at the SAMA or to seats of the board, which is exactly the opposite of the Kuwaiti and Emirati SWFs (or the central banks for that matter). This shows that the sense of ownership, which other ruling families of the Gulf expressed over their country's sovereign wealth, has not been practiced in the same manner in Saudi Arabia. Moreover, the SAMA has an excellent track record and there has never been a scandal (like that of KIO in Spain or the BCCI scandal of Abu Dhabi). This is evidence of the robust governance system in the SAMA, which has created a high level of accountability.

Data collection and procedures at the SAMA

The Saudi government, unlike the neighbouring state of Kuwait, has never introduced clear saving procedures that require the government to save a certain share of the oil income (on say an annual basis). The oil revenue surplus is allocated to the SAMA after the investment decision for current and future development projects are made at the beginning of every fiscal year. There has been no indication by the government that they intend to commit to a regular saving system. Another area in which the SAMA lacks in-place regulation is the use of external asset management companies. The SAMA uses both internal and external expertise in managing its resources. However, there is no information on the ratios of internally managed to externally managed assets.

In spite of the SAMA's well-formed information gathering and reporting system, finding information on the SAMA's foreign investments has proven to be challenging during this study. Saudi authorities seem to have been extremely concerned about political issues surrounding high profile government investments and have avoided flashy transactions, unlike other the SWFs of the Gulf, which would have made the financial news' headlines from time to time.

The new Saudi SWF

The Saudi government announced the launch of a new government investment vehicle named *Sanabil el-Saudi* (SES) in July 2008. The fund was established in the form of a joint-stock company with US$5.3 billion, and it is fully owned by the Public Investment Fund (PIF) of Saudi Arabia. The Saudi authorities have not disclosed detailed information on the SES's strategy, the purpose of its establishment or how it differs from the SAMA in those respects. Public announcements surrounding the establishment of the SES stated that it is a long-term and risk-taking investor, which is managed independently from the PIF, with heavy reliance on the use of external advisors in management strategies. The governor of the SAMA at the time of its establishment, Mohammad Al-Jasser, said in January 2008 that the SES was a Saudi government initiative to enter the SWF market slowly to avoid any backlash in places such as the USA and parts of Europe, where there is 'too much populist bias against emerging markets sovereign wealth funds' over the transparency and accountability of state-owned funds (Roberts, 2008).

In April 2008, the secretary general of the PIF, Mansour Al-Maiman, shared more information about the SES's investment strategy. In his interview with the *Financial Times*, Al-Maiman introduced the general investment strategy of SES as being similar to some of the world's large SWFs, such as Norway's Government Pension Fund, and Singapore's GIC. He described the difference between this fund and its counterparts to be the particular focus of SES, taking into account 'the specific requirements of Saudi Arabia' with more typical frameworks for SWFs to optimize risk-adjusted returns and portfolio diversification to a level that it is acceptable to the Saudi financial authorities. Al-Maiman believed that the SES will help further by enhancing development of the country's financial services sector and building Saudi nationals' asset management skills (England, 2008a).

Therefore, based on Al-Maiman's and Al-Jasser's statements, the new Saudi SWF, unlike the SAMA, is expected to have a highly diversified portfolio of investments similar to other GCC sovereign wealth funds. In order to avoid potential controversy in the markets, the initial size of the SES's investments will be significantly lower than those made by other GCC SWFs. In terms of asset classes, the SES is expected to engage more in riskier investments with higher rates of return (such as equities) as opposed to the SAMA's heavy investments in government bonds and dollarized deposits in foreign banks.

In regards to the governance and management structure of the SES, there have been limited information provided to the public by the Saudi authorities. In April 2009, the secretary general of the PIF announced that the SES would start operating, with heavy reliance on its external advisors (Yahoo, 2009). There is no further explanation on the external advisors of the SES. Ashby Monk, in one of his posts on the Oxford SWF Project's blog, clarified that using external advisors for management of the SES is a fine way for the Saudi government to proceed in the short-term because:

> First, the difficulty of setting up an effective investment vehicle should not be underestimated. The governance and competencies required necessitate outsourcing the investment function, at least in the short term. Second, in this tumultuous market, it is better to have a scapegoat for any initial bad investments (see China Investment Corporation). By outsourcing investments, the SWF could simply replace the investors in case of poor performance, and the new SWF will retain domestic legitimacy. Conversely, if the fund started investing its own money from the outset, bad investments could result in a loss of mandate altogether. Finally, investing internationally may spark some concern on the part of target countries; independent consultants making the investment decisions may alleviate any political concerns of recipient countries.
>
> (Monk, 2009b)

As it is mentioned above, the initial size of this fund is relatively moderate in comparison with some of the Gulf sovereign funds, particularly given that Saudi oil revenue far exceeds that of its neighbours. One of the reasons for the Saudi authorities, who have managed the conservative SAMA portfolio for many years, would be to build up a track record and perhaps gain experience in managing a small-size diversified portfolio of investment, before increasing the allocated fund. Moreover, as Al-Jasser mentioned, there is a strong desire in the Saudi government to avoid a similar backlash to that which other SWFs experienced. As the country is suffering from high unemployment and income inequality, the Saudi government may also have concerns about the public reaction to high-profile investments abroad. Moreover, in order to increase the AUM of the SES, transactions will need to be made from other government accounts including the SAMA. Given that the major share of Saudi foreign assets are held in US government bonds, to divest large sums of these assets in favour of less liquid investments would have a strong signalling impact on both American and Saudi economies (Bahgat, 2008). Therefore, it is well justified for the Saudi government to start the new SWF with a smaller share of its sovereign assets.

Conclusion

The SAMA has served as the main sovereign wealth management organization in the Saudi financial system (in addition to its role as the country's central bank). Even though the Saudi government has struggled with massive budget deficits, in the light of debt reduction policies (since 2004) coupled with the growth of oil price in the global commodity markets, the Saudi government has managed to place a large sum of the country's oil revenue in the SAMA foreign reserves account.

The investment strategy of the SAMA has not followed the same pattern as other GCC CSWFs as the SAMA does not have a diversified portfolio of investments and the assets under its management are mainly concentrated in low-risk asset classes with lower return. The main share of the SAMA's assets is held in US dollars and this mirrors the country's close political alliance with the USA over the past decades. This trend is not likely to change for the foreseeable future for the following reasons:

1   The conservative investment pattern and risk aversion of the SAMA protects its assets from significant loss on the value of its investments, as it happened during the 2008 global financial crisis.
2   The Saudi–US political and economic links are expected to remain strong enough for the Saudi government to continue its support for the US dollar.
3   There is no alternative to the US dollar in the financial and oil markets.
4   Unlike its counterparts in the Gulf region, the SAMA has not gained experience in managing a diversified portfolio of assets. Therefore, it is unlikely that it will engage in risky investment projects, particularly at a time of volatility in the markets.

Given the SAMA includes some of its foreign holdings in annual government budget reports, the organization has practiced a more transparent governance pattern in comparison with other GCC commodity-based funds. Like other GCC SWFs, the ruling elite directly appoints the SAMA's senior managers. However, the royal family members have not filled any senior management positions at the SAMA since it was established. All in all, the SAMA has managed to maintain a high degree of organizational stability.

The Saudi government has recently initiated policies to set up a diversified government investment fund with a long-term investment horizon and profit maximization strategies. The reason for taking such a measure is that the Saudi financial system is not flexible enough for a major reallocation of assets by the SAMA to increase portfolio diversification, and it may limit the ability of Saudi government to act quickly. The launch of SES can be seen as the authorities' intention to create a small investment institution in order to practice risk-taking investment strategies and to develop expertise. It is therefore expected that over time the government will gradually expand its risk-taking investment strategies in order to reach a level to be able to compete with other GCC funds.

Note

1   Phone interview with Professor Hussein Askari, 12 February 2010.

5 The United Arab Emirates' sovereign wealth funds

Introduction

The government of the richest emirate of the UAE, Abu Dhabi, established the second oldest SWF of the Gulf (after the KIA) in 1967. The discovery of oil in the early 1960s made a huge impact on Abu Dhabi's government income, from US$75,500 in the mid-1940s to US$84 million in 1967 (Mann, 1964: 18–32). The increase in government revenue highlighted the importance of establishing a government investment institution to manage the vast surplus income of the emirate. The Abu Dhabi Investment Board (ADIB) was established in 1967 to manage the increasing excess oil revenue. It was structured as an organization within the department of finance of Abu Dhabi and its headquarters was in London (Al-Otaiba, 1977: 22–41).

In 1971, another government organization, Abu Dhabi Investment Administration, was established to manage the surplus revenue of Abu Dhabi in parallel to the ADIB, but with a higher level of independence from the department of finance. As the oil income increased from US$952 million in 1973 to US$5278 million in 1974 (Ghanem, 1992: 26–35), the Abu Dhabi Investment Administration took sole power in the management of Abu Dhabi's sovereign wealth.

In 1976, the administration's operations were further developed and its name was changed to the Abu Dhabi Investment Authority (ADIA). Since 1976, the ADIA has remained the main SWF of the government of Abu Dhabi and has inherited a fairly high degree of independence from the ministry of finance in comparison with its predecessor, the Abu Dhabi Investment Administration. With the growth of oil revenues since the establishment of the ADIA, however, the government of Abu Dhabi has established a number of other government investment institutions to manage smaller portions of the surplus oil income.

The government of Dubai also has been active in creating a number of sovereign investment vehicles to manage the government's assets. It is worth noting that the SWFs of the UAE, as are discussed in this chapter, are not limited to those owned by the government of Abu Dhabi. After Abu Dhabi, Dubai is considered to be the second richest emirate within the UAE. Dubai's natural resources have been rather limited and its oil production had been considerably lower than Abu Dhabi (see Figure 5.1). For that reason, the sovereign wealth management institutions

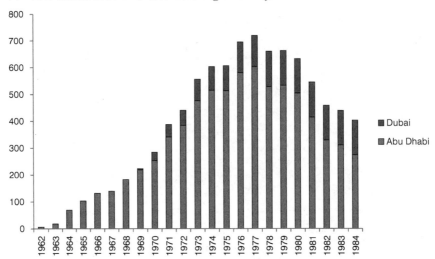

Figure 5.1 Abu Dhabi and Dubai annual oil production, 1962–1984 (million barrels)
Source: Central Bank of the UAE, Statistical Bulletin (1978 and 1985)

of Dubai have not been financed solely by oil surplus incomes, and have relied heavily on leverage. That said, due to the important role of Dubai's economy in the overall economic performance of the UAE, Dubai government investment vehicles are reviewed in this chapter.

UAE political and financial structure

Understanding the structure of the federal government in the UAE is essential in order to provide an inclusive view of the structure of the country's government investment institutions (in Dubai and Abu Dhabi). The political composition of the UAE consists of seven federal monarchical emirates and the government organizations created in the light of the federal monarchical system, including the SWFs, reflect the characteristics of the country's political power structure.

Under the UAE federal constitution, the natural resources and wealth of each emirate is the property of that emirate. Each emirate exercises authority over all matters that are not within the assigned jurisdiction of the union government, including the right to manage the natural resources and the wealth generated from them.

The highest federal authority in the UAE is the Federal Supreme Council (FSC) comprising the rulers of the seven emirates. The FSC is in charge of all the policy making at the federal level and ratifies federal laws (UAE Cabinet, 2012). Abu Dhabi and Dubai hold the highest power within the federal government; as such all the decisions of the FSC must be approved by their emirs and at least three of the other five emirates. Traditionally, the federal president has always been the leader of Abu Dhabi. Sheikh Khalifa bin Zayed Al Nahyan was elected for a five-year term by the FSC in 2004 (soon after he became the emir of Abu Dhabi).

The UAE has various institutions for the legislative, executive and judicial branches of the federal government; in practice, the ruling families of the larger emirates, particularly Abu Dhabi, influence most of the decisions made at the federal level, with a fairly low level of transparency at times. At the local level also, particularly in the financial institutions (i.e. SWFs), weak transparency of information has been an element of institutional behaviour in the UAE.

Abu Dhabi is the largest emirate, representing 86 per cent of the land area and most of the coastline of the UAE, it produces around 90 per cent of the total oil of the country, and it has been the major financier of the federal budget (Shaheen and Hassan, 2010). The second largest emirate of the UAE, Dubai, accommodates around one third of the population of the UAE in only 5 per cent of the country's land. As its oil production has fallen (since the 1980s) Dubai has started a transition to an economy based on trade and services. Dubai had been moving towards achieving an equal level of financial power to Abu Dhabi. However, the economic crisis in Dubai has changed this equation in favour of Abu Dhabi.

Abu Dhabi's SWFs

The government of Abu Dhabi has the largest SWF of the GCC, through which the emirate invests the surplus crude export income. Such a strategy has protected the Abu Dhabi economy from increasing liquidity (ultimately leading to higher inflation), as well as generating investment returns. Moreover, the emirate's SWFs are set up to support diversification of the economy from the petroleum sector, and national wealth preservation. Abu Dhabi's flourishing economy, like many other GCC countries, is already suffering from double-digit inflation. Therefore, distribution of wealth amongst the citizens in the form of grants, as it traditionally used to be done, is not a feasible option for the government anymore. Instead, the government uses its SWFs to transfer the emirate's crude income to other types of financial assets. The government of Abu Dhabi has particularly focused on diversification of the national economy from the oil sector, via transfer of technological development for the domestic non-oil sector, as one of the core investment strategies for its various SWFs. Such a strategy has been a key characteristic of Abu Dhabi SWFs (and to a greater extent the Dubai SWFs), which differentiates these funds from those of Saudi Arabia and Kuwait, where the major focus is to generate income (for current and future generations) through investments abroad.

As of 2011, the emirate of Abu Dhabi controls six major sovereign wealth management institutions. A summary of these institutions is given in Table 5.1. As is demonstrated in the table, each of these institutions has its own individual investment interest, which varies from private equity and real estate to tourism and the petrochemical industry. However, one major characteristic that all these institutions share is their source of funding. All the government investment vehicles of Abu Dhabi are funded from the emirate's crude export income. Moreover, another major attribute of these organizations is that they are all ultimately seeking a mutual goal, which is to strengthen the emirate's position

Table 5.1 Abu Dhabi main SWFs

Name	Description	Sector focus
ADIA	Largest SWF, invests the Emirate's surplus revenues mainly into financial assets abroad, providing capital diversification for the economy	Multiple sector asset management
Mubadala	Primary business development company of Abu Dhabi. Its mandate is to support economic diversification and development of Abu Dhabi	Oil & Gas, Energy & Industry, Real Estate & Hospitality, Infrastructure, Services, Aerospace, Information, Communication & Technology, Healthcare
Invest AD	Initially part of ADIA, it is now a separate entity, it has a greater focus on investments within the Middle East and North Africa (MENA) region	Private equity, real estate, infrastructure

Source: Field research

in regional and global markets. Finally, these institutions are designed to help diversify Abu Dhabi's economy from the risks posed by volatile oil markets, as well as to secure and maintain the prosperity of Abu Dhabi for future generations.

The ADIA is the oldest institution amongst the major sovereign wealth management vehicles of Abu Dhabi, while Mubadala is the youngest. Although the ADIA and Mubadala have a fundamental difference in the size of their assets, as the ADIA is the largest SWF of Abu Dhabi with estimated total AUM of between US$300 billion and US$800 billion (depending on different estimates at various periods), they share some important characteristics. Both of the organizations have highly diversified portfolios and they have managed to establish their brands as highly prestigious organizations within the global financial world. Both of the institutions are seeking to contribute to the diversification strategy of Abu Dhabi; while the ADIA has remained focused on profit maximization as its major investment policy, Mubadala has been actively engaged in projects that contribute to the social and technological development of Abu Dhabi.

The main focus of this chapter will be on the ADIA and Mubadala, the two highly diversified government investment vehicles of the government of Abu Dhabi. The two organizations have engaged in high profile investments, which have often become a matter of scrutiny in the global financial world. The scale of the activities of the two organizations will provide a good understanding of the emirate's wealth management policies.

The source of government income in Abu Dhabi

More than four fifths of Abu Dhabi's income comes from oil revenue collected by the Abu Dhabi National Oil Company (ADNOC) and the fourteen companies

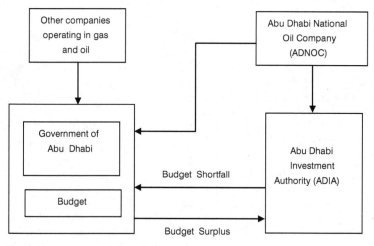

Figure 5.2 Source of funds from the government to ADIA
Source: ADIA Annual Review (2009)

under its umbrella. The company does not publish financial statements, but is estimated to produce just less than three million barrels of crude every day (http:// www.adnoc.ae). Under the terms of concessions that date back to 1978, ADNOC pays US$1 per barrel, regardless of the oil price on the market, to its joint venture partners such as BP, Mitsui, Shell and France's Total. After paying its own costs, ADNOC then pays an undisclosed percentage of its generated income to two of Abu Dhabi's largest funds: the ADIA and the Abu Dhabi Investment Council (ADIC) (Wayne, 2008).

UAE does not have an official wealth saving programme like the one in Kuwait. Therefore, the allocated funds from the surplus oil income to the emirate's sovereign wealth management institutions may vary each year (depending on the crude export income of the respective year). The flow of oil and gas revenues in Abu Dhabi is shown in Figure 5.2. Arnold Wayne wrote in an article published by a local newspaper, *The National*, that 70 per cent of surplus oil revenue is transferred into the ADIA's account. The ADNOC's costs are known to be significantly lower than its royalty and tax earnings. Therefore, up to 95 per cent of the ADNOC's gross revenue is speculated to be surplus. The ADNOC has two affiliate companies; the Abu Dhabi Gas Liquefaction Company (ADGAS) (http://www.adgas.com), which is a joint venture between the ADNOC, Mitsui, BP and Total, and the Abu Dhabi Gas Industries (GASCO), which is another ADNOC's joint venture with Shell and Total (http://www. gasco.ae). The two joint ventures of the ADNOC pay royalties and tax to the government of Abu Dhabi. The payments from the ADGAS and the GASCO therefore contribute to the government's income, in addition to the ADNOC's direct earnings, which are transferred to the government accounts (the ADIA and the ADIC) (Wayne, 2008).

Table 5.2 A summary of ADIA's development history

Year	Event
1967	Creation of Financial Investments Board of Abu Dhabi under the Department of Finance. Under the Mandate of UBS, Robert Fleming, Morgan Guarantee Trust, and Indosuez.
1976	A decision was made by the government to separate ADIA from the government as an independent organisation. The following departments were created within ADIA: Equities and Bonds, Treasury, Finance and Administration, Real Estate, Local and Arab Investments.
1986	ADIA started investing in alternative strategies
1987	Equities and Bonds Departments became regional (North America, Europe and Far East)
1988	Number of employees exceeded 500
1989	ADIA started investing in private equity
1993	ADIA started formal asset allocation process with a set of benchmarks and guidelines, number of employees exceeded 1000
1998	Started investing in inflation-indexed bonds
2005	Dedicated allocation to small caps within equities, and investment-grade credit within fixed income
2007	Started investing in infrastructure sector; moved into new headquarters building

Source: www.adia.ae

Introduction to the ADIA

The ADIA, the largest government investment institution of the government of Abu Dhabi and, by many estimates, the largest CSWF in the world, was established in 1976 and is wholly owned by and subject to supervision by the government of Abu Dhabi. It has an independent legal identity with full capacity to act in fulfilling its statutory mandate and objectives. (Table 5.2 demonstrates some of the major developments in the history of the ADIA.)

Five years after its establishment, the ADIA went through some fundamental changes (under a law known as Law No. 5 of 1981) that defined the roles and responsibilities, ownership and the management of the ADIA. According to the official website of the ADIA, the authority's current constitutive document is Law No. 5 concerning the reorganization of the ADIA. There is no information about how the ADIA's system was different before the ratification of Law No. 5. The authority has been highly secretive about its developments and changes over time; however, the application of Law No. 5 seems to have given the ADIA a higher level of freedom and independence of 'operation' from the government financial system (i.e. the Abu Dhabi Ministry of Finance). That said, the government of Abu Dhabi has closely monitored the ADIA's operation, while maintaining separate accounts for the ADIA and other government accounts (particularly the emirate's budget).

According to the ADIA's 2009 annual report, as a result of the application of Law No. 5: 'ADIA carries out its investment programme independently and without reference to the Government of the Emirate of Abu Dhabi or the Government's other "affiliates" that also invest funds on behalf of the Government of the Emirate of Abu Dhabi' (ADIA, 2009). Moreover, the law has defined the ADIA's objective:

> ...to receive funds from the Government of Abu Dhabi allocated for investment, and invest and reinvest those funds in the public interest of the Emirate in such a way so as to make available the necessary financial resources to secure and maintain the future welfare of the Emirate.
> (International Working Group of Sovereign Wealth Funds, 2008a)

Therefore, the ADIA's assets are invested and managed separately from other government investment vehicles, and the sole strategy of the ADIA is to maximize profit on current and future investment projects in order to secure an avenue of income for the future generations of Abu Dhabi.

Separation of the ADIA from other government investment institutions has provided it with a strong shield from scrutiny and assisted the authority in avoiding public disclosure of information both domestically and internationally (Ghanem, 1992). The government has not set clearly defined regulations for the withdrawals from the ADIA's account. Although the ADIA's charter in principle forbids withdrawals from its account, Abu Dhabi officials acknowledge borrowing from the fund when money is tight.

The ADIA has developed immensely over the years of its operation. Starting a few decades ago from a significantly smaller organization (ADIB), the ADIA has developed into the largest government investment institution of the Gulf. The ADIA has emerged as a major financial player just as Abu Dhabi is racing to become one of the regional energy, tourism and cultural centres. The authority has had a long and prestigious history in the global financial world, which it is likely to maintain for the foreseeable future.

The political controversy over the SWFs triggered by the financial crisis of 2008 encouraged the ADIA to open up to the public. The ADIA's contribution to the establishment of the International Working Group (IWG) of SWFs in partnership with the IMF had been a huge step towards a more transparent operation of the organization. In May 2008, the ADIA agreed to co-chair the IWG along with the IMF. The working group comprised representatives from twenty-six countries, and was created to help providing a better understanding of the SWFs' strategy, frameworks and governance practices, and to confirm that their investments were made only for commercial purposes. The outcome of the IWG's work was twenty-four Generally Accepted Principles and Practices (GAPP) for the operation of the SWFs, also known as the Santiago Principles (the IWG and the international debate over the SWFs will be discussed in detail in the final chapter).

The ADIA signed up to be a full observer of the GAPP; there have been visible impacts on the way in which the ADIA communicates with the outside world. In 2009, the ADIA published its first report in over three decades of operation.

Having said that, the organization has a long way to become a fully transparent SWF yet (like the one owned by the government of Norway).

The size of assets held by the ADIA

The ADIA has been reluctant to disclose information on various aspects of its activities to the public. The authority has avoided any official disclosure of the size of its AUM. Therefore, almost all the available information on the ADIA's assets is based on speculation and guesswork. By the end of the 1990s, the AUM of the ADIA were estimated to be between US$120 and US$150 billion (Richards, 1999). Analysts speculated in 2007 and 2010 that the ADIA's assets amounted to somewhere between US$500 billion (*New York Times*, 2010) and US$1000 billion (Das, 2008). The difference between various estimates for the ADIA's AUM proves that due to a lack of official information, the estimates may be overstated. Rachel Ziemba and Brad Setser, in a study that was conducted in 2009, argued that the size of the ADIA's assets had been overstated, sometimes by as much as 100 per cent. Ziemba and Setser deemed that the ADIA was hit hard by the fall in global equities. Therefore, as many of the same factors that had worked in its favour from 2004 to 2007 (i.e. a high allocation to equities, emerging market and private equity) worked against it in 2008. They estimated that the external assets of the ADIA were likely to be less than US$400 billion (and could be as low as US$300 billion) in 2009 (Setser and Ziemba, 2009). The Sovereign Wealth Institute estimated the ADIA's total assets to stand at about US$627 billion in 2012 (SWF Institute, 2012).

Although, the size of the ADIA's assets is not clearly known, there is no doubt that the ADIA is one of the largest SWFs in the Gulf region. One can find two reasons to justify this assumption. Firstly, Abu Dhabi's oil and gas production has never been interrupted by regional conflicts (Heard, 1999) (which has been the case for Kuwait and Saudi Arabia). Secondly, the ADIA's assets are not used to meet the spending requirements of the government of Abu Dhabi (ADIA, 2009). Although in accordance with Law No. 5, at the time of financial difficulties the ADIA is obliged to provide the government with the necessary financial resources to secure and maintain the welfare of the emirate, the history of Abu Dhabi economic development proves that there have not been many instances in which any major transfer of assets from the ADIA's account has been needed. This has indeed been the opposite to the cases of the KIA and the SAMA (as discussed in the previous chapters).

As noted above, all the available information about the size of the ADIA's assets is based on speculation and educated guesswork. Often there have been enormous differences between various estimates. All the available estimates have been either:

- based on a simple calculation in which the annual government income is calculated as: income = (production * average annual price) – government costs
- or/and, by following up the ADIA's major acquisitions in each year.

The latter is less reliable as the ADIA, like most of the Gulf SWFs, has maintained a strict investment policy of holding small equity stakes to remain below disclosure requirements. Moreover, the ADIA's reliance on external managers makes it more difficult to map all its acquisitions.

All in all, with the oil price standing at about US$100 per barrel, Abu Dhabi is expected to at least produce a US$50 billion surplus every year. Given the emirate's small population, even the most extravagant investment and welfare policies will hardly make any impact on the size of the ADIA's assets (Thomas, 2008). Therefore, in light of the oil prices (between 2008 and 2011), the ADIA has indeed been one of the largest CSWFs in the world.

Governance of the ADIA

The supreme governing body at the ADIA is the board of directors. The board holds ultimate control over all the ADIA's affairs and businesses. It is composed of a chairman, managing director and eight other board members, all of whom are senior government officials appointed by an *amiri* decree for a duration of three years, subject to renewal (Zawya, 2007). The managing director is the chief executive in charge of the ADIA's management affairs and operational decisions. He is responsible for carrying out the strategic policies as well as legally representing the ADIA in its relationships with third parties. The managing director is vested with financial independence and the power to make decisions in respect to investment proposals.

An investment committee (composed mainly of the heads of the several investment departments) provides advice to the managing director with investment proposals put forward by the investing departments. According to the ADIA's 2010 report, the committee has thirteen members (including the chairman and the deputy chairman) and it comprises senior executives from across departments at the ADIA. The investment committee aims to operate in such a way that maintains the ADIA's independence from the government and/or other government investment vehicles in Abu Dhabi (www.adia.ae).

In addition to individuals and committees dealing with the management and investment decision making of the ADIA, the authority has an internal audit department to oversee the operations of various departments and report back to the managing director. The internal audit department evaluates the ADIA's internal control systems to ensure the safety of the assets; it also provides an additional layer of security to ensure all transactions are undertaken in accordance with the ADIA's policies and procedures. ADIA's board of directors also has an audit committee of its own, and appoints two external audit firms to act jointly to audit the ADIA's annual accounts. Both the internal audit department and the external auditors report their findings to the audit committee of the board (ADIA, 2009). In addition to the investment committee, there are other departments whose roles include supporting the managing director (the strategy unit, evaluation and follow up, internal audit and legal departments). The structure proves that the ADIA indeed benefits from being professionally formed.

Table 5.3 Members of ADIA's Board of Directors (as of February 2012)

Name	Position
Sheikh Khalifa bin Zayed Al-Nahyan	Chairman
Sheikh Mohammed bin Zayed Al-Nahyan	Vice chairman
Sheikh Hamed bin Zayed Al-Nahyan	Managing Director
Sheikh Mansour bin Zayed Al-Nahyan	Member of the board
Sheikh Sultan bin Zayed Al-Nahyan	Member of the board
Sheikh Mohammed bin Khalifa bin Zayed Al Nahyan	Member of the board
Mohammed Habroush Al Suwaidi	Member of the board
Dr. Jua'an Salim Al-Dhaheri	Member of the board
Hamad Mohammed Al Hurr Al-Suwaidi	Member of the board
Khalil Mohammed Sharif Foulathi	Member of the board

Source: ADIA Annual Review (2010)

The ADIA has repeatedly alleged that it maintains a high level of independence from the government of Abu Dhabi. However, with more than half of the members of the board of directors being from the Al-Nahyan family, the independence of the ADIA from the government of Abu Dhabi does not seem to be effortlessly fulfilled (see Table 5.3). There is no indication of the track record of the board members on the ADIA's official website; but with a basic internet search one comes to the conclusion that most of the members of the board are key political figures in Abu Dhabi.

The chairman of the ADIA's board of directors (as of February 2012) is the ruler of the emirate of Abu Dhabi, Sheikh Khalifa bin Zayed Al-Nahyan, who is also the president of the UAE. The ADIA's vice chairman, managing director, and three other members of the board are members of the ruling family.

Sheikh Mohammed bin Zayed Al-Nahyan, the crown Prince of Abu Dhabi and Deputy Supreme Commander of the UAE Armed Forces serves as the vice president of the ADIA. In addition to his role at the ADIA, he has also been the chairman of the Abu Dhabi Executive Council, which is responsible for the development and planning of the emirate of Abu Dhabi and is a member of the Supreme Petroleum Council (SPC). Moreover, he serves as a special advisor to the president of the UAE, Sheikh Khalifa, his older brother. Sheikh Mohammad also serves in other official positions, including the head of Abu Dhabi Council for Economic Development, which is the economic policy advisory council in Abu Dhabi, the chairman of the Mubadala Development Company, the head of the UAE Offsets Program Bureau and the head of the Abu Dhabi Education Council.

The next key position at the ADIA is the managing director. Between 1998 and March 2010, Sheikh Ahmed bin Zayed Al-Nahyan, a half-brother of Sheik Khalifa, was the authority's managing director. He died in a plane accident in Morocco in March 2010 (*The Telegraph*, 2010). Less than one month after the death of Sheikh Ahmed, another younger half-brother of Sheikh Khalifa, Sheikh Hamed bin Zayed, was appointed as the managing director of the ADIA. Prior to his appointment, Sheikh Hamed was the head of the Abu Dhabi Crown Prince's Court and the chairman of the Higher Corporation of Specialized Economy Zones (Salama, 2010).

Another member of the board who is also a younger half-brother of Sheikh Khalifa is Sheikh Mansour bin Zayed. He started his political career in 1997 and was first appointed as chairman of the presidential office by his father Sheikh Zayed. After the death of his father, he was appointed as first Minister of Presidential Affairs of the UAE, which was created by merging the Presidential Office and the Presidential Court. He was appointed as Chairman of the Ministerial Council for Services, which is a government entity attached to the cabinet. In addition to this, Sheikh Mansour served in various other high profile government capacities including as the chairman of First Gulf Bank, International Petroleum Investment Company, Abu Dhabi Judicial Department, the National Centre for Documentation and Research, Emirates Foundation, Abu Dhabi Food Control Authority and Abu Dhabi Fund for Development, the vice chairman of the Abu Dhabi Education Council, a member of SPC, and the chairman of the Khalifa bin Zayed Charity Foundation.

Sheikh Sultan bin Zayed Al-Nahyan is the second son of Sheikh Zayed, founder of the UAE, also on the board of directors of the ADIA. Sheikh Sultan started his political career in 1990, and served as Deputy Prime Minister of the UAE until 2009. In addition to that, he has held various other official positions including the President's Representative, the chairman of the Media and Cultural Centre, the Emirate Heritage Club, Zayed Centre for Coordination and Follow-Up, and as a member of the SPC.

Finally, as demonstrated in Table 5.3, another of the ADIA's board members who is also from the Al-Nahyan family is Sheikh Mohamed bin Khalifa Al-Nahyan. Sheikh Mohamed is the son of Sheikh Khalifa the ruler of Abu Dhabi. He has served in other key government positions and is the chairman of the Department of Finance and a member of the Executive Board of Abu Dhabi.

The rest of the members of the board are elected from among the highly influential individuals who are closely linked to Al-Nahyan and, like the rest of the members, have been serving in a number of other high profile positions within the government of Abu Dhabi. Mohammed Habroush Al Suwaidi is a board member of the ADIC, SPC, and Al-Ahlia Insurance Co, and advisor to the president of the UAE. Jua'an Salim Al-Dhaheri is the president of the Abu Dhabi Social Services and Building Department, deputy chairman of the board of National Bank of Abu Dhabi, board member of the SPC, and a member of the Abu Dhabi Executive Council. Hamad Mohammed Al Hurr Al-Suwaidi is a board member and director of the ADIA, a board member of the Mubadala Development Company, the chairman of the Abu Dhabi National Energy Company (TAQA), under-secretary of the Abu Dhabi Finance Department, chairman of the board at Emirates Power Company, director of the board at Oasis International Leasing, the General Industry Corporation, the Health Care Authority, the National Company for Tourism, member of Abu Dhabi Executive Council, member of the board of Union National Bank, Abu Dhabi Water and Electricity Authority, the GIC

Group, and finally a member of the SPC. Khalil Mohammed Sharif Foulathi is the chairman of the Board of the UAE Central Bank.

In addition to the official members of the board, Sheikh Ahmed delegated significant executive power to a French money manager named Jean-Paul Villain. Villian has played a significant role in the investment strategy and asset allocation management of the ADIA. Serving as the head of strategy at the ADIA, Villian is reportedly the most senior foreign-born executive at the authority and was ranked by *Arabian Business* as the third of the fifty most influential expatriates in the Gulf region in 2010. Villian joined the ADIA in 1982 (and has been working for the ADIA since then except for a brief period in the mid-1980s) and gained the trust of the Abu Dhabi ruling family. In addition to his commitments at the ADIA, Villian has also been a board member of the Abu Dhabi Commercial Bank since 2004 and a member of the investment committee of the Abu Dhabi Benefits and Retirement Fund (*Arabian Business*, 2010a).

As discussed above, the largest SWF in the world is managed by the people who are at the top of almost all the key political and economic institutions within the government of Abu Dhabi. All the board members of the ADIA are either members of the SPC or the Al-Nahyan family, or both. Therefore, it is not far from reality to say, 'the ADIA is an investment organization, run by top-ranked politicians'. The close link between the ADIA and Abu Dhabi political elite makes the authority far from being independent from the government, despite what the ADIA's official statements have repeatedly indicated. However, Abu Dhabi government officials have repeatedly emphasised that the ADIA's investments have never been held for non-commercial purposes. In 2008, Abu Dhabi's director of international affairs, Yousef Al-Otaiba, wrote an open letter to the US treasury secretary and other western financial officials, saying: 'it is important to be absolutely clear that the Abu Dhabi Government has never and will never use its investment organizations or individual investments as a foreign policy tool' (*The Economist*, 2008).

The government of Abu Dhabi is trying to turn Abu Dhabi into a regional hub for energy, finance and culture in the Gulf. Such a transition requires the Abu Dhabi's government institutions to have a good track record, as well as the development of various economic sectors. The ADIA has indeed been playing a significant role in this, with some high profile investments in Western financial institutions (mainly since 2008), as well as going into partnership with the IMF in establishing the IWG, both of which may well be motivated by the boost they bring to Abu Dhabi's global reputation. The ADIA has not taken any measures to leverage its financial power for political purposes and it is unlikely to do so, for the foreseeable future. Nonetheless, the strategic decisions through which the ADIA has been aiming to support the government's agenda in building a new identity and credibility at the regional and global level may not have always served the commercial interest of the organization (Clark, 2009). In other words, even though the ADIA's governance is focused on commercial profit maximization, the organization has been actively working in line with the major economic and political strategies of the government of Abu Dhabi.

Table 5.4 The key events in the BCCI scandal

Date		Event
1976		New York regulators rejected the BCCI's offer to buy a New York bank
1978		A US affidavit showing that Bank of America was holding 30% of BCCI's total shares is critical of BCCI's lending
1980		Bank of England rejected BCCI's request for a full UK banking licence
1983		International banking supervisory bodies in Basel were concerned about the BCCI and made arrangements for dealing with anomalies in a responsibility sharing agreement
1985		Treasury fiasco. Auditors failed to uncover the fraud and the Bank of England agreed BCCI's transfer of its treasury from London to Abu Dhabi
1986		Ernest and Young wrote to the BCCI to complain about exclusive management power and the weakness of its systems and controls
1987		Basel supervisors from eight countries created a working group to oversee BCCI
1988		BCCI was indicted for money laundering in Florida
1990		Price Waterhouse uncovered false practices and reported them to the Bank of England. Regulators approved a bail-out from Abu Dhabi to save BCCI from collapsing. US and Luxembourg gave BCCI deadlines to move its operations
1990	March	Bank of England reported that Palestinian terrorist accounts were held by BCCI
	November	Auditors seized files detailing fraud
1991	January	Bank of England reported $600million of unrecorded deposits
	March 4	BCCI commissioned Price Waterhouse report which led to the shutdown in July
	July 5	Shutdown

Source: Mitchell et al. 2001

The Bank of Credit and Commerce International scandal and its impacts on the ADIA

In early 1990s, the UAE experienced a major financial scandal in which the Bank of Credit and Commerce International (BCCI) lost hundreds of millions of dollars (*The Independent*, 1992). The ADIA had a 10 per cent share in BCCI. The scandal caused tremendous financial and reputation damage to the ADIA. The BCCI was a Luxemburg-registered company that was closed down in 1991 due to large-scale financial fraud (see Table 5.4).

The controversy of the BCCI started in the early 1980s, as a result of which BCCI's headquarters was moved from London to Abu Dhabi. In 1990, Sheikh Zayed Al-Nahyan, who was a founding shareholder in BCCI, had purchased

77 per cent of the BCCI's shares and planned to restructure the bank's system. An audit commissioned by the Bank of England alleged major fraud by the BCCI in the same year. The audit triggered the closing of most of the bank's branches worldwide and had important impacts on the UAE financial sector. The BCCI had a £5.6 billion deficit at the time of its closure. It was the 'largest financial fraud of the world' (BBC, 1991) to that date.

The government of Abu Dhabi has always stated that it was a victim of the BCCI fraud, not the perpetrator. However, due to the high involvement of the Abu Dhabi government in the bank's operation, the reputation of the country's banking system suffered from the negative effects of the scandal for some time. In addition to this, as a result of the involvement of influential members of the Al-Nahyan family with the bank, who at the same time held high management positions at the ADIA, the reputation damage of the BCCI outrage was significant on an individual level.

Two key figures involved in the BCCI's operations were a Pakistani banker named Agha Abedi, one of the founders of the BCCI, and Ghanim Al-Mazroui, a UAE citizen, who served as a financial adviser to Sheikh Zayed for more than fifteen years. Al-Mazroui was the secretary general of the ADIA at the time and a member of the board of directors of the BCCI. The two men were heavily involved in creating and managing a network of foundations, corporations and investment vehicles for Abu Dhabi's ruling family (Richards, 1999), while the BCCI acted as a bank to those organizations. The BCCI managed a variety of Abu Dhabi's government portfolio accounts, and provided members of the ruling family with personal services. The bank, therefore, maintained a solid relationship with the government and the ruling family in Abu Dhabi (Davidson, 2005: 23–44).

The Al-Nahyan family became embroiled in regulatory investigations, although no charges were ever brought against them (Thomas, 2008). Twelve executives of the BCCI were sentenced to jail in 1994 (Hauser, 1994). The investigations by the Abu Dhabi government continued after the BCCI was closed down as a result of which Al-Mazroui was arrested and held in custody. He was released soon after that and placed at the head of Abu Dhabi's working group dealing with the BCCI. The appointment of Al-Mazroui with the background of close involvement with the BCCI as the head of the government's working group for investigating the scandal created massive public controversy (Davidson, 2005).

The BCCI scandal affected the strategy and governance of ADIA. The most significant impact of the BCCI experience on ADIA is that the authority's reluctance for sharing information with outsiders has been reinforced. ADIA has never been a fully transparent organization. Nevertheless, Abu Dhabi government's conservative information disclosure strategy may well be a defense mechanism to protect the reputation of the organization and the ruling family at the time of a potential crisis (like the BCCI incident) in the future (Fletcher Research, 2010). Moreover, the monopoly of the ADIA's management by a handful of members of the ruling family and their close allies amongst a limited number of non-family members with a long history of working with the government may well be another effect of the BCCI experience on the governance of the ADIA. Such policies

Table 5.5 ADIA's portfolio* overview by asset class and region (2010)

	Asset Class	Share of the portfolio (%)
Asset Class	Stocks in developed markets	35–45
	Stocks in emerging markets	10–20
	Small-cap stocks	1–5
	Government bonds (fixed income)	10–20
	Credit	5–10
	Alternative investment**	5–10
	Real estate	5–10
	Private equity	2–8
	Infrastructure	1–5
	Cash	0–10
Region	North America	35–50
	Europe	25–35
	Developed Asia	10–20
	Emerging Markets	15–25

* This indicates what ADIA refers to as the 'neutral benchmark' ranges within which allocations can fluctuate; hence they do not total 100%.
** Alternative investment comprises hedge funds and managed funds.

Source: ADIA's review (2010)

may well have been applied in order to avoid assigning high ranked management positions to any outsider who may not act as loyally towards the ADIA as the members of the ruling family or their closest local allies.

The ADIA's investment strategy

According to the ADIA's 2010 annual review, shown in Table 5.5, the highest share of its portfolio is in stocks of developed markets (up to 45 per cent), stocks in emerging markets and government bonds (each up to 20 per cent), cash and credit (each up to 10 per cent). The lowest share of the assets has been allocated to small-cap stocks and infrastructure (each up to 5 per cent).

Investments in each of the above mentioned asset classes are managed by specific departments within the ADIA:

• External and internal equities form the largest share of the ADIA's assets in equities both in developed and emerging markets. These allocations are made either directly (internal equity) or through external managers (external equity). In total, the ADIA operates more than sixty external equity mandates.
• Private equities receive up to a maximum of 8 per cent. The authority's investment in private equity started in 1989 by focusing on investments in

primary funds, secondary and distressed funds and selected co-investments alongside external managers. Generated returns of the ADIA private equity investments are monitored against a group of peers over a trailing six-year period in order to identify and invest in equities, which outperformed over ten years.

- Real estate makes up to 10 per cent of the ADIA's assets. The investments are made through 'a collaborative approach that includes joint ventures with experienced local investors and extensive use of third-party fund managers, whose performance is monitored by ADIA's in-house team' (ADIA, 2010).
- Alternative investments form up to 10 per cent of the ADIA's portfolio. The department of alternative investments at the ADIA has three main asset class focuses: managed future (managed both externally and internally), hedge funds (managed only externally) and commodities (managed only externally) (ADIA, 2010).
- Fixed income and treasury. After equities, the highest share of the ADIA's assets is invested in fixed income instruments (up to 20 per cent). These assets are managed both internally and through external managers. In addition to money markets, the department's investments can be grouped into four broad categories: global government bonds, global inflation-linked bonds, emerging market bonds and global investment-grade credit (ADIA, 2009).
- Infrastructure investments form the smallest share of the ADIA's portfolio (up to 5 per cent). The authority entered the infrastructure market in 2007. As the portfolio overview shows, there is still a relatively cautious approach toward infrastructure investments at the ADIA. The aim of investments in this type of assets is to provide a stream of relatively stable returns and cash flows. Its primary strategy is to acquire minority equity stakes alongside proven partners, with an emphasis on developed markets but an ability to look at emerging markets on an opportunistic basis (ADIA, 2009).

In terms of currency allocation and geographic distribution of the assets, the ADIA has a relatively heavy focus on developed markets. As is shown in Table 5.5, up to 85 per cent of the total assets under the ADIA's management are invested North America and Europe. Investments in Asian and emerging market currencies are growing gradually.

The ADIA's risk framework

Managing risk plays a central role in the ADIA's strategic and day-to-day decision making. Perhaps in the aftermath the financial crisis of 2008, the ADIA, like many other GCC sovereign investment vehicles, has started taking more vigilant actions in terms of risk management and diversification strategies. An investment services department deals with risk monitoring at the ADIA. The managing director carries direct responsibility for risk management (with assistance and advice from various committees within the organization) (ADIA, 2009).

According to the ADIA's annual reports in 2009 and 2010, the risk management system is formed to allow for both pre-trade and post-trade compliance checking and is divided into four main categories:

- Settlement risk: an operations control function designed to identify operational risk. Other measures are also taken such as using only approved brokers and counterparties for trading and breaking up duties across key processing areas.
- Business continuity risk: this includes general awareness and education for staff and all levels of management, as well as the development and regular review of business continuity plans.
- Reputational risk: all of the employees must adhere to the ADIA Code of Ethics and Standards of Professional Conduct, which are designed to help manage potential conflicts of interest and cover several areas, including pre-approval of personal account trading, disclosure of outside business interests, and disclosure of gifts or benefits received. The ADIA subjects employees to rigorous selection criteria, including background checks. Its Code of Ethics and Standards of Professional Conduct is not published on its website; however, from the brief mention of the code and the areas which it covers on the website, it seems to be a standard code of practice that is followed in any given international financial institution. It is worth noting that this study did not find similar codes of conduct in other Gulf SWFs which are reviewed in this book
- Regulatory risk: the ADIA's compliance officers, in-house lawyers and key staff work closely with front office departments to ensure that the ADIA responds to changes in market regulations and legal requirements.

As has been noted above, the global financial crisis of 2008 has increased the ADIA's risk management awareness. This may well be as a result of the rather unsuccessful experience of the ADIA's acquisition of Citibank. The authority has been the only SWF that has made a legal claim on the deal with Citigroup, and has accused it of fraud at the time of the deal. Other SWFs that hold shares in Citigroup reported high returns on their investments. The KIA reported 36.7 per cent return on the recent sale of its US$4.1 billion shares of Citi. The Government of Singapore Investment Corp. also reportedly made a US$1.6 billion profit when it sold about half of its stake in Citigroup after converting its holdings from preferred shares to ordinary shares (Critchlow, 2009). In addition to this, partnership with other SWFs globally in order to diversify the investment risks has been on the ADIA's agenda since before the financial crisis of 2008. In 2006, the ADIA and the Mubadala Development Company agreed to take up joint investment projects with their Singaporean counterpart, Temasek Holdings, 'helping both sides to bring together resources and expertise from all three parties for mutual benefit' (Haider, 2006). All in all, the authority has employed a sophisticated risk management strategy that has significantly developed throughout over three decades of operation.

Invest AD

Invest AD is one of Abu Dhabi's small SWFs and it was established upon ratification of an emiri decree in 1977. The company was established initially under a different name, the Abu Dhabi Investment Company, and was rebranded in 2009. The company gradually developed throughout three decades of actively operating as a government investment company in Abu Dhabi. Invest AD initially operated under the patronage of the ADIA. In 2007, however, it started a new mandate to manage third-party funds in addition to its existing assets, which were entrusted to it by the government of Abu Dhabi. In the same year, the company was removed from the patronage of the ADIA and began to operate under the umbrella of the ADIC. The company is now owned by the ADIC and its strategy is aligned with Abu Dhabi 2030 Vision.

At the time of its transition in 2009, Invest AD was trusted with all the domestic investments of the ADIA. Since then, the ADIA no longer invests locally. In addition to investment within the UAE, Invest AD is actively operating in many countries across the Middle East and North African regions. The company is focusing on three core areas of financial operation: asset management, private equity and proprietary investments. The rebranding of the company was an important step in the development of Invest AD and it reflected the evolution of the company's business model. Invest AD began to offer a new range of services to third-party investors in 2007. Therefore, rebranding was to create a new identity to signal this important change. Nazem Fawwaz Al-Kudsi, the chief executive officer (CEO) of the company, explained the choice of the new brand name as: 'Invest AD was chosen as our new name because it reflects exactly what the company wants to do – attract investment to great opportunities in the Middle East and Africa'(MacDonald, 2011).

Investment strategy of Invest AD

Under its asset management services, Invest AD offers investors access to securities markets across the Middle East and emerging Africa through equity funds and discretionary managed accounts, and also provides sub-advisory services to other fund managers. Asset management at Invest AD operates various funds. Each of these funds has a particular geographic focus for their investment:

1 UAE Total Return Fund: this fund is designed to provide the investors access to leading stocks in the UAE (Invest AD, 2010d).
2 Emerging Africa Fund: this fund invests mostly in equities in Nigeria, Morocco, Egypt, Kenya, Mauritius, Botswana, Ghana, Zambia, Namibia, Tunisia, Algeria, Uganda and Tanzania, as well as equity securities listed on the *Bourse Régionale des Valeurs Mobilières* regional exchange (which includes the equities of companies in Ivory Coast, Benin, Burkina Faso, Guinea Bissau, Mali, Niger, Senegal and Togo). It also invests in other

Table 5.6 Invest AD board of directors

Name	Position
Khalifa M. Al-Kindi	Chairman
Nasser A. Al-Sowaidi	Deputy chairman
Khalifa S. Al-Suwaidi Mohamed Ali A. Al-Dhaheri Khalaf S. Al-Dhaheri Salem M. Al-Ameri Hashem F. Al-Kudsi	Board members
Salem Mohamed Al-Ameri (chairman) Abdirizak Ali Mohamed (member) Clive Gallier (member)	Audit committee

Source: http://www.investad.com/en/article/about-us/board-of-directors.html

equities, including South Africa, as well as those listed on international stock exchanges (Invest AD, 2010a).

3   GCC Focus Fund: this is an investment trust fund, which invests at least 70 per cent of its assets in the equities companies listed in the GCC, or on financial instruments that provide a return on such equities (Invest AD, 2010b).

4   Iraq Opportunity Fund: the fund channels capital into various areas of the Iraqi economy that will benefit from liberalization, government spending on infrastructure and FDI. The banking sector, which is forecast to see strong growth as small- and medium-sized enterprises seek capital growth, is considered as an opportunity by this fund (Invest AD, 2010c).

5   Libya Opportunity Fund: the fund was established to invest in listed Libyan companies, in sectors such as banking, insurance, manufacturing and telecommunications. The fund was suspended as a result of the crisis in Libya in 2011 (Zawya, no date).

Governance of Invest AD

A board of directors is the main governing body of Invest AD (see Table 5.6). Like other government organizations in Abu Dhabi, Invest AD also has a few members from the local families with close links with Al-Nahyan, such as Al-Suweidi and Al-Dhaheri. As of February 2012, the CEO of the company who deals with day to day operations at Invest AD is Nazem Fawwaz Al-Kudsi. Al-Kudsi has worked for the ADIA and various financial institutions globally. Al-Kudsi was also a member of the Water & Electricity Sector Privatization Technical Evaluation Group, playing an important role in Abu Dhabi's early privatization initiatives. Al-Kudsi took the lead at Invest AD in 2008 (Invest AD, no date).

An introduction to the Mubadala Development Company

The Mubadala Development Company is a government-owned investment company that was established in 2002. The company's focus is on long-term and

Table 5.7 An overview of Mubadala Development Company's business units (as of 2010)

Business Unit	Strategy
Oil and gasoil	To leverage technical, commercial and inter-governmental relationships. To expand regional activities. To establish Mubadala as a globally competitive oil and gas, energy and petroleum (E&P) company
Energy and industry	To capitalize Abu Dhabi's natural resources. Development of energy-linked infrastructure (including utilities). To make investments that focus on basic industries. To build an export-oriented industrial sector
Real estate asmd hospitality	To develop residential, commercial and retail real estate and to invest in luxury hospitality sector to increase Abu Dhabi's appeal as travel destination
Infrastructure	To develop, invest in, own and operate concession-based infrastructure (through public, private partnerships (PPPs)), particularly in health and education
Services	To develop new business ventures in services-based sectors (finance, maritime, transportation, defence, and logistic services)
Aerospace	To establish and develop aviation and aerospace industry in Abu Dhabi
Information, communications and technology	To focus on creating an information, communications and technology cluster and establish a local technology footprint
Healthcare	To enhance the private healthcare infrastructure
Key initiatives / investments	To establish Abu Dhabi as one of the leading global centres for renewable energy, (through minority investments and joint ventures, e.g. with GE)

Source: field research communications and interviews

capital-intensive investments that deliver strong financial as well as social benefits for the emirate of Abu Dhabi, through partnerships with global leading companies to facilitate the transfer of knowledge and expertise (Mubadala, 2010). In a message published in Mubadala's 2008 financial statement, Sheikh Mohammad bin Zayed, the chairman of the company, highlighted the role of the company in the diversification of the Abu Dhabi economy 'through the patient and robust support of its shareholder', which means that Mubadala is able to take a long-term perspective in its projects both locally and internationally (Mubadala, 2008).

The word 'Mubadala', which is the Arabic translation of 'exchange', represents the mission of the company well. Mubadala was established to invest in foreign companies in exchange for a transfer of their expertise to Abu Dhabi. Involvement in the social development of Abu Dhabi is a core mandate of Mubadala's institutional strategy. Reflecting the mandate, each investment at Mubadala is required to demonstrate contributions to the economic and social development of Abu Dhabi. Due to the investment mandate of Mubadala for transferring new technology and know-how to further develop the technology sector in Abu Dhabi,

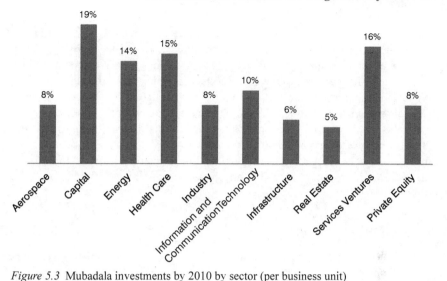

Figure 5.3 Mubadala investments by 2010 by sector (per business unit)
Source: *Mubadala* Annual Report (2010)

the company has a highly diversified portfolio of assets. Various in-house business development units manage Mubadala's assets (see Table 5.7).

Mubadala's investment strategy

The sharp focus of Mubadala on technological advancement and reduction of economic reliance on oil in Abu Dhabi is demonstrated in the company's portfolio of investments. According to Mubadala's 2010 report, over 30 per cent of the company's investments are held in aerospace, health care, information and communication technology, and industry (Mubadala, 2010) (see Figure 5.3). According to Mubadala's 2009 financial statement, the energy, and oil and gas industry assets of the company decreased to 15.5 per cent in 2009 from 23.1 per cent in 2008, 'highlighting *Mubadala*'s commitment to diversifying' (Mubadala, 2009).

Nearly 66 per cent of the assets are invested in the Middle East region (Mubadala, 2010), which is in contrast to some other GCC funds like ADIA and the KIA. Moreover, in the aftermath of the financial crisis of 2008, while some of the Gulf SWFs (such as the KIA and the ADIA) engaged in investments in collapsing Western financial institutions, Mubadala chose a different approach by remaining focused on domestic and regional investments.

As noted above, the social mandates are a significant element of Mubdala's investment strategy. In order to facilitate the transfer of technology to Abu Dhabi, joint venture investments have always been preferred at Mubadala, instead of straight equity purchases. There has, however, been further emphasis on joint venture investments since the financial crisis. This makes Mubadala an active investor, which is able to influence how the businesses are managed (Barbary and Chin, 2009).

By the end of 2010, the real estate sector had the lowest share in the company's investment portfolio (5 per cent). The real estate investment by the Abu Dhabi government investment vehicles (including Mubadala) was driven by the strong government ambition to further develop the real estate sector in competition with Dubai, the leading emirate of the UAE for its real estate and tourism industry until its financial collapse. According to a forecast by the Abu Dhabi Urban Planning Council, there would be a 20 per cent oversupply in real estate market across the asset classes (residential, retail and office) (Abu Dhabi Urban Planning Council, 2010), which would have a significant negative impact on the sale prices and rents in Abu Dhabi. In order to balance the market the government started to decrease the real estate investments and this strategy was mirrored in Mubadala's portfolio of investments.

Governance of Mubadala

Governance and management of Mubadala is, like other government investment engines of Abu Dhabi, dominated by the ruling family. Five out of the seven members of Mubadala's board of directors are also members of the Abu Dhabi Executive Council. The board is chaired by Sheikh Mohammad bin Zayed Al-Nahyan, the crown prince of Abu Dhabi. As of February 2012, two of the board

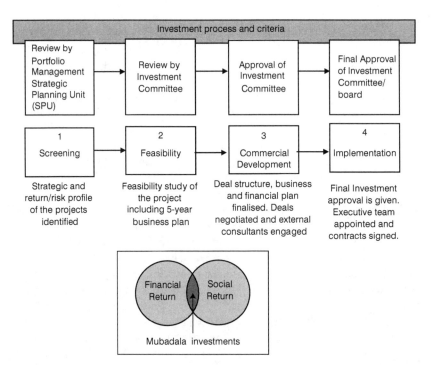

Figure 5.4 Investment process and investment criteria at Mubadala
Source: Field research

members of Mubadala are also on the board of ADIA (Sheikh Mohammad bin Zayed Al-Nahyan and Hamad Al-Hurr Al-Suwaidi). Such appointment can create a higher level of coordination between ADIA, Mubadal, and the government of Abu Dhabi. The company's portfolio includes various high profile strategic assets and projects closely aligned with the government's development strategy and the highly diversified investment strategy of Mubadala is directed by the Abu Dhabi Economic Vision of 2030 (Abu Dhabi Government, 2009).

Mainly Western experts form the middle management team at Mubadala. Various units of the company deal with the specific technical issues of the day to day investment and management operations. Figure 5.4 demonstrates details of the investment decision making procedures at Mubadala.

In the field research of this study, which was undertaken in 2010, Khaldoon Khalifa Al-Mubarak, the CEO and managing director of Mubadala, was repeatedly referred to as the most senior, influential individual who makes most of the company's day to day operational decisions. Like many other senior individuals in the government of Abu Dhabi, Al-Mubarak holds other positions in addition to his role at Mubadala, most important of which is his membership of the executive council.

As of February 2012, he is the chairman of the Abu Dhabi Executive Affairs Authority, which provides strategic policy advice to the chairman of the Abu Dhabi Executive Council, of which he is also a member. In addition to this position, he has held various other senior government positions including chairman of the Emirates Nuclear Energy Corporation, Abu Dhabi Motorsports Management, the Abu Dhabi Media Zone Authority and Emirates Aluminium (EMAL), deputy chairman of the Urban Planning Council, a member of the Abu Dhabi Council for Economic Development and a board member of First Gulf Bank, Ferrari SpA, and ALDAR Properties. Al-Mubarak holds a degree in economics and finance from Tufts University, Boston, USA (Mubadala, 2012).

Historically, the governance and management at Mubadala had strong links with the politics of Abu Dhabi. This is directly as a result of a strong link between the creation of Mubadala and Sheikh Mohammed bin Zayed's offset initiative. Offsets involve a large foreign purchase by a government – the buyer – of which the import price is 'off-set' by the seller. Offsets are a reciprocal agreement between foreign firms and the government of Abu Dhabi, as compensation for large government procurements. Offsets are often associated with arms transfer, thus distinguishing them from the categories above (which tend to embrace commodity or industrial goods) (Nanakorn, 2009: 172). Such a link has made the company a strong tool, both to reshape the political economy of Abu Dhabi and to raise Sheikh Mohammed's influence within Abu Dhabi's political elite.

The role of individuals and the potential for their influence in the governance of Abu Dhabi's government investment institutions is greater than in the other Arab SWF case studies in this book. Often the power struggle between various individuals within the political elite has been mirrored in the arrangement of senior managers in Abu Dhabi's government investment vehicles. A good example of this kind is the ADIA's management reshuffle in April 2010, which mirrors the power struggle between Sheikh Mohammed and Sheikh Khalifa. In the new arrangement of the ADIA's senior management, while Shaikh Khalifa remained in final control of the ADIA, allies of Sheikh Mohammed, as well as himself, were moved into more influential positions. This has been arguably a strategic move by Sheikh Mohammed to balance his power in the ADIA with Sheikh Khalifa's previously undisputed hold.

Emirate Investment Authority

A new sovereign wealth initiative at the federal level in the UAE was announced in late 2007. The new investment institution is called the Emirates Investment Authority (EIA). The organization is responsible for government investments on behalf of the UAE government (in contrast with the ADIA, Mubadala and Invest AD that only manage the assets of the emirate of Abu Dhabi). As noted above, according to the federal law of the UAE, each of the seven members of the UAE is entitled to manage their wealth independently. Abu Dhabi, the most well endowed emirate, has traditionally utilized the surplus oil revenues within the emirate. A small share of Abu Dhabi's wealth has been distributed amongst other emirates through the form of subsidies, extended loans or grants. In order to have a more efficient wealth management system (at the federal level) a federal investment authority has been established. There is very little coverage on the development of this initiative (which to some extent might reflect the tendency to keep the EIA low profile; *Arabian Business*, 2011). But the establishment of a federal fund may well act as a driver for closer federal cooperation and union among the ruling elites of the seven emirates (http://www.eia.gov.ae/index.htm).

The governing body of the EIA is a board of directors with eight members, chaired by Sheikh Mansour bin Zayed Al-Nahyan – who also sits on the board of directors of the ADIA. The headquarters of the EIA are located within walking distance of the ADIA's iconic building in Abu Dhabi. All in all, despite the lack of information revealed about the newly established federal fund, it is most likely that Abu Dhabi, the major financier of the EIA, holds the main share of the organization's control. Table 5.8 presents the EIA senior management team. As shown in Table 5.8, the governance of the EIA is very much dominated by senior individuals from Abu Dhabi and Dubai. It seems that in practice and despite the purpose of establishment of the EIA, which is to incorporate all seven members of the UAE, smaller emirates and less financially privileged ones have not been included much in the management team.

There has been very little media coverage and publicity on the EIA. One commentator, Tristan Cooper, a senior sovereign analyst at Moody's Middle East Ltd was quoted as saying:

> The Emirates Investment Authority is certainly an interesting initiative and symbolizes the drive for closer federal coordination and unity among the upper reaches of government…the UAE federal budget is rather small compared with the overall consolidated fiscal position of the country and it

Table 5.8 EIA's senior management (as of February 2012)

Name	Position at EIA	Other positions
Sheikh Mansour bin Zayed Al-Nahyan	Chairman	Board Member and Director of ADIA/ Chairman of the International Petroleum Investment Company (also manages the Falah Fund)/ Minister of Presidential Affairs for President Sheikh Khalifa bin Zayed Al-Nahyan in the UAE Federal Cabinet/ Chairman of the First Gulf Bank/ Member of the Board of Trustees of the Zayed Charitable Humanitarian Foundation/Chairman of the Emirates Horse Racing Authority
Mohammad Abdullah Al-Gergawi	Deputy Chairman	Minister of State for Cabinet Affairs
Rashid Mubarak Al-Mansouri	Chief Executive Officer	Board member of Central Bank of the UAE, Abu Dhabi National Company for Building Materials, Emirates Telecommunication Corporation, and Arab International Bank
Khadem Al-Qubaisi	Board Member	Board Member of the First Energy Bank / Managing Director for the International Petroleum Investment/ Chairman of Tabreed/ Chairman of Aabar Investments PJSC
Soud Ba'alawy	Board Member	Executive Chairman of the Dubai Group
Abdul Hamid Saeed	Board Member	Chairman of Assel Finance/ Board member of First Gulf Bank
Hashim Al-Dabl	Board Member	CEO of Dubai Properties/ Board member of Dubai Holding
Eisa Al-Suwaidi	Board Member	Director for Far East Equities at ADIA/ Director of Abu Dhabi National Oil Company for Distribution/ Chairman of Arab Banking Corporation – Egypt/ Director of Arab Banking Corporation/ Board member of the International Petroleum Investment Company

Source: www.taighde.com

Table 5.9 Development timeline at the EIA (as of February 2012)

Date	Timeline
November 13, 2007	Emirates Investment Authority created by Royal decree
January 9, 2008	Board of Directors appointed
March 23, 2008	First Board of Directors meeting held
June 1, 2008	Second Board meeting held and Rashid Mubarak Al-Mansouri appointed as CEO
July 21, 2008	First investment with a bond sale by First Gulf Bank

Source: www.taighde.com

tends to be close to balance from year to year...unless significant amounts of extra revenue are injected into the federal budget by individual emirates or assets are transferred from existing funds such as ADIA, it is difficult to see how the EIA will build up substantial amounts of cash for investment over the short to medium term.

(Sleima, 2007)

As noted, there has not been significant news coverage on the EIA since it was established in 2007 – a conscious decision by the UAE authorities to keep the investments of the EIA low key. Table 5.9 gives a timeline for the institutional progress of the EIA. There is not much information on investment activity of the fund. In 2011, Paul Oliver, the head of financing at the EIA told *Arabian Business* that the fund is looking to invest in opportunities that help the government of the UAE in 'creating a financial services hub in the UAE, and clearly healthcare, education, food in the broader sense like processing' (*Arabian Business*, 2011). All in all, the EIA seems to be rather in line with the overall UAE federal government development vision, focusing on the financial, health care and education sectors. As discussed in detail above, Mubadala is a great example of the government's emphasis on development of these sectors in Abu Dhabi. Therefore, the replication of a similar investment interest at the EIA highlights the federal government's effort to create a cohesive development strategy across the country that can include the less financially privileged and smaller emirates.

An introduction to Dubai's sovereign wealth investment institutions

Similar to Abu Dhabi, the government of Dubai has established various investment institutions. These investment vehicles have heavily relied on borrowing and leverage, and they are not fully financed from commodity income surpluses like the SWFs of Abu Dhabi. For that reason one may argue that these funds may not fit well into the definition of commodity-based SWFs. This book, however, considers these institutions as SWFs for the following reasons:

1   As defined in the previous chapters, the major source of financing the investments of the SWFs is commodity export income. Although the government of Dubai has used leverage for financing their SWFs over the past decade, the early source of wealth for the government of Dubai, as well as the primary source of funds for these investment vehicles, has been oil revenue. As shown in Figure 5.1, oil production in Dubai started in late 1960s and it had significantly increased through 1970s and early 1980s forming the main source of the government's key income for financing the development projects, which led to establishment of the government investment vehicles of Dubai.

2   Based on the definition of SWFs in this book, the CSWFs (like the KIA and the ADIA) were established to save the country's wealth for future generations. Dubai's government investment institutions have also been established to

generate revenue for the years to come after the end of oil production (which has evidently arrived much earlier than in other oil-rich countries of the Gulf, such as Kuwait and neighbouring emirate of Abu Dhabi).

3   Another aim of some (commodity-based) SWFs, such as Mubadala, has been to help the national economy to diversify from the oil sector. Dubai's state-owned investment institutions have contributed heavily in the diversification process of Dubai's economy (which is demonstrated in their highly diversified investment portfolios).

Another reason for reviewing Dubai SWFs in this chapter is to highlight the ways in which the national wealth has been managed in Dubai, in comparison with what is practiced by the government of Abu Dhabi. As has been discussed above, the emirate of Abu Dhabi plays an important role in the federal government of the UAE. Dubai is the single competitor with Abu Dhabi in both political and economic contexts. Exploring Dubai government-owned investment institutions gives a clearer outlook for the future role of both Abu Dhabi's and Dubai's SWFs in the economic development of the UAE, at a local, regional and international level. Moreover, studying Dubai's sovereign wealth investment engines also underlines the differences between the two emirates in various aspects including the visions of the rulers, the management style of the local elite, business culture, and sectoral focus.

Because of Dubai's limited oil resources, the government of Dubai has opened the economy to inflow of investments (internationally) and has pursued a leverage-led growth model. Dubai's vision for establishing a globally known brand name has focused on the development of the various sectors of Dubai's economy, including services, tourism, real estate and banking. Most of these development projects were financed by heavy foreign borrowings. Dubai's government investment institutions comprise several companies with highly diversified portfolios, from real estate to ship repair and marine-related activities. In this section, three major Dubai government investment funds will be reviewed: Dubai World, Dubai Holding, and the Investment Corporation of Dubai (ICD).

Dubai World

Dubai World was launched in 2006. The company is a conglomerate with a highly diversified portfolio of investments, which owns various enterprises across sectors including transport, finance and investment, maritime and shipbuilding, and real estate internationally. Dubai Ports World is one of the companies forming Dubai World's investment portfolio. It is one of the largest marine terminal operators in the world and was established through the merger of the UAE-based Dubai Ports Authority with Dubai Ports International in September 2005 (http://webapps. dpworld.com/portal/page/portal/DP_WORLD_WEBSITE). Another company that is included in Dubai World's portfolio is Economic Zones World (EZW). It is a developer and operator of economic zones, technology, logistics and industrial parks (http://www.ezw.ae/). Istithmar World is a private equity firm that is also part of the investment portfolio of Dubai World and it was founded in 2003. Its activities include various investments including those in the financial services, industrial and real estate sectors through a number of investment methods including majority and minority stakes, joint ventures, listed equities and debt securities (http://www.istithmarworld.com/). Drydocks World, which is a ship repair, vessel conversion and offshore constructions company, is also a part of Dubai World's investment projects, with branches in Indonesia, Singapore, Scandinavia and Japan (http://www.drydocks.gov.ae/en/default.aspx). Finally, Dubai Maritime City is a Dubai World investment initiative, a man-made island that is to become a multipurpose maritime centre to create a newly designed environment for the global maritime community (http://www.dubaimaritimecity.com/).

In addition to the projects mentioned above, Dubai World had a number of other business ventures that had to be restructured after the financial crisis. Nakheel was a real estate company, engaging in development projects in the residential, retail, commercial and leisure sectors inside the UAE. Nakheel World was established in 2006. The company went through a massive recapitalization in the aftermath of Dubai's financial crisis (http://www.nakheel.com/en). In May 2011, *Arabian Business* reported that Nakheel 'will be carved out of parent company Dubai World and become a government-owned entity by June' 2011, after its programme for restructuring U$10.8 billion debt is complete. The company was at the heart of Dubai World's debt problem, which started in November 2009. 'Nakheel's inability to meet its obligations, in the wake of a property collapse and the global credit crunch, left it with billions of dirhams in unpaid bills to contractors and suppliers' (Bladd, 2011). Limitless, also a real estate developer, which was established in 2005 and had projects in the UAE as well as a number of other countries in the Middle East and Asia, including Hong Kong, Vietnam, Saudi Arabia, Jordan and Russia (http://www.limitless.com/en-GB/home.aspx) was a part of Dubai World's investment portfolio. In July 2011, however, *Arabian Times* reported that Limitless was excluded from Dubai World's restructuring plan. The company was a vehicle for most of Dubai World's overseas property investments and it has 'rolled over a US$1.2 billion loan owed to one syndicate of banks several times'(*Arabian Times*, 2011).

Dubai World has been one of the most indebted and problematic government investment institutions of Dubai, which went through organization restructuring. One of the most important initiatives for restructuring Dubai World was the reshuffle of the senior management team, particularly the change of the company's chairman. Dubai World had been managed since its establishment in 2006 by Sultan Ahmed bin Sulayem, one of Sheikh Mohammed bin Rashid's (the ruler of Dubai) closest allies. Upon the financial breakdown of the company, Sheikh Mohammed issued a decree on 12 December 2010 restructuring the board of directors of Dubai World, and appointed his uncle, Sheikh Ahmed bin Saeed Al-Maktoom, to the chairmanship of the company. Sheikh Ahmad had managed Emirate Airline for many years and had a proven, prominent track record in Dubai's government-owned businesses. In addition to these positions he is also the president of Dubai Civil Aviation and chairman of the Higher Committee that oversees Dubai World.

In addition to appointing the new board member, the decree of the ruler of Dubai on 12 December 2010 stated that the board of directors will

> ... study the reports submitted to it on the activities of the Dubai World and its subsidiaries, and their financial positions and will take appropriate action. The jurisdiction of the Board also includes the approval of plans restructuring the company and its subsidiaries and to decide the draft annual budget and final accounts, in addition to the ratification of financing operations and borrowing from financial institutions against financial guarantees to them. The Board will also approve the sale, purchase and leasing of real estates, stocks, bonds, other securities and other property belonging to the institution or its affiliates. The Board will also propose the formation of corporate boards of the subsidiary firms, and the appointment of auditors for the Dubai World and its subsidiaries. The decree stipulated that the Board shall hold its meetings at the invitation of the chairman once at least every two months and whenever the need arises.
>
> (http://www.dubaiworld.ae/board-of-directors/)

The statement quoted above from the official website of Dubai World shows that the company has indeed learned from its past mistakes and is taking restrictive and monitoring measures that will minimize the risk of the similar crises. Moreover, the restructuring of Dubai World's senior management and the tighter control of the board members on investment activities of the company, defined in Sheikh Mohammad's decree, proves that company is heading towards becoming a more conservative investor than it was before 2009. A more cautious investment strategy will be applied in Dubai World in order to recover from the financial and reputational damages to Dubai. Also, the appointment of Sheikh Ahmed as the chairman of Dubai World is a sign of the ruling family's strong will to take control of the company in the future, in order to avoid similar circumstances.

Dubai Holding

Dubai Holding is a government investment vehicle in Dubai focusing on a number of investment verticals including the property, business parks, hospitality and financial sectors. There is no reliable data on the actual size of the total AUM for the holding, which is believed to be essentially in the private ownership of Sheikh Mohammad bin Rashid, Dubai's ruler (Woertz, 2011: 151). The chairman of Dubai Holding is Mohammad Al-Gergawi, minister of cabinet affairs for the federal government of the UAE. Below, the four main investment verticals of Dubai Holding are reviewed:

1 Hospitality: Jumeirah Group is a hospitality company, which became a member of the holding in 2004 and is a main pillar of Dubai Holding investments in the hospitality sector (http://www.jumeirah.com/en/Jumeirah-Group/About-Jumeirah-Group/Portfolio/).

2   Business Parks: TECOM Investments is the spearhead of the holding in its business park vertical. It is active in media, education, life sciences and clean technology (http://www.tecom.ae).
3   Investment: Dubai Group and Dubai International Capital (DIC) are the two companies that form the investment vertical of Dubai Holding. Both companies are leading institutions in financial services (http://www.dubaigroup.com/aboutus/default_en_gb.aspx).
4   Property: Dubai Properties Group (DPG) is a property development and property management company comprising Dubai Holding's property vertical (http://dubaipropertiesgroup.ae).

Investment Corporation of Dubai

The Investment Corporation of Dubai (ICD) is a major investment institution of government of Dubai and was established in 2006. The ICD has a highly diversified portfolio comprising investments in the financial, transportation, utilities and energy, industrial and real estate sectors. As of February 2012, one third of the companies in which the ICD holds investments (roughly thirty companies in total) is in the financial sector and only one company is in the energy sector (Emirate National Oil Company). The company is heavily involved in investments in industrial sector: it has six industrial companies in aluminium production, engineering, mineral water production and cold store. Members of the ruling family dominate the senior management of the ICD. Four out of six members of the board of directors of the ICD are from Al-Maktoum and company's chairman is Sheikh Mohammad bin Rashid Al-Maktoum, the leader of Dubai.

Having reviewed the SWFs of Abu Dhabi and those owned by the government of Dubai, one could easily find some similarities and differences between the SWFs of the two emirates. The major difference between the SWFs of Dubai and those of Abu Dhabi is in their source of capital. As noted above, the government of Dubai has mainly relied on leverage to finance the sovereign wealth investment institutions, while Abu Dhabi government-owned investment funds are exclusively managing surplus oil incomes. A key similarity between the government-owned investment institutions of Dubai and those of Abu Dhabi lies in their investment strategies. Both emirates own CSWFs with highly diversified, often ambitious portfolios of investments. A key mission for the government-owned investment funds of both emirates is to support the economic development and diversification policies of the government.

Another key factor in common between the government investment institutions of Dubai and those of Abu Dhabi is their similar governance and management patterns. A majority of senior management and key positions in Dubai SWFs are allocated to individuals from the ruling family or those who have a close personal relationship with them. However, in contrast with Abu Dhabi government organizations, where almost all the board seats and chairmanship positions are held by the ruling family members, the number of senior managers and board members in Dubai SWFs who are not from Al-Maktoum family members is relatively high.

The financial crisis and the Dubai government's investment vehicles

The impact of the 2008 global financial crisis on Dubai government-owned business entities has been huge. Given the leverage-led growth of Dubai SWFs, the business model that has been followed by Dubai conglomerates to some extent brings back the memory of what had been practiced by the Korean *Chaebols* before the financial crisis of 1997. In both cases, high levels of foreign borrowing coupled with aggressive investment regimes in extremely diversified portfolios of assets led to a financial crisis. In addition to the foreign borrowing and diversified, often risky, investments, Dubai's government enterprises' heavy involvement in the domestic real estate market has caused major damage to these organizations. At the peak of the crisis when the expatriate labour that created the real estate bubble in the city of Dubai started to fly out of the country due to the high number of jobs being lost, the propery bubble burst. This has caused a sharp decline in demand for housing, and ultimately led to massive losses in the real portfolio value of Dubai SWF's real estate investments.

The global financial crisis has in many ways affected institutional investors around the world. Reviewing the commodity-related funds in the previous chapters of this book shows that the CSWFs have more or less been forced by the crisis to shift away from risky investments in Western banks and businesses, in order to focus on their domestic economies (to support local banks and businesses), while in Dubai most of the state-owned investment engines have been rather active locally since before the crisis. In other words, Dubai SWFs were at the heart of the domestic economy at the time of the crisis. This is in contrast with other SWFs, which held the majority of their assets outside their country of origin and were able to transfer some of those assets to support the domestic economy in the aftermath of the crisis. Moreover, CSWFs have suffered from losses on both their investments and their oil incomes, as a result of the decline in the price of oil. However, there was a constant inflow of capital into their accounts from oil exports. Given the reliance of Dubai SWFs on leverage, a major struggle for Dubai state-owned businesses after the crisis was to attract foreign investors to refinance their portfolio (in the absence of oil income).

After the collapse of some of Dubai's SWFs, the government has taken various steps in stabilizing the economy including creating a financial support fund for state-linked businesses. In order to finance this fund, US$10 billion was borrowed from the UAE Central Bank as part of a broader US$20 billion bond programme. It was planned to use the borrowed cash to help companies owned or linked to the government to refinance debts and settle the bills, as well as to push the maturity of the debt further away, and buy more time (Kerr et al., 2010).

The government of Dubai was prompted to provide financial support to the state-owned entities through borrowing, while facilitating reforms to protect the long-term viability of those entities. The establishment of this fund will be an important step towards bringing stability and confidence to the revised business plans of the government, particularly in the real estate sector. In addition to the newly established governmental financial support fund, some state entities have attempted to borrow from foreign institutions. Since the crisis struck, for example, the ICD has been able to raise US$6 billion from international banks (Kerr, 2009).

Accumulation of massive debt by Dubai conglomerates has highlighted the necessity of changes in the operation of Dubai SWEs, particularly in their investment strategy. Some of the state-owned investors have already responded to this need by a shift in asset management and investment strategy in the aftermath of the recent crisis. In September 2008, when the crisis peaked in equity markets globally, the Dubai Group announced that it would focus on financial assets in equity and insurance markets globally (Franco, 2008). Moreover, the government of Dubai has been seeking to streamline its commercial assets to reduce costs in response to the global economic downturn. The restructuring plan has become the core of the post-crisis cost efficiency policies of the government. Deep staff cuts have taken place in most of the government-related entities, particularly in Dubai Holding (Kerr and Khalaf, 2009).

The crisis has affected the relationship between Dubai and Abu Dhabi. Abu Dhabi's assistance for paying Dubai's massive debt strengthened the role of Abu Dhabi in the balance of economic power within the UAE. Dubai's debt was not payable neither by the inflow of the emirate's oil income nor foreign borrowing. Instead, the neighbouring emirate was called upon for a rescue package. Abu Dhabi's financial support of Dubai imposed extremely high reputational costs on the government of Dubai. Over the night, the iconic 828 metre (previously named) Burj Dubai, which was the flagship of the growth and success of the emirate, showing off in the skyline of the city of Dubai, was renamed Burj Khalifa (after the ruler of Abu Dhabi) as a sign of appreciation for the generous support of the government of Abu Dhabi in restructuring Dubai's debt.

All in all, the leveraged-led growth model of Dubai has slowed down significantly since the 2008 global financial crisis. Even though some of the Dubai government investment entities have ended up in massive debt and organizational restructuring, they have been the main engines of Dubai's development and they are likely to remain powerful economic pillars in the emirate in the future. Being the main economic and political competitor to Dubai, Abu Dhabi has in many ways won the power struggle within the UAE after the financial collapse of the Dubai government entities. This may well extend the process of recovery in Dubai from a political point of view.

Conclusion

Being the major oil producer of the UAE, Abu Dhabi has become the financial engine of the country. For many decades Abu Dhabi has played a key role in providing the federal government's budget. The emirate created a number of sovereign wealth investment institutions to manage the surplus oil revenue. The largest sovereign wealth fund of the UAE, and by some estimates the largest one in the world, the ADIA, has been the front-runner of these organizations, followed by Mubadala and Investment AD. Each of these investment institutes has an individual investment mandate and operation strategy. The ADIA has been actively focusing on international investments seeking high return; Mubadala has been investing domestically to support technological advancement of Abu Dhabi; and Invest AD has a more regional focus in the Middle East and North Africa.

All the sovereign wealth management institutions of Abu Dhabi are managed directly by members of the ruling family and individuals with close links to the ruling family. The close links between domestic politicians and those who are running the emirate's investment institutes (seeking commercial profit) is why the issue of transparency of operation and governance of these organizations has been controversial. The government of Abu Dhabi has become an active collaborator of the international initiative to promote transparency of SWFs that was launched in 2008. As a result of this contribution public disclosure of information by Abu Dhabi funds has improved significantly since 2009.

The next wealthiest emirate of the UAE is Dubai, and in this chapter we have seen that the government of Dubai has applied a different economic model from that of Abu Dhabi. Even though the basis of Dubai wealth was oil income, the emirate applied a heavy foreign borrowing strategy in order to promote economic growth and establish Dubai as a successful and globally known brand name to attract foreign investments. The global financial crisis, however, had a significant impact on Dubai, leading to massive losses by major government investment institutions. The government of Abu Dhabi stepped in to bail out the Dubai sovereign wealth management institutions. The intervention of the government of Abu Dhabi has further strengthened the position of Abu Dhabi in the political and financial balance of power within the UAE. Dubai's experience of sovereign wealth management has not been as successful as its neighbouring emirate.

The debate over transparency of operation of Dubai sovereign wealth management organizations in the emirates financial breakdown has been intense. Often the governments of the GCC countries have failed to draw a distinct line between the private wealth of the ruling elite and the national wealth. In the aftermath of the crisis, some of the SWFs of both Dubai and Abu Dhabi have shown improvement in the level of information shared with the public. Some of these organizations released their first ever published annual report in the years immediately after the crisis (2009–10).

The UAE federal government has initiated the creation of a federal SWF that is capable of harmonizing the UAE financial policies. In contrast with Dubai and Abu Dhabi SWFs, the activity of the federal government's SWF has kept a very low profile and there has not been much publicity and public disclosure of information of the EIA's operations.

Dubai and Abu Dhabi sovereign wealth management organizations have played a significant role in the domestic social and economic development of their emirates while creating an international reputation as a safe haven for foreign investments. Given the massive crude resources, the country is expected to further develop, while the engine for development (at the federal level) will be Abu Dhabi (where there is the highest concentration of natural resources across the country).

The ruling families (in Dubai and Abu Dhabi) will continue to hold the ultimate power in the management of the country's SWFs (both at local and federal levels) while the smaller emirates will expect to receive more generous financial packages from the two richest emirates in the UAE.

6   Iran's experience of sovereign wealth management

Introduction

Like other oil-rich economies of the region, Iran has remained dependent on crude export income to finance the government expenditures (Economist Intelligence Unit, 2012). In contrast with other countries of the Gulf region, the Iranian government is not an active international investor. While Iran's neighbours in the Gulf have invested a significant share of their oil revenue in various asset classes internationally, Iran has chosen to direct a major share of the country's oil wealth domestically. Such a policy choice has aimed to boost non-oil growth in the public and private sectors. In practice, however, these investments have not been efficient and the contribution of the non-oil sector in Iran's economic growth has not shown significant improvement over the last two decades. High government expenditure on food and energy subsidies, and the limited flow of foreign direct investments as a result of the economic sanctions on Iran, have also had a negative impact on the country's non-oil GDP growth and the country has remained heavily reliant on oil revenue

Between 1948 and 1979, a large share of the government's oil income was spent locally on infrastructure and development projects. Following the Islamic revolution, the country then went through eight years of devastating war between 1980 and 1988 and, during this period, a major share of oil income was spent on covering the costs of war. As a result, most of the development projects were abandoned. In the aftermath of the war the reconstruction and development projects were restarted, which absorbed a considerable share of oil income while the rest was used to finance the government budget deficit that had been accumulated during the war. During the post-war reconstruction period, oil price fluctuation was a key challenge for the government. As such reconstruction and development projects were affected by the oil price changes and any price decrease caused delays in the progress of those projects. In order to protect the country from the volatility of the oil markets, the government's third economic development plan proposed the establishment of an Iran Foreign Exchange Saving Account (IFESA).

The IFESA was created in 1999 at the beginning of the former president Seyed Mohmmad Khatami's second term in office. In his keynote speech in the parliament (Majlis), Mr Khatami told the Iranian members of parliament (MPs), who were about to give their votes of confidence to his proposed cabinet, that over the past few years he and the minister of finance had been 'extremely worried about the country's financial affairs and could not sleep at night as the country only had enough wheat reserves for domestic consumption for three days due to lack of sufficient foreign reserves' (Iran newspaper, 2001). The IFESA, which was established as an oil stabilization fund, therefore represented what was historically one of the important steps to have been taken by the Iranian government to manage the country's oil revenues since the discovery of oil in the country.

Compared with its neighbours in the Gulf, Iran had lagged behind in the establishment of an oil stabilization fund. As noted in previous chapters, some of the largest CSWFs of the Gulf were created three to five decades earlier than Iran's IFESA. Iran's oil revenue management policies have, however, been affected by one key factor: the country's large population. In this respect there has been some similarity to Saudi Arabia, which has the largest Arab population of the Gulf. However, the Saudi government has maintained a strong political and financial relationship with the West, particularly the US, while Iran–US relations were effectively ended in the aftermath of the Islamic Revolution. Therefore, Iran started its sovereign wealth management policies not only with decades of delay compared with its Arab counterparts in the Gulf, but with the management policies of its SWF's heavily influenced by its political relationship with the Western world, which limited Iran's access to the global financial systems and restricted Iran's sovereign wealth management in the global markets.

Iran's IFESA has mainly applied an inward-looking investment policy, details of which are discussed later in this chapter. It has sought to protect the Iranian economy against the fluctuations in oil prices (like all the SWFs of the GCC) and to promote production and growth domestically (similar to some of the SWFs of the UAE). The key difference between the IFESA and the SWFs of the Arab countries of the Gulf lies in its international investment activities. The IFESA has not been active in the international financial system as its counterparts in the Gulf have been, mainly due to Iranian economy's significant absorptive capacity, lack of access to international creditors, large domestic capital demand and high government expenditure (including food and energy subsidies) and international financial sanctions led by the West.

The Iranian government established a new SWF, called the National Development Fund (NDF), in 2011 to replace the IFESA. The NDF holds all the assets that were previously managed by the IFESA. Details of the Fund's institutional organization, governance, asset management and savings policy are reviewed at the end of this chapter.

The financial relationship between the government and the National Iranian Oil Company

Before the Islamic Revolution

Prior to the revolution in 1979, the National Iranian Oil Company (NIOC) was the main institution responsible for managing the oil sector in Iran on behalf of the government. All offshore and onshore operations were carried out either by the NIOC directly or by other companies contracted by the NIOC, and the revenue generated from oil exports was paid to the company. The NIOC was also in charge of managing the financing of the oil sector's development projects and production facilities. The government was the major shareholder of the NIOC and received some of the oil income in the form of shareholder's interest. Another form of contribution by the NIOC to the state's revenues was by paying tax to the government. In addition to the income from oil exports, the company generated revenue by collecting concession fees and royalties from the foreign companies operating in Iran's oil sector. One per cent of all concessions and royalties were saved in the NIOC's account while the rest was paid to the government (Moini and Haji Mirzaee, 2005).

1979–2000

In the aftermath of the revolution, the Revolution Council changed the relationship between the government and the NIOC. All foreign companies were forced to leave the country and the concession fees were abolished. All export revenues during this period were paid directly to the government as well as all the domestic crude sale income. Therefore, the only source of income for the NIOC was income generated from selling refined product in the domestic markets. This caused a major budget deficit for the NIOC. To reduce the company's massive budget deficit, since 1987 the NIOC has been permitted to export 200,000 barrel of crude oil per day to cover its expenses (in addition to collecting generated incomes from selling refined products domestically) (Majlis Research Centre, 2009b).

2000–2004

The third government economic development plan authorized the NIOC to receive the revenues generated in the domestic markets from crude oil sales, as well as income generated from selling offshore and refined oil and gas products in the domestic markets, while the government collected the export revenues. The aim of this exercise was to increase crude production capacity and to boost export income for the government. However, increased local automotive production meant that domestic oil consumption and imports of refined products also increased; thus, not only did oil exports not increase but aggregate exports also declined because the allocation of a large share of the crude production was exchanged with refined products from other countries.

2004–2009

The fourth government economic development plan, which began in 2004, redefined the relationship between the government and the NIOC. The income generated from selling 6 per cent of land-based oil exports and 11 per cent of oil exports transported by sea was allocated to the NIOC. In addition, the government was authorized by the Majlis to allocate additional funds to the NIOC from the assets held in reserve to cover the company's budget deficit (Majlis Research Centre, 2009b).

After the revolution of 1979, the government changed the relationship between the NIOC and the ministry of petroleum, although the structure of this change has not been clear. In January 2012, the senior inspector for oil affairs at the Iranian general inspection authority (*Sazaman-i Bazrasi Kul-i Kishvar*), which is a government regulatory body, told Bazar Khabar (one of the largest financial news agencies in Iran) that there had been a loophole in the legislation and clarification of oil affairs had been a challenge for the parliament for over three decades. One of the key criticisms of the NIOC, made by the MPs, concerned the lack of transparency in the company's financial operations. Pricing methods and the NIOC's total income have not been clearly stated in the annual budgets and this has been a matter of controversy between the NIOC and the Supreme Audit Court (Khabar Bazar, 2012). In 2011, the IMF published a report, which included a diagram to explain the flow of oil and gas income in the Iranian economy (Figure 6.1) that clarified the flow of capital earned from oil and gas exports, but did not give further information on the NIOC's financial relationship with the government.

The IFESA

Iran's SWF, the IFESA, was established in 1999. Shortly after the establishment of the SWF, the country's oil income started to surge, thanks to the crude markets. The government's oil income increased significantly between 2000 and 2004. Actual oil income increased from 5 per cent above the estimated level in 2000, to 44 per in 2004 (Majlis Research Centre, 2005a). The increase in oil price encouraged the government to commit to saving all the surplus incomes (what was earned above the estimated levels) in the IFESA throughout the third economic development plan (2000–2004). According to MRC report, the government set three main aims for its saving strategy: firstly, to protect the country against oil shocks; secondly, to reduce the government's reliance on oil incomes; and thirdly, to support and strengthen (non-oil) private sector growth (Majlis Research Centre, 2005a).

The fourth economic development plan (2005–2010) included a clearer government saving policy which was more consistent in comparison with the third economic development plan. The role of IFESA was highlighted further by the fourth government development plan. As such article 1 of the plan defined the functions of the IFESA as follows:

- From 2005 until the end of the fourth development plan, total surplus oil income will be kept in the IFESA.
- At the time of a budget deficit, the government is allowed to use the assets of this account only if the oil export income drops below the estimated levels of each annual budget.
- The government is not allowed to use the assets of the IFESA to finance non-oil budget deficits.

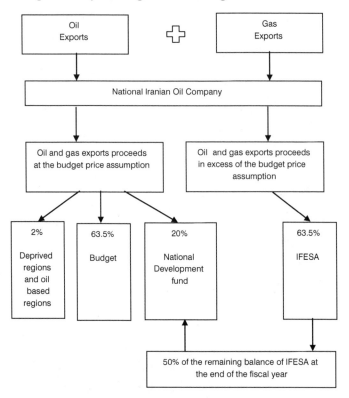

Figure 6.1 Distribution of Iran's oil revenue (as of 2011)
Source: IMF (2011), Country Report 11/241

- The government is allowed to invest a maximum of 50 per cent of the assets of the IFESA in development projects in the industrial, mineral, agriculture, transport services (including tourism), and information technology sectors. The investments must take the form of loans that are extended through national and foreign banks after sound reviews and a risk analysis by their respective ministries, in order to prove the profitability of the projects.
- A minimum of 10 per cent of the assets of this account must be allocated to private projects in the agriculture sector. These assets will be transferred to the Agriculture Bank to be distributed in the form of loans to agricultural projects aimed at promoting agricultural exports.
- Should the government use the assets of the account, all transactions must be stated in the annual budgets.
- All decisions concerning the operation of this account must be proposed by the organization of planning and budget, the central bank, the ministry of finance and approved by the cabinet (Majlis Research Centre, 2007).

According to report number 7114 of the MRC, the initial plan for establishing Iran's SWF was to create separate accounts (managed by the same government

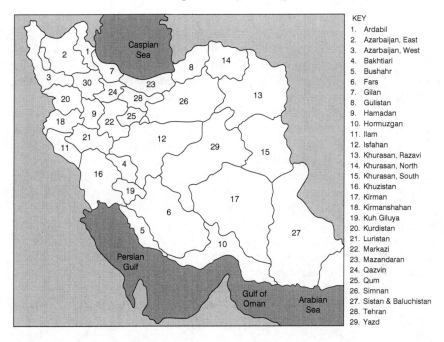

KEY
1. Ardabil
2. Azarbaijan, East
3. Azarbaijan, West
4. Bakhtiari
5. Bushahr
6. Fars
7. Gilan
8. Gulistan
9. Hamadan
10. Hormuzgan
11. Ilam
12. Isfahan
13. Khurasan, Razavi
14. Khurasan, North
15. Khurasan, South
16. Khuzistan
17. Kirman
18. Kirmanshahan
19. Kuh Giluya
20. Kurdistan
21. Luristan
22. Markazi
23. Mazandaran
24. Qazvin
25. Qum
26. Simnan
27. Sistan & Baluchistan
28. Tehran
29. Yazd

Figure 6.2 Sketch map of Iran showing provinces until 2005

body) for the government's oil revenue in riyal and in foreign exchange currencies (US dollars at the time), to maintain the balance of the government's oil revenue inside and outside the domestic economy. In practice, however, the report said that only the foreign exchange account was created and its resources were merely used to extend loans to domestic private and state funded investment projects, which mostly were inefficient and non-profitable (Majlis Research Centre, 2006).

Governance of the IFESA

At the time of its establishment, a board of trustees comprising the head of the organization for planning and budget, the minister of finance, the governor of the central bank, and two other ministers chosen by the president managed the IFESA. In March 2006, the government reshuffled the members of the board of trustees of the IFESA. The new arrangement of the board included the president's deputy for planning and strategic supervision, who replaced the head of the organization for planning and budget; the minister of finance; the minister of industry and mining; the minister of employment and social affairs; the first deputy of the president; the governor of the central bank; the minister of trade; and the head of the organization for cultural heritage (Majlis Research Centre, 2007).

The government's decision to change the arrangement of the IFESA's board was part of a major restructuring plan in which the organization for planning and budget, established sixty years earlier, was dissolved. The main role of the organization for planning and budget had been to harmonize the government's planning across the country, supervise the implementation of the government plans and oversee the government's expenditures through those plans. The government's decision for closing down the organization was criticised by many political figures in Iran. The government produced no obvious justification for the decision; nevertheless there was no pressure from the supreme leader or from the Majlis to reverse it (BBC Persian, 2007). One can argue that President Ahmadinejad's decision to reshuffle the board of trustees of the IFESA followed by dissolving the organization of planning and budget was merely to give the President's Office more power over the country's economic affairs and specifically the government's budget and expenditures.

In 2008, the cabinet proposed another change in the governance of the IFESA. According to the BBC Persian service, the government announced that the board of trustees of the IFESA had been dissolved and the responsibility for the governance of the IFESA was transferred to the government economic commission in order to conduct a 'fundamental reform, removal of parallel institutions and procedures, which delayed the government's economic decision-making process and policy implications' (BBC Persian, 2008). At the same time, the government also renamed the IFESA the Iran Foreign Exchange 'Fund' (*Hamshahri*, 2008a). The change of governance of Iran's SWF to the government's economic commission, which was headed by President Ahmadinejad who had the right to appoint and dismiss the members (including the minister of finance, the governor of the central bank, the president's first deputy and a few other secretaries of the president), assigned the ultimate governance control of the fund to the president. The move was criticized by some of the MPs but did not lead into any disruption in the restructuring of the governance of the country's SWF (BBC Persian, 2008).

Investment strategy of the IFESA: a failed attempt to increase non-oil production

The IFESA's investment strategy and spending regime was designed to allow the government unlimited withdrawal facilities from the account when the price of oil fell below the levels estimated in the development plans. In addition, initially the IFESA was planned to allocate a maximum of 50 per cent of its total assets at any given time to private sector businesses in the form of loans (*Hamshahri*, 2008b), to boost the production and growth of non-oil industries in the private sector. Such an investment strategy, in principle, was to support a gradual diversification of the Iranian economy from oil income and increase the capacity of the private sector. Therefore, in this respect the IFESA's investment strategy was similar to those of some of the GCC countries as it was ultimately aiming to support long-term economic diversification.

In practice, however, the private sector did not benefit from the allocated 50 per cent of the IFESA's total assets (see Figure 6.3) and most of the investments were directed to public-sector projects. In 2009, Bahman Arman, a former member

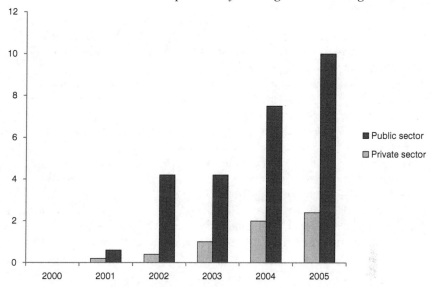

Figure 6.3 IFESA's financed project, public and private sector 2001–2005 (US $ billion)
Source: MRC (2005a) Report No. 8126

of the board of ttrustees of the IFESA told Fars News Agency (an Iranian state-owned news agency) that the Iranian economy did not have a developed industrial sector. This is why only a small share of the account's assets had been allocated to industry. The same applied to the private sector. The number of projects with absorption capacity for investment of US$100 million and above in the private sector was rather low in comparison with those of the public sector. He added that another reason for limited investment activity of the fund in the private sector was the 'inefficiency and bureaucracy of the government-owned banks' (Fars News Agency, 2009b).

Another reason for the low benefit from investments in the private sector from the IFESA's assets was the high interest rates on long-term deposit holdings by local banks. Because of these, many private sector businesses applied to the IFESA for loans, but instead of investing these loans in business units, which would contribute to non-oil production growth, they kept the credit in long-term savings accounts at local banks to generate interest in return. While the IFESA loan interest rates were set at 9 per cent annually, the local banks offered a 23 per cent return on five-year deposit holdings. Therefore, the private sector loan applicants, in many cases, never invested the loans in projects that generated production and growth as it was commercially more profitable and indeed easy to generate return when they deposited their cash in banks for a fixed five-year term. Low interest rates for loans were initially set to boost private sector borrowing and production. However, the domestic banks' high interest rates for long-term holding deposits have undermined the efficiency of the loans as they were not technically helping the non-oil private sector (Majlis Research Centre, 2006). Although keeping interest rates high at the local banks was the government's policy, to encourage domestic saving, to control outflows of private sector capital and to help the national banks safeguard their balance sheets, eventually the central bank had to decrease the local banks' interest rates to 14 per cent per annum in 2010 and 12.5 per cent per annum in 2011 (*Hamshahri*, 2011).

The next factor that contributed to the low benefit from the private sector's borrowing from the IFESA was corruption in the key institutions involved in the lending process. Since the eligibility criteria for projects when applying for these loans were broadly defined, in practice any application had a high chance of receiving credit. In many cases neither the profitability of the projects nor the credibility and track record of the applicants were examined in a rigorous manner.

Three private sector entrepreneurs who were interviewed for this study recounted similar stories about their experience of the loan application procedures (see Figure 6.4). One interviewee said: 'having personal contacts and "Wasta" – someone with a position in one of the institutions involved in the procedure who can breach the rules or influence the final decision – could change the decision

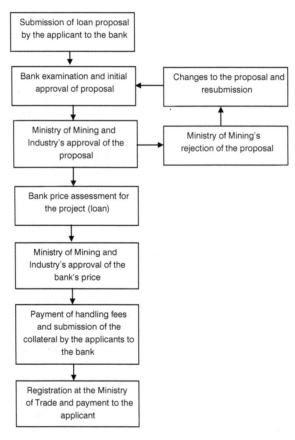

Figure 6.4 Loan application procedure at IFESA
Source: MRC (2005a) Report No. 7607

for any application.' Another interviewee also mentioned how, in many cases, employees of the bank to which the first proposal for a loan was submitted would increase the total amount approved for the loan in exchange for an off-record payment of a percentage of the loan in cash from the applicant.

The application review procedures at the IFESA (during the Khatami administration) depended on the amount of credit that was applied for. Loan proposals for less than US$20 million required approvals from the ministry of mining and industry and the banks (as is shown in Figure 6.4), while applications for more than US$20 million required the approval of the board of trustees of the IFESA and the final decision was made directly by them. After 2005 (during the Ahmadinejad administration), the government changed the loan application procedures, as follows:

- Applications for less than US$10 million were reviewed by the ministry of mining and industry as well as the bank.
- Applications of between US$10 million and US$50 million were reviewed by a group of 'senior financial analysts' (the arrangement of the group is not specified in the documents).
- Proposals over US$50 million were reviewed by the senior financial analysts, the president's advisors and the board of trustees (Majlis Research Centre, 2005a).

With the change of application procedures in 2005, technically any large payment from IFESA could be made to any given project, if the president approved the payment. The financial operations of transferring the funding to the companies, receiving collateral and letters of guarantee, and following up the repayments of the loans in the event of a company default were the bank's responsibility. All in all, lack of clear procedures for repayment, lack of a coherent evaluation process, and low accountability and follow-on procedures to further

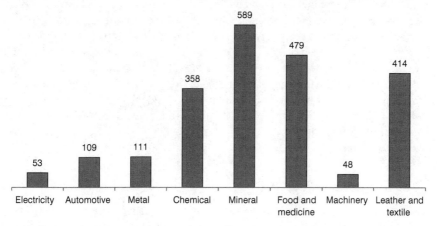

Figure 6.5 A review of projects financed by IFESA until September 2005
Source: MRC (2005c) Report No. 7607

assess the development of the investments have left a vacuum in the investment strategy of the IFESA leading to low efficiency of capital, and poor return.

Sectoral concentration of investment projects

Although the IFESA investment strategy was to support the diversification of the Iranian economy from the petroleum sector, there has been no balance in distribution of investments by the IFESA across the sectors: the most significant concentration of investment has been in the mineral sector (see Figure 6.5). Cement production companies were the main industries in this sector and received a large share of allocated investments from the IFESA. US$1.07 billion of all the financed projects between 2000 and 2005 were in cement production companies. This was as a result of a combination of domestic demand in infrastructure projects as well as demand in neighbouring countries, particularly Iraq and Afghanistan, who were both emerging from long-lasting devastating years of war. Consequently, the demand for construction material in reconstruction projects in both countries was at a significantly high level.

Geographical concentration of the IFESA's investment projects

As the data published by MRC shows, the majority of the investment projects funded by IFESA loans were located in areas in physical proximity to the capital, Tehran. The Iranian government has historically focused more on development projects in regions with lower risks of political instability. The Sunni minority population, which is concentrated in the western and eastern provinces along the borders with Iraq and Pakistan (Ilam, Kurdistan, Sistan and Baluchistan), have historically received a very small share of government development expenditure. Over the past century, the ethnic minorities have had clashes with the central government in Tehran. Therefore, it has somehow been embedded in the Iranian government's culture (before and after the revolution) to avoid investments in the areas in which the ethnic minorities (Kurds, Arabs, Sistans and Baluchis) reside. As Table 6.1 shows, the investment projects in provinces where the majority of the population are from religious and/or ethnic minorities received the smallest share of the allocated funds from the IFESA (Ilam, Kurdistan, Sistan and Baluchistan: 0.4 per cent, 0.7 per cent and 1 per cent, respectively), while projects in Tehran received the highest share of funds (about 18 per cent) followed by its neighbouring provinces Isfahan, Qazvin, Markazi and Simnan (which received 9.4 per cent, 6.4 per cent, 5.9 per cent and 4.9 per cent, respectively).

The size of assets of the IFESA

As noted above, Iran's oil revenue had shown a significant increase between 2000 and 2004 (during the third government economic development plan). Despite the fact that the government had committed to deposit its total surplus oil income, a

Table 6.1 Number of funded projects by IFESA in each province (2000–2005)

Province	Number of projects	Share of total number of projects
Ilam	4	0.4
Kuh Giluya	5	0.5
Kurdistan	6	0.7
Bakhtiari	7	0.8
Sistan & Baluchistan	9	1.0
Bushahr	10	1.1
Hurmuzgan	10	1.1
Ardabil	11	1.2
Hamadan	13	1.4
Gulistan	14	1.5
Kirmanshahan	20	2.2
Luristan	21	2.3
Qum	23	2.5
Kirman	25	2.7
Khuzistan	26	2.9
Azarbaijan, West	28	3.1
Gilan	31	3.4
Fars	33	3.6
Zanjan	34	3.7
Mazandaran	38	4.2
Azarbaijan, Eest	41	4.5
Yazd	43	4.7
Simnan	45	4.9
Khurasan	52	5.7
Markazi	54	5.9
Qazvin	58	6.4
Isfahan	86	9.4
Tehran	165	18.1
Total	912	100.0

Source: Majlis Research Centre (2005c), Report No. 7607

large share of the assets were withdrawn to be spent on maintaining the balance in the domestic foreign exchange markets and keeping the value of the riyal, financing the government's deficit, and investments in government projects. About US$9 billion of the government's petrodollars was spent to cover the government's riyal expenses (Majlis Research Centre, 2009a).

Table 6.2 IFESA's activities 2000–2007 (US $ million)

Description	2000	2001	2002	2003	2004	2005	2006	2007
Inflow								
Surplus foreign exchange income	5,944	1,848	5,596	5,400	1,0207	1,2806	21,174	12,322
Deposit interest	–	312	282	6246	175	216	380	149
Loan pay backs	–	417	33.3	40	196	156	252	158
Loan interest	–	–	2	3	5	15	25	19
Outflow								
Loan to private sector	–	158	598	1,075	1937	2,313	5,512	5,202.
Share of loan to private sector in total assets (%)	–	19	12	20	21	19	24	37
Government budget spending	–	656	2,100	1,947	4,732	8,051	1,7761	8,785
Share of government spending in total assets (%)	–	81	41	36	50	67	76	63
Total assets (left in the account end of each financial year)	5,944	7,298	8,082	8,843	9,478	3,411	3,215	–1,939

Source: Majlis Research Centre (2009), Report No. 9913

The most radical move by the government in regards to the IFESA was in November 2005, when they transferred 30 per cent of the assets of the IFESA to a fund called the 'Mihr-i Raza' fund, the aim of which was to empower civil society, encourage capacity building, job creation and poverty eradication, and support marriage among young Iranians, particularly in poorer areas (Aftab News Agency, 2005). Such investments have never been in IFESA's mandate. Prior to 2005, the assets held in IFESA were only invested in the non-oil industry and agriculture sectors.

In 2007 and 2008 the government withdrawals from the IFESA exceeded the deposits into the account. As it is shown in Table 6.2, the new mandate, which was introduced in 2005, incresed the withdrawal of IFE assets and led to negative figures for total assets left in the account end of both financial years. In 2007, the government withdrew about US$37 billion from the IFESA, which was US$20 billion above the government's proposed budget (Mardomsalari, 2008). According to MRC, the central bank estimated in 2008 that the IFESA's total assets stood at US$12.8 billion, while the government's total deposit to the IFESA in the same year was US$24.106 million (MRC 2009c).

The government has been particularly secretive in sharing information about the size of the assets under the management of the IFESA. In October 2009, Mahmood Bahmani, the Governor of the Central Bank of Iran (CBI) at the time, told Fars News Agency that Iran's foreign exchange reserves were over US$100 billion and the country's gold reserves had reached a historically high level. He added that while most of the economies of the world had been affected by the financial crisis of 2008–2009, Iran's aggregate export level had shown a 10 per cent growth in 2009, which had an extremely positive impact on the size of country's sovereign assets (Fars News Agency, 2009a). One year later, in 2010, Bahmani told Tabnak News (another state-run news agency) that the government does not reveal information on the size of the IFESA assets because otherwise the Islamic Republic's 'enemies' would plot to take over the country's resources (Tabnak, 2010). Bahmani's comment may well have been a prediction of the US and EU economic sanctions, which in 2011–2012 led to the freeze of some of the country's foreign exchange assets. But regardless of the prediction of the CBI for Western economic sanctions, the officials used various reasons to justify the government's secretive attitude in regards the size of assets held by the IFESA. In 2011, Trend News Agency, in confirming Bahmani's earlier statement about the size of IFESA assets, quoted Shamsedin Hosseini, the minister of finance, who said that Iran's foreign exchange reserves including those held by the CBI were about US$100 billion (Trend, 2011). Finally, recently the IMF came up with an estimate of over US$104 billion for the size of the IFESA's asset in the financial year 2012–2013 (IMF, 2011a).

As noted above, the government has been reluctant to share information about the activities of the IFESA. This has caused massive controversy between the Majlis and the government as well as in the public media. The critics of the President Ahmadinejad's government have raised the issue in various political debates inside parliament, in the Farsi speaking media of diaspora, and in local television channels and newspapers. President Ahmadinejad and his administration have been frequently accused of mismanagement of the Iranian economy, which led to parliamentary action in 2012. He was summoned by the Majlis to answer a series of question specifically regarding his government's economic policies (*New York Daily News*, 2012). However, such parliamentary actions and general economic policies and the public debate are not likely to have any impact on the government's information sharing strategy for the foreseeable future.

One key factor about the future of sovereign wealth management in Iran is the effect of Western economic sanctions on Iranian foreign exchange assets. Economic sanctions are expected to significantly impact Iran's foreign currency reserves. Given the tightening of the sanctions on Iranian financial and oil sectors, the government will face further challenges in receiving the petrodollars as the international financial transactions to Iran will be highly restricted. Moreover, as a result of oil embargos, it is predicted that Iran will experience an oil export decline, which will boost the already existing budget deficit (Torchia, 2012). Therefore, a combination of these factors will leave very little room for Iran's sovereign wealth accumulation over the coming years.

The scandal of Tehran Urban and Suburban Railway Company

One of the most controversial debates between the government and the Majlis over the size of the assets held by the IFESA concerned the case of the Tehran Urban and Suburban Railway Company (TUSRC). The company is owned by the Tehran Municipality and is in charge of the construction and operation of Tehran's underground public transport. Mohsen Hashemi, son of the former Iranian President, Akbar Hashemi Rafsanjani, had managed the company for seventeen years. The TUSRC was scheduled to receive US$2 billion from the government's assets held in the IFESA in 2009, to import new trains in order to develop the underground public railway network and to cover some of the company's operating costs, so that it would be able to provide subsidized services to Tehrani residents.

In 2010, the project was put on hold when the government refused to make the payment that had been approved by parliament in 2009. An initial plan was drawn up to make the payment from the IFESA but the government later said that the payment was to be made only from the NDF. The NDF was a new fund created to replace the IFESA, as announced in the fifth development plan. At the time when this condition was put forward by the government the fund had not even been established, and the government announced therefore that no payment would be made before the fund had been set up and was fully operational.

The government's refusal to make the payment to the TUSRC became a source of controversy between the government of President Ahmadinejad and the Majlis. Moreover, it coincided with a period of intense political conflict between President Mahmoud Ahmadinejad and former President Hashemi Rafsanjani. Since the 2009 presidential election, when former president Hashemi supported Ahmadinejad's opposing candidates, the disagreement between the two had intensified. In various occasions, including in public statements broadcasted by the state-owned television channels, President Ahmadinejad attacked Hashemi and his allies (including his children who have held various senior government positions for many years) and accused them of financial corruption, favouritism and betraying the fundamental principles of the Islamic Revolution.

In July 2010, *Ettelaat* (a state-owned newspaper that is also available online) quoted Mousa Al-Reza Sarvati, a member of the budget and planning commission of the Majlis, commenting on the overdue payments to TUSRC:

> Linking Tehran Metro's payments to the establishment of the National Development Fund is irrelevant. All the oil export income surplus of US$65 per barrel should have been transferred to the account. Therefore, the government's claim of lack of sufficient funding in the account to make overdue payments to this project is not valid. The government cannot refuse obeying the law while it refuses to answer the enquiry of the Majlis on this topic. Even if the government has legitimate reasons for its refusal, it must be discussed in the Majlis and the decision must be made there. Should the government refuse to obey the law, we will invite the ministers who are related to this case for an official enquiry.
>
> (*Ettelaat*, 2011)

The debate over the TUSRC payment intensified in summer 2010. The Majlis discussed holding an official enquiry among ministers who had played a role in the government's decision in the financial dispute with the TUSRC. Mohammad Hoseini and Hamid Behbahani, ministers of finance and transport at the time, were the two cabinet members who would have been called in by the Majlis if the majority of the MPs had voted for an enquiry. According to the constitution, when ministers are invited to such an enquiry they must obtain a vote of confidence from the majority of Majlis members. If, after the enquiry, the majority of members had not voted for that minister, he would lose his ministerial position and the president would need to find a replacement.

There was an intense debate inside the Majlis over the TUSRC controversy. On the one hand, some MPs criticized the government openly for its lack of cooperation in this particular case with another government body (Tehran Municipality). The political disagreement between the government, the Tehran Municipality and the TUSRC was referred to as a clear case of violation of the law. Moreover, the delay that resulted in the development of Tehran's underground public transport projects because of the overdue payment to the company was heavily criticized as it directly affected the welfare of Iranian citizens. On the other hand, some of the MPs argued that allocation of such funding to one single project that would benefit only the citizens of the capital was unjust.

The Majlis ratified a bill for the delayed payment to the TUSRC in July 2011. According to the constitution, the Council of the Guardians must also approve any bill approved by the Majlis. In the Iranian legislative system, although the council acts like an upper house and does not introduce bills, it is able to block bills that are passed by the Majlis, which acts as the lower house. In this instance, the council did not approve the bill regarding the payment to the TUSRC. Again, according to the constitution, when there is disagreement between the Council of the Guardians and the Majlis (e.g. the council does not approve a bill which the Majlis has approved), the bill will be sent to the Expediency Discernment Council (EDC) for review.

It is worth mentioning that President Ahmadinejad was greatly supported at the time by the supreme leader, Ayatollah Khamanei, although later in 2012 political disagreement between the two surfaced on a number of issues. The general consensus at the time when the Council of the Guardians, which is mainly comprised of members of clergy who are traditionally amongst the closest allies of the supreme leader, rejected the ratified bill sent by the parliament, was that the refusal was as a result of Ayatollah Khamenei's influence in the council's decision making.

As noted, the EDC, which is a government body in Iran's political system to which the supreme leader has delegated some of his authority, was prompted to resolve the issue. The former president, Akbar Hashemi Rafsanjani, father of the CEO of the TUSRC at the time (Mohsen Hashemi) was the chairman of the EDC at the time when the EDC had to intervene to resolve the issue to fulfil its constitutional role. Therefore, when the EDC gave its vote of approval to the TUSRC's bill in February 2010 the government remained disinclined to execute the bill and refused to make any payment, mainly because the EDC decision was seen by the government as a move by the EDC's chairman to exercise the constitutional power of the EDC in favour of his son. Shortly after the EDC had confirmed its approval, the president's secretary of parliamentary affairs declared that the government was unable to make the payment despite the EDC's decision, and that the payment would remain on hold until the government had announced the legal procedures for the operation of the NDF, which as noted above had not been established at the time.

Various Majlis members and government officials were interviewed and asked to comment on the controversy over the TUSRC. In a debate broadcasted by the state radio channel, Radio Goftogoo, between Mohammad Reza Khabbaz, a member of the economic commission of the Majlis, and Mehrdad Lahooti, a member of the infrastructure development commission of the Majlis, Khabbaz said the payment bill to transfer US$2 billion to the TUSRC was potentially a good one as it would resolve many of Tehran's public transport network problems. While given that the IFESA's assets belong to all Iranian citizens, any transfer from the account must be done carefully and the Majlis must pay extra attention to ensure the bill is not violating the equal right of the citizens to the national assets. Since the Council of the Guardians did not approve the payment, the responsibility of the Majlis was increased to ensure it would make a decision in the best interests of the public. The Majlis approved the payment bill when it did not have sufficient information on the size of the total assets held in the account. Therefore, due to lack of information on the available fund in the IFESA, the risk of a wrong decision made by the Majlis increased (Radio Goftogoo, 2010).

Another member of the parliament, Sattar Hedayat-Khah, also commented on the matter of Majilis approval of the payment to the TUSRC, underlining the fact that transferring US$2 billion from the IFESA to invest in Tehran's public transport system was unjust and 'discriminatory' to other provinces and cities of Iran and in contradiction with the constitution that emphasizes equal distribution of national wealth (Deutsche Welle Persian, 2011).

The debate in the parliament was carried until Mohsen Hashemi, the CEO of the Tehran Urban and Suburban Railway Company, resigned on 5 March 2011 (*Tehran Times*, 2011). In his resignation letter to Mohammad Bagher Ghalibaf, the mayor of Tehran, Mohsen Hashemi clearly stated that the government's reluctance to provide the promised finances was a personal attack on him because of his father's political disagreement with the government of President Ahmadinejad (Radio Zamaneh, 2011). Three days later, on 8 March 2011, the former president, Hashemi Rafsanjani, who in addition to his role at the EDC, served as the chairman of the Assembly of Experts of the Leadership since 2006, withdrew his candidacy for re-election to the assembly (Dehghan, 2011). The Assembly of Experts of the Leadership is a government body in the Iranian political system that is charged with the electing and removing of the supreme leader and supervising the supreme leader's activities. Despite the constitutional role of the Assembly of Experts of the Leadership, it has mainly been a figurehead organization without any actual execution power to dismiss the supreme leader or question his decisions. Therefore, the resignation of Hashemi was interpreted mainly as a symbolic gesture to demonstrate his disagreement with Ayatollah Khamanei, which has intensified since the 2009 presidential election when the supreme leader backed President Ahmadinejad, and Hashemi supported Ahmadinejad's reformist opponents.

The controversy over the TUSRC was just one of the political backlashes amongst members of the Iranian political elite after 2009 presidential election when the domestic power struggle in Iran deepened. The political dispute over the TUSRC's payment between the cabinet and the country's legislature highlighted the politically oriented nature of the investment strategy of the Iranian government in the management of the country's sovereign wealth. In contrast to the CSWFs of the GCC members, the Iranian government has not succeeded in promoting the commercial aspect of the country's sovereign wealth investments. The financial debate over the TUSRC was transformed into a straightforward political disagreement between the former Iranian president, Rafsanjani, who had supported the government's opposition movement in the aftermath of the presidential elections in 2009. The TUSRC case was seen as a major turning point for the balance of political power in Iran, while Rafsanjani's resignation from the Assembly of Experts of the Leadership was interpreted as a major step back for the government's opposition. In March 2011, Ahmadinejad's administration marked a victory over the reformist elite in Iran backed by Mr Hashemi Rafsanjani.

NDF

The government of President Ahmadinejad proposed the establishment of a new sovereign wealth fund. The NDF was established to receive all the assets of the

IFESA. The governance, operational strategy and savings policies of the NDF differ from those of the IFESA (http://www.ndf.ir). The goals and responsibilities of the fund are similar to those of the IFESA, but there has been another major objective added to the NDF that was not included among the goals of the IFESA, which is the intergenerational savings aspect of the fund. Like the IFESA, the NDF seeks to finance private sector projects to support non-oil growth and export. Moreover, the government has committed to keeping the NDF's management structure independent of the political elite. The initial proposals also reveal the government's plan for managing the NDF directly, as opposed to the IFESA, which was managed through the country's banking network, or CBI (MRC, 2009a).

According to the MRC, the governance of the NDF is divided between a board of trustees, a board of managers and a supervisory board. Other government bodies, including the Majlis and the EDC, have also been given a stronger role in the governance of the NDF, compared with the IFESA. The board of trustees of the fund includes the president's secretary of strategic planning, the governor of the CBI, the minister of finance, a member of the Majlis chosen by the Majlis (preferably a member of the economic commission of the Majlis), a member of the EDC chosen by the EDC, the head of chamber of commerce, industry and mining, and the head of Iran central chamber of cooperatives (which represents the cooperative sector). The board of trustees is to be the main element in the governance of the NDF, and its administrative office will be located in the central bank. A special inspector will be appointed by the board of trustees to monitor the activities of the fund constantly. The board of managers will include the governor of the CBI who is the chair of the board and two experts in finance who will be chosen by the board of trustees. The supervisory board includes three auditors chosen by the Majlis who will be responsible for supervising all the fund's activities and presenting annual reports to the Majlis. As noted above, it appears that the Majlis will have a strong role in decision making and overseeing the NDF (NDF, 2011). According to the organization chart published on the NDF's official website, the board of trustees and the board of managers both have an equal position in the management of the NDF and are above the chairman of the board of managers.

The NDF is planned to take over all the assets held in the IFESA, although it is not clear when the IFESA's activities will end, and whether or not both funds might operate actively for some time. In addition, the NDF is set to have a clearly defined savings strategy, which includes 20 per cent of annual oil revenues paid on a monthly basis, an additional 5 per cent annually in order to achieve a savings rate of 40 per cent (of total commodity revenues) in the final year of the fifth economic development plan (2011–2015), all loan paybacks (for the loans that are made to the public and private sectors from the assets held in the NDF) and the reinvestment of all investment returns (NDF, 2011).

The government's savings proposals for the NDF appear to be quite ambitious. According to MRC (2009a), the government aims to reach full financial independence from oil revenues for budgetary expenses by the end of the fifth economic development plan. Throughout this period, the government plans to completely cut subsidies and instead deposit the assets allocated to the subsidies (in previous years) into the NDF's account. Moreover, the initial proposals for the fund aim to deposit the investment and saving returns into the fund's account as well. All the returns will be kept in a separate account from the actual assets and the government will not be permitted to withdraw from the assets of that account.

Similar to the IFESA's investment strategy, the NDF aims to support the private sector. Thirty per cent of total assets under management of the fund will be invested in the private and cooperative sectors in order to increase production and efficiency in the domestic economy. In addition, 10 per cent of the total AUM of the fund is planned to be invested in the oil and gas sector. This is a new investment area in which the country's sovereign wealth management institution will operate. Investments in the oil and gas sector were not included in the IFESA's investment mandate. Furthermore, up to 20 per cent of the assets held in the fund is planned be deposited in local banks to support the domestic financial sector. Support for the domestic financial sector was also not included in the IFESA's investment mandate. Finally, the government has proposed that it will invest the rest of the NDF's assets in various financial products in international markets. For the first time since the creation of Iran's sovereign wealth investment institution, the government has committed to invest up to 40 per cent of the country's sovereign wealth in the international financial market (Majlis Research Centre, 2005b).

The government has also included other areas for investing the fund's assets, such as projects that aim to support the poor and young, newly married couples, to maintain the market balance in consumer goods, to provide affordable housing for the underprivileged, and to invest in development projects aimed mainly at strengthening schools against natural hazards (such as earthquakes) (Majlis Research Centre, 2005b).

The government's proposals for the creation of the NDF have also indicated particular procedures that will be put in place in order to maintain the transparent operation of the fund. It is suggested that the assets managed by the fund will be kept in a separate account from the CBI's foreign exchange reserves. The board of trustees will appoint an external auditing team to conduct regular auditing, and update the board and the Majlis on the operational activities of the fund. In addition, regular internal auditing will take place (internally every six months, externally every year). The fund will be committed to release regular quarterly reports (Majlis Research Centre, 2009a). There has been no information as to whether or not these reports will be made available to the public or if access will be restricted to the Majlis and the EDC only, but given the government's policies on public disclosure of information about the IFESA's activities, it seems unlikely that such information will be available to the public.

The government has put forward a much more developed proposal for the structure of the NDF than it did for the IFESA. This is probably due to a combination of factors. The management of the IFESA's assets has been criticized by the Majlis and the public, therefore the government has felt the need for a different approach in its sovereign wealth management policies. Moreover, Iran is in need of economic restructuring programmes as the economic conditions have worsened over the last few years and in comparison with other oil-rich countries of the region, Iran has lagged behind in growth and development, both in oil and non-oil sectors. Having said that, the experience of the IFESA shows that the country's sovereign wealth has been managed in a rather inefficient manner. It is therefore difficult to predict whether the NDF will operate more efficiently and with more transparency or not.

Conclusion

The Iranian government has remained highly dependent on its oil income, and Iran's sovereign wealth management has been the least developed of its kind in the Gulf region. The key issue that has contributed to the poor performance of the country's sovereign wealth management institutions is its weak legal and management systems and lack of supervision. The IFESA caused controversy between the government, the Majlis and the public on various occasions, the most publicized of which was the TUSRC scandal. Moreover, lack of consistency in the government's economic policies contributed to the weak performance of Iran's sovereign wealth management experience. After 2005, the president heavily influenced economic policy making and either ignored the orders of the Majlis or bypassed them following an intervention of the supreme leader or the Council of the Guardians. Iran lagged behind the neighbouring oil-rich countries of the Gulf partly because of the US-led economic sanctions, in place since the Islamic Revolution of 1979. While the international economic sanctions forced Iran into severe economic isolation, integration into the global financial system has proved to be one of the most important catalysts of the sovereign wealth management policies of the Arab Gulf countries. In addition to the external isolation imposed by the economic sanctions, since 2005 Iran has struggled with major internal political issues, which have impeded the sound operation of the country's domestic economic activities. A good example of this is the case of the TUSRC. While creation of a new SWF, which seeks to avoid the mistakes of the previous fund, would be a huge step for the Iranian economy, given Iran's internal and external difficulties on the economic as well as the political front, it is unlikely that the NDF will turn out to be the country's shortcut to catching up with the Gulf's larger SWFs.

7   The government pension fund of Norway

Introduction

Norway, with an oil production of 2.38 million barrels per day, is one of the world's major oil producing countries. The Norwegian economy has been struggling with two main challenges over the past few decades. Firstly, Norway has an ageing population: the proportion aged 67 years or above is predicted to increase from around 13 per cent in 2009 to 17 per cent by 2030. The ratio of the population of 67 or above relative to those aged 15–66 is expected to increase from around 20 per cent in 2009 to just over 30 per cent by 2030. Secondly, the Norwegian economy is heavily dependent on oil export incomes. The petroleum sector generates more than 50 per cent of the country's total export revenue (Economist Intelligence Unit, 2011). The share of the oil sector in government revenue of Norway is less than that of Gulf countries, nonetheless dependence on oil revenues is a challenge facing the Norwegian government. As a result, the government of Norway will need to find non-oil revenue generating sources to finance a larger volume of services to the country's ageing population.

According to the Economic Intelligence Unit, with the ageing population, regardless of the flow of oil revenue, the pension liabilities of the government are expected to greatly exceed the estimated assets of the entire government pension funds (Economist Intelligence Unit, 2011). The government will therefore need to pursue policies of prudent management of Norway's petroleum wealth. Given the structure of the Norwegian society, in which the government is responsible for the maintenance of the social safety of the population, the management of the country's public wealth is a fundamental social responsibility and a priority for the government. In order to meet pension obligations and to preserve the country's natural wealth for future generations, the government of Norway has established two government investment vehicles:

1   The National Insurance Scheme Fund, which was established in 1966 to set aside a share of the national assets to finance future social security expenditure.
2   The Government Petroleum Fund, which was established in 1990 to support the country's long-term wealth preservation strategy.

In 2006, the government renamed the National Insurance Scheme Fund and the Government Petroleum Fund to the Government Pension Fund – Norway (GPFN) and the Government Pension Fund – Global (GPFG), respectively. Both funds have often been referred together under one overarching title: the Government Pension Fund. The purpose of the Government Pension Fund has been defined as: 'to support government savings to finance the pension expenditure of the National Insurance Scheme and long-term considerations in the spending of government petroleum revenues' (Norwegian Ministry of Finance, 2009). In other words, the Government Pension Fund is a combination of the National Insurance Scheme and the Petroleum Fund and continues the responsibility of serving the government in the same way as those funds did, only with a new title.

The GPFN and GPFG are active institutional investors of the Norwegian government and they are managed separately and have different investment strategies. The GPFN investment mandate is to invest in the Nordic region only, while the GPFG invests globally. For the first two years following its establishment, the GPFG was managed by the central bank of Norway (between 1996 and 1998). In 1998, Norges Bank Investment Management (NBIM) was set up and put in charge of the management of the GPFG on behalf of the Norwegian ministry of finance. The GPFN, however, has been managed by another government organization: the Folketrygdfondet. The Folketrygdfondet is an investment institution, established by the government in 1967, and commissioned to manage the GPFN (previously the National Insurance Scheme Fund).

The GPFG has the characteristics of an oil stabilization fund and it was set up to protect the government's fiscal policy should oil prices drop or the domestic economy contract. The fund is also considered to be a tool to manage the financial challenges of an ageing population and an expected drop in petroleum revenue. The fund is designed to invest in long-term assets, but in a way that makes it possible to draw on when required. The change of the fund's name highlights its role in saving government income to finance the expected increase of the future public pension expenditures. Notwithstanding its name, the fund has no formal pension liabilities nor mandate on when the fund may be used to cover future pension costs (www.nbim.no). The fund has two main objectives Firstly, it acts as a saving mechanism aiming to distribute petroleum revenues across generations (as the petroleum resources are part of the national wealth that do not only belong to the current generation but also to future generations). Secondly, it acts as a protection measure against the fluctuation of oil prices. Although the country benefits from a rather diversified tax base, unlike the Gulf countries, the volatile crude markets can have a negative impact on the competitiveness of Norwegian internationally exposed industries. Therefore, the GPFG is designed to serve as a buffer between current oil incomes and expenditures (Birger, 2008). Based on the definition of the SWFs in this book, the GPFG is the SWF of the government of Norway and it will be reviewed in detail in this chapter.

The GPFG is integrated into the government's annual budget. The capital inflow of the GPFG includes all government petroleum revenue and net financial transactions related to petroleum activities, minus net of what is spent to balance

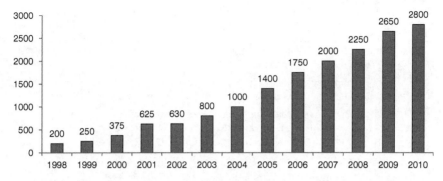

Figure 7.1 The GPFG's market value (krone billion)
Source: Government of Norway (2011) Report No. 15 (2010–2011)

the state's non-oil budget deficit. The full integration of the fund with the state budget proves that net allocations to the fund reflect the total budget surplus. Norwegian fiscal policy is formed based on the guideline that the structural, non-oil budget deficit shall correspond over time to the real return on the fund's investments, which is estimated to stand at about 4 per cent of the value of the assets. Therefore, a spending rule was established in 2001 for the GPFG, which only permits a maximum 4 per cent of the fund's return over time to be spent on the annual national budget. For that reason the market value of the GPFG's assets has constantly grown over time (Eriksen, 2006) (see Figure 7.1). This is in contrast with the savings and spending policies of the Gulf CSWFs, where their assets have been drained from time to time to cover various government expenditures including the costs imposed by regional conflicts.

The GPFG investment strategy

The investment strategy of the GPFG has gradually developed over time since it was established. The fund has been investing in equities in developed economies since 1998. In 2000, emerging markets were also included in the benchmark portfolio for equities. The benchmark portfolio for bonds was expanded in 2002 to include the non-government-guaranteed bonds (i.e. corporate bonds and mortgage-backed bonds). In 2006, the investment universe of the GPFG was further expanded. The ministry of finance expressed the intention for an expansion of the investment universe to include the small-cap sector in the benchmark portfolio for equities and to increase the equity portion of the benchmark portfolio from 40 per cent to 60 per cent. The parliament, Storting, approved of the ministry's intention (Norwegian Ministry of Finance, 2007). In 2008, the ministry decided to include property investments in the GPFG's portfolio (Norwegian Ministry of Finance, 2008b). It was also decided to expand the benchmark portfolio by including more emerging stock markets and to increase the limit on ownership stakes for equity investments in individual companies from 5 per cent to 10 per cent (Norwegian Ministry of Finance, 2008b) (see Table 7.1).

Table 7.1 Development of investment strategy for the GPFG since its establishment

Date	Development
1996	First net transfer to the fund, invested similarly to the Central Bank of Norway's currency reserves
1997	Prior to this year, the fund was wholly invested in government bonds; the ministry decides to invest 40 per cent of the fund in equities.
1998	Norges Bank Investment Management (NBIM) was set up on 1 January to manage the fund. NBIM converted about 40 per cent of the fund's bond portfolio into equities within the first half of 1998.
2000	Five emerging-market countries were added to the equity benchmark
2002	Non-government bonds (corporate and securitized bonds) added to the fixed income benchmark
2004	Ethical guidelines were established
2006	The fund was renamed from Government Petroleum Fund to Government Pension Fund-Global
2007	The Ministry of Finance decided to increase the fund's share of equity investments to 60 per cent from 40 per cent. It also decided to add small-cap companies to the benchmark portfolio.
2008	The Ministry of Finance included real estate to the fund's investment universe, with a maximum share of 5 per cent of total assets. All emerging markets were included in the reference equity index.
2009	The fund's ethical guidelines were evaluated. Its share of equity investments reached 60 per cent in June. The fund posted a record return of 25.6 per cent.
2010	The Ministry of Finance gave the fund a mandate to invest as much as 5 per cent of its assets in real estate, reducing its share of fixed-income investments correspondingly.

Source: www.nbim.no

The overall aim of the investments in the GPFG is to achieve maximum financial return with moderate risk. Similar to most of the SWF case studies in this book, the GPFG investment strategy is to diversify the fund's assets in different asset classes. In order to minimize the risk associated with investments in diversified asset classes, various risk calculation measures are in place on the basis of historical events' impacts on investment returns under the asset composition and country allocations at any given time. The crisis scenarios include different historical events during the past 100 years, such as the oil crisis of 1973–1975, the stock market crash in 1987, and the Mexican and Asian crises of the 1990s. The majority of the GPFG investments are in shares of listed companies and fixed income products with high credit ratings, given by various credit agencies like Moody's, and Standard and Poor's (Government Pension Fund – Global, 2010a) (see Figure 7.2).

As noted above the GPFG does not have any particular short-term liability. This minimizes the fund's short-term liquidity requirement and extends the investment horizon of the GPFG. Like other CSWF case studies in this book, the

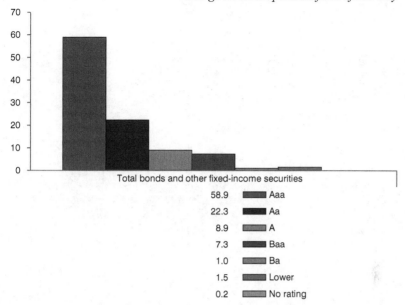

Figure 7.2 GPFG's fixed-income holdings based on credit ratings (% of portfolio)
Source: GPFG Annual Report (2010)

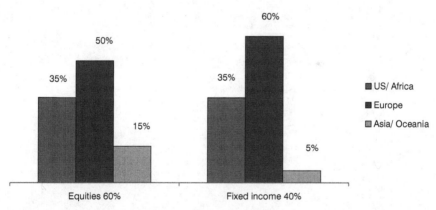

Figure 7.3 Benchmark portfolio of the GPFG (as of 2009)
Source: Ministry of Finance, (2008–2009) Report No. 20

GPFG is a rather patient investor with a long investment horizon. The fund has a formulated long-term investment strategy in which the share of investments in various asset classes and geographical regions is decided based on their expected long-term returns and risks.

As was mentioned above, the portfolio of investment of the GPFG is diversified into various sectors and geographic locations. The benchmark index for equities of the GPFG comprises almost 7,700 companies across twenty-seven countries and the benchmark index for bonds comprises more than 9,800 bonds across

Table 7.2 The largest holdings of the GPFG as of 2010 (million krone)

Equity			Bond		
Company	*Country*	*Holdings*	*Issuer*	*Country*	*Holdings*
Royal Dutch Shell	UK	19,914	US government	US	136,622
HSBC	UK	18,982	UK government	UK	91,768
Nestle	Switzerland	18,123	Federal Republic of Germany	Germany	65,155
Vodafone Group	UK	14,781	Japanese government	Japan	51,322
Novartis AG	Switzerland	13,947	Italian Republic	Italy	51,226
BP	UK	13,695	French Republic	France	49,158
Telefonica	Spain	11,667	Kingdom of Spain	Spain	23,207
Total	France	11,018	European Investment Bank	Supranational	23,163
BHP Billiton	UK	10,805	Fannie Mae	US	19,806
GlaxoSmithKline	UK	10,562	Bank of Scotland	UK	18,762

Source: GPFG Annual Report (2010)

the currencies of twenty-one countries (Figure 7.3). Equity investments in basic material and oil and gas sectors earned the highest percentage of return in 2010 (see Table 7.2 for a list of the fund's largest equity and bond holdings). As it is shown in the table the main share of the GPFG investments are held in European economies.

New investment programmes

Since 2008, the GPFG has introduced two new investment programmes, which contain investments in asset classes that had not previously been included in the fund's portfolio: real estate and infrastructure. Unlike the Gulf funds, the GPFG had not been active in real estate markets. The ministry of finance asked for Storting's approval of the plans to invest up to 5 per cent of the GPFG in real estate in 2008. Due to the poor return in the global real estate market in 2008, the ministry did not set a fixed investment plan in real estate for the following years. The new investment plans will have to be adapted to the market conditions and capacity. Therefore, in the first few years, the investments in real estate will be concentrated in a number of chosen areas. The GPFG will gradually build up a global real estate portfolio over time with a high degree of risk diversification. As is the case for real estate, the ministry of finance decided to include investments in infrastructure in the portfolio of investments of the GPFG as an element of risk diversification strategy. The decision was approved by Storting on the basis of rapid growth of the sector as a result of the large demands for infrastructure investments in emerging economies. Investments in infrastructure by the GPFG will include various assets across the sector such as water supplies, toll roads, airports and telecommunications. Storting suggested that the fund must develop investment competence in all the asset classes including infrastructure in order to maintain a good international representation in all the markets in which other institutional investors are actively investing (Government Pension Fund – Global, 2010a).

The GPFG ethical guidelines

Ethical guidelines were created for the management of the GPFG's assets on 19 November 2004. The guidelines build on recommendations made by a government-appointed committee, which presented its report in summer 2003. The committee identified the following main obligations for the management of the fund: firstly, profit maximization, secondly, exercise of ownership rights and exclusion of companies from the fund's investment universe in order to protect the rights of those affected by companies in which the fund invests (Norwegian Ministry of Finance, no date).

Exercising the ownership rights

One of the key characteristics, which differentiates the investment strategy of the GPFG from that of the other SWFs, is the active exercising of ownership rights. It focuses on two key aspects. Firstly, it focuses on good corporate governance, which includes equal treatment of shareholders, carrying responsibility and accountability to serve as board member or influential shareholder, as well as responsibility for the maintenance of well-functioning, legitimate and efficient markets in which the fund invests. Secondly, it focuses on environmental and social issues, which include ensuring zero violation of the protection of children's rights, climate change regulations and efficient water management policies by the companies in which the fund invests (Government Pension Fund – Global, 2010b).

Norges Bank is responsible for applying the ownership rights on behalf of the GPFG through voting at the general assembly meetings of the companies in which the GPFG invests. In general, Norges Bank votes in favour of the proposals forwarded by the management of the companies in which it holds a shareholder right unless the board as a whole does not satisfy the bank's expectations in maintaining sufficient independence from the company's management or major shareowners. In addition, the bank often votes against managerial salary schemes in cases where there is no obvious link between performance and reward (Norwegian Ministry of Finance, 2009).

The bank also has strict guidelines for exercising its ownership rights on various social and environmental issues such as those concerning child labour and carbon emissions. Norges Bank has prepared a document 'NBIM Investor Expectations on Children's Rights' (Norges Bank Investment Management no date a), to explain the expectations of the bank concerning children's rights to companies in which the GPFG invests. The document is designed for companies that operate in areas or sectors where there is a high risk of children's rights' violation. It has specifically targeted countries such as India, Brazil, China and West Africa (Norges Bank Investment Management, no date a). Since 2008, Norges Bank has focused on the activities of certain companies in accordance with the national climate change regulations in the USA. The Bank is also part of the Carbon Disclosure Project, which is an independent organization that gathers and publishes information on companies' emissions of greenhouse gases. Norges Bank also takes part in a petition by 135 funds calling for wealthy nations to reduce their emission of greenhouse gases in accordance with the recommendations of the UN Intergovernmental Panel on Climate Change (25–40 per cent by 2020) (Norwegian Ministry of Finance, 2009).

Exclusion of companies from the GPFG portfolio of investments

Under a number of circumstances companies may be excluded from the GPFG portfolio. Firstly, the companies that produce weapons that violate fundamental humanitarian principles in their normal use. Secondly, those that sell weapons or military material to states mentioned in the supplementary guidelines for management of the fund. Thirdly, when investment in a company entails an unacceptable risk of contributing to actions or omissions, that must be deemed grossly unethical. So far thirty-two companies have been excluded from the investment universe of the GPFG. In 2010, three companies were excluded from the GPFG: two Israeli companies and one Malaysian. Divestment from the Israeli companies, Africa Israel Investments Ltd and Danya Cebus Ltd, and the Malaysian company, Samling Global Ltd has been concluded.

- Africa Israel Investments Ltd is the parent company of several subsidiaries with interests in property development, infrastructure and energy. The company holds major shares in Danya Cebus, which is a construction company that is involved in developing settlements in occupied Palestinian territory. This company was excluded on the basis on serious violations of individual rights by the two companies in situations of war and conflict. The GPFG owned shares worth NOK 7.2 million in Africa Israel Investments at year end 2009.
- Samling Global is an integrated forest resource and wood products company that produces timber, plywood, veneer and palm oil. The exclusion of this company took place on the basis of extensive and repeated breaches of the licence requirements, regulations and other directives governing the company's forest operations in Sarawak, Malaysia and Guyana (Norwegian Ministry of Finance, 2010).

The ethical guidelines are constantly reviewed to assess whether they are satisfying their intended purpose, and maintain broad political support. As part of the evaluation process, the ministry carries out a number of activities to gather information and views from Norwegian and international stakeholders. One of the ongoing processes in reviewing the ethical guidelines is negative screening of companies from the portfolio on the basis of the companies' products. A new screening criterion is being planned to cover companies that produce tobacco. However, with respect to excluding other unhealthy or socially unbeneficial services, such as alcohol, there has not been the same degree of norm development that can provide a similarly clear anchoring nationally or internationally.

Savings regulation of the GPFG

The GPFG has a comprehensible guideline for the government savings policy and transactions of funds. The Government Pension Fund Act No. 123 of 21 December 2005 clarifies the gross revenues from petroleum activities including total tax revenues and royalties deriving from petroleum activities, revenues deriving from tax on carbon dioxide (CO_2) emissions due to petroleum activities, revenues deriving from tax on nitrogen oxide (NO_x) emissions due to petroleum activities, operating income and other revenues deriving from the state's direct financial interest in petroleum activities, central government revenues from net surplus agreements associated with certain production licences, dividends from Statoil (the Norwegian national oil company), transfers from the Petroleum Insurance Fund, government revenues deriving from the removal or alternative use of installations, and any government sale of stakes representing the state's direct financial interest in petroleum activities. In addition, the guideline sets a number of deductions that are made from gross revenues including the government's direct investments in commercial petroleum activities, operating costs and other costs directly related to the government's investments in the petroleum sector, government expenses linked with the Petroleum Insurance Fund, government expenses in connection with the removal or alternative use of installations, and any government purchase of stakes in petroleum activities (Norwegian Ministry of Finance, 2011b).

Governance and management of the GPFG

The ministry of finance is the owner of the GPFG and holds the overall responsibility for the fund. The ministry is in charge of setting strategic asset allocation and ethical guidelines. In addition, the ministry is responsible for monitoring and evaluating operational management and constant reporting to Storting. The ministry of finance designs all the guidelines for the fund, subject to parliamentary approval. The ministry has a separate Council on Ethics, which gives it advice on exclusion and negative filtration of companies based on ethical criteria.

The central bank, Norges Bank, is the manager of the fund. The bank is responsible for the implementation of the investment strategy, active management to achieve excess return, risk control and reporting, and exercising the fund's ownership rights. The bank is also responsible for providing the ministry of finance with professional advice on investment strategy. Within the central bank, there is an asset management unit, NBIM, which is in charge of the day to day management of the GPFG. NBIM was established by the central bank in January 1998 to manage the GPFG and most of Norges Bank's foreign exchange reserves. NBIM has about 290 employees in its five offices in Oslo, London, New York, Shanghai and Singapore (http://www.nbim.no). NBIM is an incorporated part of Norges Bank and it is subject to the same laws and regulations as the bank. NBIM's investment activities are governed by Storting, the ministry of finance and Norges Bank. Rules and guidelines for the fund's management are laid down by the executive board of the Norges Bank and NBIM leader group (headed by the CEO of NBIM) (see Figure 7.4). The CEO's job description is issued by the executive board of Norges Bank.

The executive board of Norges Bank

The board is the responsible body for Norges Bank's operations. It is chaired by the governor of the central bank and has seven members. The board sets all the guidelines and strategic plans for NBIM's management activities (see Figure 7.5). The members are appointed to full-time positions for a term of six years.

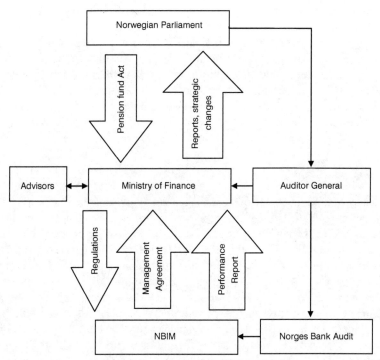

Figure 7.4 Structure of governance and management of the GPFG
Source: Martin Skancke (2008)

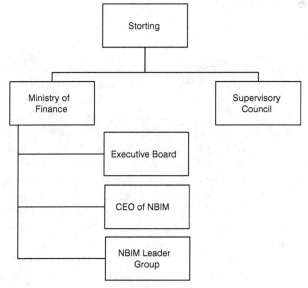

Figure 7.5 Organization structure of the GPFG
Source: Norwegian Ministry of Finance (2001a) and Norwegian Ministry of Finance 2012

Reappointment to the same position may take place for one period of a further six years. There are also five alternate members who are appointed for four-year terms (http://www.norges-bank.no). As of 2012, nearly all the members are either experienced executives with backgrounds in finance or other senior management positions, or senior academics with strong backgrounds in management and finance. This is not the same trend as in the Gulf SWFs where either individuals who have close alliances with the senior political elite of the country, or the ruling family members fill all the senior management positions on the board of the organizations.

NBIM leader group

The leader group is in charge of the management of investment operations and day to day activities of NBIM. The leader group consists of seven members. In contrast with the Gulf funds where appointment processes are based on an individual's links with the high-ranked senior political figures, NBIM appointments take place based on an individual's professional experience in the financial sector internationally. In this respect, the NBIM leader group is more similar to a private investment institution, rather than a state-owned investment organization. Moreover, unlike the Gulf CSWFs executive management teams, particularly those from the UAE, individuals from the NBIM leader group team do not hold other government positions. Such arrangement separates the political elite from those who are in charge of making investment decisions for the GPFG. This has been something that the Gulf funds have failed to accomplish. The overlap between the political and financial power in the Gulf countries is the major source of uncertainty about the non-commercial investment incentives of the Gulf CSWFs.

The GPFN

The second part of the Government Pension Fund of Norway is GPFN. The GPFN is managed by the Folketrygdfondet, which manages the fund's capital in its own name. The GPFN assets are invested in Norway, Denmark, Finland and Sweden. The basic capital of the GPFN originated primarily from surpluses in the national insurance accounts from the National Insurance Scheme, introduced in 1967, until the late 1970s. The return on the assets of the GPFN is not transferred to the treasury, but is added to this part of the fund on an ongoing basis. Consequently, there are no transfers between the fiscal budget and the GPFN nor are there any transfers of capital between the two parts of the Government Pension Fund.

The Folketrygdfondet is a company that is wholly owned by the state of Norway and has been commissioned to manage the GPFN on behalf of the Norwegian ministry of finance. It is a long-term asset manager aiming for the best investment returns on the capital within the management limits. Capital can be invested in shares listed on regulated markets in Norway, Denmark, Finland and Sweden, and in fixed income products issued by these countries. The GPFN supports government savings for financing future national insurance pension fund

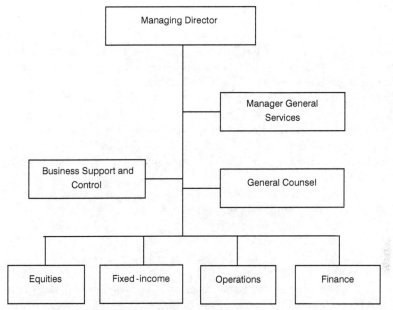

Figure 7.6 Folketrygdfondet's organization chart
Source: *Folketrygdfondet*'s website, http://www.ftf.no/en/c-225-Organazation-chart.aspx

costs. By the end of 2009 total assets amounted to 117 billion Norwegian krones (http://www.ftf.no/en/home.aspx). The Folketrygdfondet is governed by a board that is responsible for the management of the fund. The board consists of nine members who are all appointed by the the Norwegian ministry of finance for four years. The Folketrygdfondet has forty-five employees (http://www.ftf.no/en/home.aspx) (see Figure 7.6).

As of 2011, the share of equity investments in the GPFN is 50–70 per cent, while the share of fixed income instruments is 30–50 per cent of the portfolio. The majority (80–90 per cent) of the fund's investments are in Norway and 10–20 per cent is in Denmark, Finland and Sweden. The investment limit for the Folketrygdfondet is 15 per cent of the share capital or the basic capital in any single company in Norway, and up to 5 per cent of total equity capital and basic capital in any single company in the other countries of the GPFN investment universe (www.ftf.no).

The Folketrygdfondet is responsible for exercising the ownership rights through the management of the GPFN. The guidelines for the exercise of ownership and the ethical principles for investment activities of the GPFN are the same as the GPFG's: to help promote long-term wealth creation and good corporate governance. The ministry stipulates general investment strategies, while the board of directors of the Folketrygdfondet is responsible for the operational management of the GFPN.

Transparency of the Norwegian SWF

The overall management model of the fund is to maximize transparency of operation. The Norwegian SWF has been referred to as one of the most transparent commodity-based funds in the world by various organizations. All the information used in this chapter was collected from the online sources that are made available to the public by the Norwegian government. NBIM, Norges Bank, the ministry of finance and the Folketrygdfondet publish information on the size of AUM in both parts of the Government Pension Fund, and the returns, holdings, asset mix, risk management and ethical guidelines. In most of the official documents such public disclosure is emphasized as a key tool in building trust, both domestically and internationally.

Norway has thus been remarkably successful in transparent management of petroleum revenue and transferring the surplus oil export income to other types of assets globally. Given the intergeneration savings aim of the fund, a major consideration in various activities of the fund is to safeguard the wealth for the prosperity of current and future Norwegians. Therefore, it is considered an important responsibility for the managers of the fund to ensure that a favourable rate of return is produced on the wealth over time, accompanied by social and environmental sustainability. The ministry of finance has contributed to the formation of the IWG of SWFs and has supported the development of the GAPP for SWFs. The GPFG has met most of the criteria of the twenty-four principles of the GAPP (Norwegian Ministry of Finance, 2008a).

Part of the success in Norway may be as a result of the inclusion of the fund in the government fiscal balance. All the transfers to the Government Pension Fund are made after the government budget is balanced at the end of each fiscal year. This mechanism has included the transactions of the SWF on government record. This has proven to be a challenge for all the Gulf CSWFs where there are no fiscal records of the assets of the SWFs as the assets of those institutions have never been included in the government's budget (with the exception of SAMA to some extent). Moreover, the Government Pension Fund addressed the issue of the savings policy of the fund, which is one of the major challenges that most of the Gulf SWFs have been facing with regards the transparency of their operation. In all the Gulf countries, except Kuwait, there is no clear savings policy according to which the government's sovereign wealth savings commitment is designed. Iran's new NDF is aiming to overcome this issue, however, the track record of the Iranian government shows various events in the the SWF's regulations have been breached by the administration.

Another factor of success for the transparent operation of Norway's SWF is the clear governance structure and the relationship between the asset management bodies (NBIM and Folketrygdfondet) with the ministry of finance and the legislature. The decision-making process and the role of each of the organizations involved in the process are clearly defined and all the decisions are announced publicly . This is in contrast with the Gulf CSWFs where understanding the decision-making process and procedures has been rather challenging as the information is not often made available to the public.

Having an independent senior management team from the government is also another key difference between the Norwegian SWF and those from the Gulf. As is noted above, most of the senior leading team of the Norwegian fund are selected through transparent recruitment processes, which are conducted mainly on the relevance of background of the individuals with the field of international finance. This is in contrast with the Gulf CSWFs where the leading management positions and the seats of the executive boards are allocated to the members of the ruling family or those with long-term historical links with the ruling elite. In most cases in the Arab oil-rich side of the Gulf, these individuals have been chosen from amongst those who in addition to their alliance with the ruling elite have had experience in the field of international investment. However, in the case of Iran, the government has mostly failed to create a balance between political alliance and the expertise of the individuals who have been involved in the sovereign wealth management organizations.

Conclusion

The Norwegian SWF is the most transparent and well-governed CSWF in the world. Since Norway has enjoyed having a well-developed economy, democratized government institutions and a parliamentary political system for few centuries, the development in the Norwegian government institutions has been mirrored in the advancement of the governance of the country's SWF. Norwegian organization management culture has been developed ahead of the traditional individual-based management culture of the Gulf monarchies leading to a distinctive practice in the country's SWF management compared to those in the Gulf region. The members of the senior management team of NBIM are not chosen on the basis of individual links with the ruling cluster of political power in Norway, and the ethical guidelines, as well as other investment regulations, limit the influence of the members of the management team in the overall strategy of the GPFG. This is indeed in contrast with the CSWFs of the Gulf where often an extreme shift of strategy takes place as a result of management changes – a good example is Iran's SWF practice.

Another key difference between the Government Pension Fund of Norway and the Gulf CSWFs is public disclosure of information. In contrast with the other case studies in this book, in the case of the Norwegian SWF, a significant amount of the relevant information on various aspects of the fund's activities is accessible via the organizations' websites and in terms of data gathering on the Norwegian SWF, the use of secondary information for this chapter was rather minimal. A good example of the difference between the Gulf CSWFs public disclosure of information and the Norwegian SWF is the public disclosure of the size of the AUM of the funds. Estimating the size of AUM of the Gulf CSWFs has been one of the major challenges of the studies on this topic. In some cases, there has been a huge difference between the various estimates done by analysts from different organizations, while the GPFG's market value is published on a dedicated page of the official website of NBIM and updated on a quarterly basis.

All in all, the Norwegian government has proven to be successful in the development of the country's sovereign wealth management institutions. Storting has set clear rules for operation of the GPFG and supervision procedures and there has been no record of corruption in the GPFG, while the governments of the Gulf countries often failed to introduce clear guidelines for various aspects of their SWFs' operation leading to financial scandals and loss of assets as a result of mismanagement. Even though there are some fundamental differences between the Norwegian government's structure, management culture and organizational behaviour and the Gulf's CSWFs, the latter can still pick up lessons from the experience of the Norwegian SWF, particularly as there has been a huge emphasis by the Western host governments on the issue of transparency and good governance of the SWFs.

8 The challenge of transparency for sovereign wealth funds

Introduction

The issue of the transparency of SWFs has become one of the current challenges facing the global financial system. The role of these funds in the international economic structure has been highlighted as a result of financial globalization. Emergence of these institutions into the global financial system has put them in a position in which the SWFs are capable of influencing political and economic stability and market competitiveness internationally, in particular the countries in which they invest. By 2008, the financial assets owned or controlled by governments internationally were calculated to be as high as $US15 trillion, or about 8 per cent of global financial assets (Truman, 2008b). Given the significant asset size of the SWFs, they would arguably have huge potential to influence global markets. Moreover, given that the ownership of the AUM of these funds belongs to their sponsoring governments, the rise of the SWFs has prompted a new economic model: 'state capitalism' (*Economist*, 2008), which has principally been the by-product of a combination of centrally planned economies and global free market doctrine. In addition to their size, lack of clear information about these funds has further emphasized their position in the global financial system and had been a key challenge for the policy makers of their host economies. As highlighted in the previous chapters, most of the Gulf SWFs reviewed in this book avoid public disclosure of the assets' size and strategies, and lack a coherent governance system in which the withdrawal and accumulation rules, investment management policy and reporting measures are clearly defined. Furthermore, despite the importance of SWFs in domestic policy management, the role of these funds in their domestic economies is often not clear. Understanding how the funds are integrated into domestic fiscal policy frameworks has, therefore, been a challenge.

Reviewing some of the largest CSWFs in the world in the previous chapters, one can characterize the SWFs as government owned investment institutions with a tremendous amount of AUM with highly secretive operation systems. From 2005 to 2008, understanding the role of SWFs in the global financial system became a political debate. Discussion of the potential risks of sovereign wealth investments was triggered by the forced withdrawal of two deals, both of which had involved the acquisition of an American company by a sovereign wealth investor (a Chinese company and an Emirati company) between 2005 and 2006. Advanced economies in the West found themselves at the heart of the argument over identifying the optimum response to the growing strength of SWFs in the world economic network. Their discussions prompted Western countries receiving SWF investments to see whether the mechanisms that they had put in place to minimize potential risks to their economies associated with such investments were in fact sufficient.

Although SWF investment behaviour has resembled that of private and commercial entities, there are concerns that these funds might have non-commercial objectives or might target strategic assets in the host economies. This perception has fuelled resistance to SWF investments, particularly those that are thought to jeopardize the national security of their host sovereigns. Another concern regarding the non-commercial investment objectives of the SWFs has been raised on the back of their potential market distortion impact given their financial strategies are presumably guaranteed by their sponsoring governments (Kimmit, 2008).

Various aspects of the funds' activities prompted tighter regulation considerations by host countries (mainly those in the West with more liberated financial regulations) in which major shares of the SWFs' investments have been held. In order to ensure the adequacy of their supervisory mechanisms, the governments of the host countries, with the support of multilateral organizations such as the IMF and the OECD, have begun procedures to design and embrace best practices for these institutions that will enhance their accountability and transparency. Such procedures aim to increase understanding of how the funds operate in their domestic economies, as well as in the countries in which they invest. The initiative, however, raised concern amongst the SWFs' sponsoring governments over potential unfair economic and political barriers and protection policies by their host sovereign nations. This chapter will look at the initiatives, how it has been developed and the outcomes that were achieved through the international effort for promoting transparency of the SWFs, in the context of the Gulf CSWFs.

What does transparency mean for the Gulf CSWFs?

Understanding the Gulf CSWFs has proved challenging for the international financial markets. The inadequate public information on Gulf SWFs' operation has caused huge uncertainty about their impact on the global financial system. Figure 8.1 indicates the key area of ambiguity of the funds' activities: the failure to provide information to the public about the structure of the funds' relationship with various domestic and foreign entities, as well as into intra-organizational relationships within the SWFs.

The nature of the funds' relationships with each element of the environment in which they operate, plays an important part in forming the role of these institutions in the global financial context. The key areas of connection between

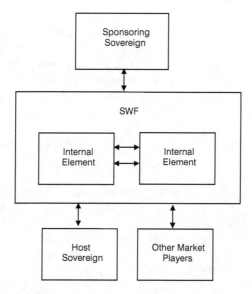

Figure 8.1 SWF's relationship with the surrounding environment
Source: author

the funds and their surrounding environment, include the fund's relationship with the sponsoring sovereign nation; the intra-organizational relationships within the sovereign wealth investment institutions; the fund's relationship with the host sovereign nation; and the fund's relationship with other market players. Providing adequate and accurate data to clarify the position of these institutions in relation to the surrounding environment is indeed expected to be a responsibility of their sponsoring sovereign nation which they have frequently failed to deliver.

The relationship between the fund and the sovereign sponsor is one of the central issues surrounding the transparency of the SWFs. Reviewing the experience of the Gulf sovereign wealth management practices highlights a historical lack of available and adequate information by the governments of the Gulf on issues such as flow of funds, savings and withdrawals' regulation, decision-making processes and strategy.

Another aspect of the funds' operation is intra-organizational relationships within the funds, where there is a lack of information on their practice of corporate governance. There is a shortage of data that can clarify the relationship between various elements within the funds. This is particularly important as it clarifies the extent to which the funds' investment strategies are influenced by their sponsoring sovereigns. The controlling influence of the sponsoring governments over directors, legal principles relating to fiduciary responsibility, and avoidance of conflicts of interest in the Gulf funds has been unknown in much detail. It is assumed that the sponsoring sovereign holds unlimited control over the above-mentioned elements of corporate governance of the funds. Lack of good corporate governance practice has been a key question in the debate over the non-commercial investment objectives of the funds. Moreover, lack of independent auditing processes in place for most of the Gulf funds underlines the lack of transparent information on the connection between the state and government organisations with the country's SWF. Their internal auditing procedures appear vague and in some cases, for example Iran SWF, there are no external audits of the funds' financial statements. Furthermore, most of the internal audit reports are not published, and there are no clear provisions for ensuring the integrity of operations. Nor is there a well-defined framework within the legal structure of the sponsoring countries to describe the institutional context in which the operational procedures, objectives, role, scope and responsibilities of the funds and their subsidiaries are carried out.

With regards to the funds' relationship with other market players, the size of the assets of the funds is a key factor, which due to lack of transparency and the limited availability of statistics has usually remained unclear. Most of these funds are not captured in macroeconomic data sets and there is no regular and timely publication of accurate data on the size, sources and the composition of assets and liabilities, or on the type and class of the assets. This is why most of the available financial data on these funds is based on no more than speculation and guesswork, mainly produced by other market players, and there are often huge differences between the data produced by various sources. Another area of information that explains the funds' activities in relation to other market players is the figures that relate to the shareholdings of the funds. To avoid the obligations of regulatory notification requirements, and/or reporting ownership interest to the invested companies and regulating bodies, acquisitions of shares in publicly traded companies by these institutions are often kept under certain thresholds (5 per cent in the USA, 10 per cent in the EU) (IMF, 2009).

In addition, there is the significant risk that the funds potentially impose on market integrity. GCC funds, like other market players, are capable of insider trading and other forms of market manipulation. Due to the ownership of these funds, it may be more difficult for the rules of market integrity to be enforced against these institutional investors. In other words, given that the owners of these funds are the governments, they are potentially capable of utilizing their political power in the interests of their commercial objectives, which might jeopardize the integrity of international financial markets. Similar to above mentioned aspects of the Gulf SWFs' activities, the extent to which the Gulf sovereign wealth management institutions' operations are committed to maintaining market integrity is not clear, which has, in some cases, led to financial fraud. The KIA's website offers a good example for rules, procedures and code of conduct of the organization to address the issue of violation of market integrity. The KIA code of conduct is stated 'to be respected and honoured by its staff without restricting appropriate flexibility, and aim to set exemplary standards for professional behaviour, prudence' (www.kia.gov.kw). The code of conduct and other relevant documents for the KIA are not publicly available. The KIA also encourages the staff 'to devise appropriate benchmarks, set realistic targets, and be responsible for their performance' (www.kia.gov.kw). Again, the details of what conduct comprises 'responsible performance' at the KIA have not been defined in the information made available to the public by the authority via its website.

The lack of transparent information is likely to divert economic analysis and has the potential to mislead policy makers of both the sponsoring and the host economies of the funds as well as other global market participants. A report published by the Bank of England in 2003 argued that in order to maintain the transparency of the financial organizations, the distribution of information must be coherent and open, while disclosures may need to be selective (Gai and Shin, 2003). The findings of this study, however, show that an element of distrust has been born amongst the host sovereign nations as a result of the lack of (or selective) distribution of information. Some individuals within the political establishment of the sposoring governments of the funds must surely have had full access to the details of the SWFs' operation information, though limited public access to such information has raised suspicions about the various objectives of these funds.

There is an opposing view, which believes that these funds have so far done nothing to violate the trust of their host sovereign nation. That is why the argument about lack trust as a result of lack of information is not relevant. This view suggests that instead of creating trust in host economies, these funds must seek ways through which they can gain legitimacy, as legitimacy is what the funds are lacking as far the host countries are concerned. Ashby Monk, in a paper entitled 'Recasting the Sovereign Wealth Fund Debate: Trust, Legitimacy, and Governance', notes that institutional legitimacy occurs when 'organizational procedures, structures and principles align with the values, norms and expectations of the society in the environment in which the organization seeks legitimacy'. He points out that for the SWFs, 'gaining legitimacy is synonymous with gaining access to operate and invest in a given country or market' (Monk, 2009a). It is rather challenging to draw a line between legitimacy and trust as Monk did in his paper. Firstly, as discussed above, the principles and procedures of the funds' relations with the other entities in the environment in which they operate are unclear, so are their intra-organization relations. Thus, in the absence of information, it is difficult to evaluate whether or not those values and structures align with the expectations of the host society should it be in relation to the issue of trust or to the issue of legitimacy.

Secondly, a counter-example to Monk's argument is the case of GCC SWFs. Historically the Arab Gulf sponsoring sovereign governments of these SWFs had been the closest allies of the Western powers in the region. Now one may ask: 'Would such alliance have been formed, in its existing form, should the West not see those Arab governments as legitimate?' Indeed, regardless of the correlation between the political and economic alliance between the West and the Arab Gulf states, in some cases they have had difficulties in accessing certain markets in the host countries of their Western allies. Therefore, the issue of lack of information about these funds was not raised merely on the basis of the legitimacy of their sponsoring government. To the contrary, lack of trust has played a significant role in the transparency debate.

Now, regardless of trust or legitimacy, let us look at what are the key factors contributing to the non-transparent reputation of these organizations. Firstly, the Gulf governments that were historically built around the monopolized authority of the ruling families (vested in them by the former colonial power in the region) have never felt obliged to act in a transparent manner domestically. The Iranian government also has never exercised transparent financial policies (despite the different political system of Iran to those of the GCC). Inevitably, the sponsoring sovereigns of the Gulf SWFs have avoided disclosure of information to the public. The best example is Kuwait, where clauses 8 and 9 of Law No. 47 of 1982 concerning the KIA clearly prohibit general disclosure to the public of any information related to the KIA's work, while also setting out the 'penalties' for unauthorized disclosure of information to the public (www.kia.gov.kw). Secondly, in the case of the Gulf funds, there is a huge data deficit. The data collection system in the region is relatively underdeveloped; therefore, there is a 'lack of data' rather than a lack of 'transparency of data'. In some areas of the funds' relations with their surrounding environment, there are no clear procedures embedded in the legal system of the sponsoring countries. In other words, the issue of lack of available information to the public stems from a lack of a strong legal and institutional framework, while from the Western perspective the Gulf sponsoring governments have the law and procedures in place but they do not share them with the public.

How did the debate start?

The debate about the need for greater transparency of SWFs was triggered by two proposed transactions by two foreign companies in the USA. The companies themselves were not SWFs, but their major shareholders were SWFs. One of the transactions, which was proposed in June 2005, involved the Chinese National Offshore Oil Company (CNOOC), 70 per cent of which is owned by the Chinese government. The second controversial transaction was proposed by Dubai Ports World (DPW), a subsidiary of Dubai World, one of the Dubai SWFs.

The CNOOC failed deal

On 7 June 2005, the CNOOC made an offer of US$18.5 billion to acquire the Union Oil Company of California (Unocal). Unocal is a California-based oil company founded in 1890. The next bidder was the Chevron Oil Company offering US$16 billion. The offer led to an intense discussion among American politicians, and the debate was also made public by the media. On 17 June 2005, two Republican representatives from California, Richard W. Pombo and Duncan Hunter, wrote to President Bush expressing their concern about the effect of CNOOC's bid for Unocal on US jobs, energy production and energy security (Timmons, 2005), and questioned the transaction on the grounds of national security (Barboza and Sorkin, 2005). On 24 June 2005, the *New York Times* published a report on the ongoing negotiations between Unocal and CNOOC, quoting Michael O'Hanlon, an international military specialist at the Brookings Institution: 'It does raise questions about how much of the country we are willing to sell to a Communist country that we might be fighting someday... I'd be surprised if we really fall on our sword to prevent the sale' (Wayne and Barboza, 2005). In August 2005, domestic policy makers, whose fears of losing control over strategic US oil resources were fuelled by Chevron lobbyists in Washington, ultimately forced the CNOOC to withdraw its bid. In response to the US government's reaction to the bid, CNOOC issued a statement after the withdrawal, saying that such unprecedented political opposition had been '...regrettable and unjustified... This political environment has made it very difficult for us to accurately assess our chance of success, creating a level of uncertainty that presents an unacceptable risk to our ability to secure this transaction' (MSNBC, 2005). Shortly after this, Chevron completed its acquisition of Unocal.

The controversy of DPW

A few months after the CNOOC scandal in August 2005, DPW approached another American company, wanting to buy the British ports operator, Peninsular and Oriental Steam Navigation Company (P&O) (BBC, 2006). P&O managed ports in eighteen countries, including six major East Coast ports in the USA: New York, New Jersey, Philadelphia, Baltimore, New Orleans and Miami. DPW notified the Committee on Foreign Investment in the United States (CFIUS) about its intentions to acquire P&O, and CFIUS duly agreed to DPW's acquisition of P&O. However, the CFIUS's approval of the deal caused negative reactions amongst US domestic policy makers. Several lawmakers, including Peter King, a Republican representative of Long Island, who was also chairman of the House Homeland Security Committee, and Senator Charles Schumer, criticized the speed of the approval process, claiming that there had been insufficient scrutiny of the security ramifications of the deal for the US (McGeehan, 2006). The Congress demonstrated American patriotism by opposing the acquisition, and the CFIUS was criticized further for approving the DPW transaction without a full investigation. The UAE was referred to as a state supporter of terrorism, and concern was raised over the possibility of the company being infiltrated by terrorists. On 22 February 2006, President Bush strongly supported the decision to approve the DPW transaction approval and released the following statement:

> The administration, as required by law, has reviewed the transaction to make certain that it does not in any way jeopardize national security. Under the process conducted by the Committee on Foreign Investment in the United States (CFIUS), officials carefully reviewed the national security issues raised by the transaction and its effect on our national security. Twelve Federal agencies and the government's counterterrorism experts closely and carefully reviewed the transaction to make certain it posed no threat to national security.
>
> (The White House, 2006)

P&O's shareholders approved the sale in early March 2006 and DPW voluntarily submitted to a further forty-five days of investigation by the CFIUS. At the same time, the Democrats were pushing for amendments to reform the legislation and to ensure that no UAE-related company would have any control over US port operations. The amendment, sponsored by Schumer, would block not only the Dubai deal, but also any other US port deals with companies wholly owned or controlled by any foreign government that had recognized the Taliban in Afghanistan between 1996 and 2001. DPW finally had to withdraw from the deal; a statement was released by the company's chief operating officer, Edward H. Bilkey, and read in the Senate by Senator John Warner: '...because of the strong relationship between the United Arab Emirates and the United States and to preserve that relationship, DP World has decided to transfer fully the U.S. operation of P&O Operations North America to a United States entity' (Porteus, 2006).

The CNOOC and DPW episodes ended with the forced withdrawal of both companies, although the reaction of the US administration to the two cases was somewhat different. The Chinese government-owned CNOOC did not receive the same support from the White House as DPW. According to Professor Gordon Clark of Oxford University, who was interviewed during the field research of this project, there is, generally speaking:

> ...less pressure on investments by the rich Arab states from the US government. The reason for this is that the US policy makers believe that the Chinese would never have grown as high and fast without the American support during the Cold War. The US had tried to split China from the Soviet Union for decades by supporting the Chinese economic liberalization process. Now, it is time for the Chinese to show their support of the US.

The second point raised by Professor Clark concerning the rationale for the US-led transparency debate was 'the economic nationalism of a group of American domestic policy makers' who saw foreign investments in the US, in any shape or form and regardless of the sponsoring country of those investors, as a potential threat to the national security of the USA.

Both deals were initiated within a few months of the US Congressional mid-term elections in November 2006. This coincidence made the Congress rather eager to demonstrate that they would not be out-manoeuvred by President Bush, the CFIUS or the Chairman of the Joint Chiefs of Staff; the Democrat and Republican parties were also both seeking recognition for taking a stronger stand on national security issues (Winfield Bean, 2010).

Foreign investments in the USA

For several decades foreign investment in the USA has been causing anxiety among American politicians, and various measures have been taken to protect the national interest that have continued to develop over time. All these measures are concerned with the broadly defined term 'national security', and have been dealt with through the following procedures:

- The CFIUS: in 1975, President Gerald Ford signed an Executive Order for the establishment of a committee to review certain investments by foreign investors in the USA. At that time there was no explicit concern about direct or indirect control of American businesses by foreign governments. In 2006, there were approximately 10,000 merger transactions in the USA, of which 1,730 involved a foreign party and which only required review by CFIUS. None of these transactions was blocked by CFIUS (Kimmit, 2008).
- The Exon-Florio Amendment: in 1988 an amendment was made to the previous regulation on foreign investments in the USA to empower the president to investigate foreign investment deals in American businesses that would jeopardise national security.
- The Byrd Amendment: in 1993 Senator Robert Byrd raised concerns with CFIUS over the sufficiency of new amendments for protecting American security. As a result of this, Section 721 of the Defence Production Act was altered. The change required the investigation of investments by foreign governments that could affect national security.
- The Foreign Investment and National Security Act (FINSA): in 2007, FINSA was mandated to establish new standards for bringing CFIUS's investment review procedures under more direct congressional supervision.

The OECD regulation for foreign investments

While the USA has been developing regulations for foreign investments that are concerned specifically with America's national security, the OECD has been working to develop international rules relating to foreign investment. The principal OECD instruments for regulating international capital movements are:

- Codes of Liberalization: including the Code of Liberalization of Capital Movements, and the Code of Liberalization of Current Invisible Operations, which promote non-discriminatory liberalization of capital movements (OECD, 2008a).
- Declaration and Decisions on International Investment and Multinational Enterprises: these contain agreements among member countries for cooperation on a wide range of issues related to international investments. Four elements are included: national treatment, guidelines for multinational enterprises, international investment incentives and disincentives, and conflicting requirements (OECD, 2000).

The issue of protecting national security in the OECD's member countries has also been considered. Existing investment codes recognize the right of countries to protect their important security interests. The 'Freedom of Investment,

National Security and "Strategic" Industries', which was reviewed in March 2008, emphasised the need for:

> ...further clarification of the content and best practices regarding the implementation of the three guiding principles, especially regarding 'accountability'. It will also explore the interaction of investors' transparency and governance practices (e.g. adequate disclosure) with recipient countries' efforts to design and implement policies that efficiently address national security concerns while preserving the open investment environment.
>
> (OECD, 2008b)

In addition, a separate group at the OECD had been working on the existing OECD guidelines for the Corporate Governance of State-Owned Enterprises and exploring the extent to which these were relevant for the SWFs (OECD, 2005).

The EU regulation on foreign investments

Despite the EU's rules on the free movement of capital, the debate about sovereign investments has reached Europe. Most of the European politicians have promised to keep their economies open to all investors, sovereign or otherwise. They have welcomed SWF investments to link both the oil-producing countries and the emerging markets of Asia more closely with the EU. Thus, Article 56 of the European Commission Treaty prohibits 'all restrictions on the movement of capital between Member States and between Member States and third countries' (www.ec.europa.eu). While the EU legal framework does allow investment reviews to protect national security, the European Commission tries to prevent member states from blocking acquisitions for protectionist reasons. The European Court of Justice is the judiciary body for dealing with alleged actions by member countries that can limit the free movement of capital. Even so, most of the EU countries have various rules in place to protect the strategic sectors of their economies from investments that have national security implications. Most of these regulations are concerned with foreign investments in defence, media and infrastructure. In the EU, legal regimes are very diverse, for example:

- The British government, like the US government, can veto almost any deal, though this has never happened in the way that it did in the US.
- France has strict controls in its defence and security sectors but none in other industries.
- Germany introduced a framework similar to that of the CFIUS in 2008.
- The Netherlands has no such processes at all (Veron, 2011).

There have been several examples of unfriendly European attitude towards the SWFs. In July 2007, a bid by Barclays for ABN-Amro ended unsuccessfully after the China Development Bank and Singapore's Temasek had taken a large stake in the UK bank (Fletcher, 2007). In the late 1980s the British authorities asked the KIA to reduce its stake in BP from 22 per cent to below 10 per cent. In Germany, when Neptune Orient Lines (controlled by Temasek) attempted to buy Hapag-Lloyd in 2008, workers took to the streets to demonstrate against feared job losses. The company was then sold to a German consortium (Reuters, 2008a).

In response to the controversy over state-owned investment institutions entering the EU, a number of proposal have been made. EU Trade Commissioner Peter Mandelson suggested in 2007 that so-called 'golden shares', which in certain circumstances give their owners veto rights, could be used to protect strategic assets in the EU against foreign takeovers (Ahmad, 2007), while a report on SWFs commissioned in 2008 by the French government suggested that 'European regulation on foreign investment should be founded on the principle of reciprocity' (Barysch et al., 2008).

Unlike the US and European economies, Australia and New Zealand have been far more welcoming to SWFs. Asian SWFs and those from oil-exporting economies have substantial investments in these two economies. SWFs of Singapore have more commercial assets in Australia than the Government of Australia (http://www.swfinstitute.org/fund/gic.php).

How transparent are the Gulf SWFs?

The debate over fears of negative influence from the GCC SWFs on the host economies has been driven mainly by a lack of understanding of the structure, governance, legal framework, and operational procedures and policies of these institutions. A number of factors have contributed to the rise of uncertainty amongst the host sovereigns including:

1   The limited available information on the investment activities (size of assets, investment strategy, etc.) of the funds.
2   Senior management positions in these institutions have been monopolized for decades by members of the ruling families or those closely linked to them, which confirms the strong government influence on the operational policies of these institutions.
3   There have been a few financial scandals in the Gulf CSWFs over large-scale corruption in handling the volumes of assets (the KIA in Spain, the BCCI's links with the ADIA, and the IFESA's poor performance in the domestic markets) which have a negative reputational impact on the funds.
4   The national laws and regulations for managing these organizations are unclear, and in most cases there are no procedures in place to monitor transactions in and out of the funds' accounts which produce publicly available data.
5   Reporting and auditing procedures among the sovereign management institutions in the Gulf region are not disclosed.
6   The role of the CSWFs in domestic policy frameworks is not clear, and the funds' assets and activities are not included in macroeconomic data sets.

7   Historically, public sectors in the Gulf countries have been known to be inefficient, and public administration has remained underdeveloped. The growing financial power of the public sector in the region is a potential threat for wider inefficiencies and corruption that can spread throughout the international financial network.

All in all, there has been a sense of uncertainty over the funds' management of their assets in the international markets. There is concern over the probability that the sponsoring sovereigns of the Gulf SWFs will manage their sovereign wealth investments in pursuit of political objectives. This has raised a number of national security concerns, particularly in the aftermath of the post-2001 terrorist incidents in the West. Furthermore, the Gulf countries have failed to draw a distinct line between their political and financial elites. In all of the Arabian Gulf countries, the sovereign wealth investment institutions are managed by either members of the ruling family who are close in rank to the ruler, or by those who are not a royal family members but are directly appointed by the monarch.

Finally, the rising financial power of the Gulf's sponsoring sovereigns puts these countries in a position from which they are capable of promoting state-owned or state-controlled national champions as global champions. Potentially this can lead to political conflicts and economic distortions between countries (Truman, 2008a). However, the sponsoring governments of the funds seem to be aware of the implications of their actions. As has happened in the past, with Middle Eastern governments like Iran and Libya, if the sponsoring sovereigns take any action at a time of probable political crisis that would indicate their intention of using their assets for political leverage, they will lose their access to Western markets and are likely to receive strong reactions from the recipient.

Measuring transparency of Gulf CSWFs

Various methods have been designed for measuring the level of transparency of SWFs. The most popular ones are the Truman Scoreboard and Linaburg-Maduell. Both methods introduce an index for the transparency of each fund, and these indexes are calculated from a series of yes/no questions. The sum of the scores for all the answers about each fund represents the index for transparency of that fund.

Truman Scoreboard

In 2007, Edwin Truman from the Peterson Institute for International Economics created a scoreboard for SWFs, which ranked the funds based on systematic and regularly available public information. The scoreboard covers four basic categories: (1) structure, (2) governance, (3) transparency and accountability, and (4) behaviour. Within each category there is a set of yes/no questions, the answers to which score between 1 and 0 (or sometimes 0.5 and 0.25). In total Truman asks twenty-five questions.

Structure

1 Is the SWF's objective clearly communicated?
2 Is the source of the SWF's funding clearly specified?
3 Is the nature of the subsequent use of the principal and earnings in the fund clearly stated?
4 Are these elements of fiscal treatment integrated with the budget?
5 Are the guidelines for fiscal treatment generally followed without frequent adjustment?
6 Is the overall investment strategy clearly communicated?
7 Is the procedure for changing the structure clear?
8 Is the SWF separate from the country's international reserves?

Governance

9 Is the role of the government in setting the investment strategy of the SWF clearly established?
10 Is the role of the manager in executing the investment strategy clearly established?
11 Does the SWF have in place and publicly available guidelines for corporate responsibility that it follows?
12 Does the SWF have ethical guidelines that it follows?

Transparency and Accountability

13 Does the SWF provide at least an annual report on its activities and results?
14 Does the SWF provide quarterly reports on its activities?
15 Do regular reports on the investments by the SWF include the size of the fund?
16 Do regular reports on the investments by the SWF include information on the returns it earns?
17 Do regular reports on investments by the SWF include information on the types of investments?
18 Do regular reports on the investments by the SWF include information on the geographic location of investments?
19 Do regular reports on the investments by the SWF include information on the specific investments?
20 Do regular reports on the investments by the SWF include information on the currency composition of investments?
21 Are the holders of investment mandates identified?
22 Is the SWF subjected to a regular audit?
23 Is the audit published?
24 Is the audit independent?

Behaviour

25 Does the SWF indicate the nature and speed of adjustment?

(Truman, 2007)

In 2009, Truman revised the scoreboard and added eight more elements; after adding a number of questions to the previous list of twenty-five and also removing a few, his 2009 scoreboard included thirty-three questions.

In the elements concerning structure, question 5 in the guidelines on fiscal treatment was removed from the 2007 scoreboard and replaced by a question on whether or not the SWF has a 'clear legal framework'. Three questions were also added to those concerning the governance of SWFs:

- Is the role of the governing body of the SWF clearly established?
- Are decisions on specific investments made by the managers?
- Does the SWF have internal ethical guidelines?

Among the elements concerning transparency and accountability, a question about regular reports on the types of investments of the SWFs was deleted and the following questions were added:

- Does the strategy use benchmarks?
- Does the strategy use credit ratings?
- Are the holders of investment mandate identified?

Finally, three further questions were added to the section on behaviour:

- Does the SWF have a policy on the use of derivatives?
- Does the SWF have a policy on the use of leverage?
- Does the SWF have an operational risk management policy?

(Truman, 2010)

Linaburg-Maduell Transparency Index

The Linaburg-Maduell Transparency Index was developed in 2007 at the SWF Institute by Carl Linaburg and Michael Maduell, who based their index on ten essential principles for disclosure of information on SWFs to the public. The scores for each question depend on the answer (yes is equal to 1 and no is equal to 0), is between 0 and 1. The SWF Institute recommends a minimum rating of 8 for a fund to be recognized as adequately transparent. The process is ongoing and the ratings may change as additional information is released. The principles include the following:

1 Fund provides history including reason for creation, origins of wealth, and government ownership structure
2 Fund provides up-to-date independently audited annual reports
3 Fund provides ownership percentage of company holdings, and geographic locations of holdings
4 Fund provides total portfolio market value, returns, and management compensation

5 Fund provides guidelines in reference to ethical standards, investment policies, and enforce of guidelines
6 Fund provides clear strategies and objectives
7 If applicable, the fund clearly identifies subsidiaries and contact information
8 If applicable, the fund identifies external managers
9 Fund manages its own web site
10 Fund provides main office location address and contact information such as telephone and fax.

(SWF Institute, no date b)

Abu Dhabi SWFs' transparency efforts

There has been a significant improvement in the Gulf CSWFs' transparency score since 2007. As Table 8.1 shows, two of Abu Dhabi's sovereign investment institutions, the ADIA and Mubadala, have recorded an impressive increase in the number of points that they gained in 2009. Mubadala's points improved from 3.75 in 2007 to 59 in 2009, and the ADIA's score improved between 2007 and 2009 from 0.5 to 11.

The government of Abu Dhabi has actively invested in creating and maintaining a positive reputation for the emirate's CSWFs particularly since the purchase by the ADIA of 4.9 per cent of Citigroup in 2007. The ADIA, like DPW, is a SWF and Abu Dhabi is a member of the UAE as is Dubai, but the experience of DPW in 2005 was one which the government of Abu Dhabi will never wish to repeat (Abdelal, 2009). The size of the stake in Citigroup purchased by the ADIA was below the legal threshold for mandatory disclosure, but it would have been extremely difficult for the ADIA to keep the deal confidential in the US financial climate at the time when the deal was closed (Sidel, 2007).

The attitude of American domestic policy makers at the time of the financial difficulties of 2007 was not the same as it had been in 2005. Commenting in 2007 on the ADIA–Citi deal, Senator Schumer, who had actively lobbied against the DPW deal in 2005, remarked that:

> It seemed to me that this is good for Citigroup, it's good for jobs in New York. It bolsters their capital position, allows what is fundamentally a very strong company to weather a difficult time. My worries relate to when there is a very strong security interest as in the ports deal or if they are buying an entity that is not purely an economic one. They have made those assurances and have lived up to them in the past.

(Timmons and Werdigier, 2007)

In responding to the welcoming position in the US, the ADIA was obliged to take a friendly and transparent approach. In January 2008, the ADIA hired a US public relations company, Burson-Marsteller, mainly to help them form a strategy to deal with the banks and the US Congress. James Lake, a former official in the

Table 8.1 Comparison of sovereign wealth fund scoreboards (2007–2009)

Fund's name	Score 2007	Score 2009	Change in percentage points 2008–09	2007–09	Linaburg-Maduell Transparency Index 2010
Norway	23.0	97	5	5	10
KIA	12.0	63	15	15	6
Mubadala	3.75	59	45	47	10
Istithmar	3.5	15	3	2	n/a
ADIA	0.5	11	3	7	3
SAMA	Truman does not calculate an index for SAMA as it does not have an identifiable structure which is independent from the central bank				2

Source: Edwin Truman (2010) and Sovereign Wealth Institute website

Department of Commerce under US presidents Ronald Reagan and George W. H. Bush, was Chairman of Burson-Marsteller when the deal between the ADIA and Burson-Marsteller was signed, and is believed to have played an important role (Kerr and Khalaf, 2008).

Shortly after, in March 2008, the US Treasury coordinated the creation of principles for investments of SWFs into the USA. Hamad Al-Hurr Al-Suwaidi, a member of the board, and Hareb Masood Al-Darmaki, an executive director, both from the ADIA, worked directly with Secretary Paulson on this initiative (Wayne, 2008). In May 2008, the IWG of SWFs was established. The ADIA became a founding member of the IWG and Hamad Al-Hurr Al-Suwaidi became co-chair and undersecretary of the group. In October 2008 the IWG published the SWFs' GAPP, which are also known as the Santiago Principles (see Appendix A).

Generally accepted code of conduct for SWFs

Debate over the practice of SWFs concluded that the best way forward would be to develop a voluntary code of principles for SWFs, which would clarify that investment decisions were driven by the financial and economic considerations, not political motives, of these institutions.

History of the GAPP

The creation of a code of conduct for SWFs in November 2007 was initiated at the Roundtable of Sovereign Asset and Reserve Managers, organized by the IMF. The IMF's roundtable was attended by senior-level delegates from central banks, finance ministers and sovereign asset managers from twenty-eight countries. It was planned that the IMF, in identifying sound practices to be followed in the management of SWFs, would take the views of the sponsoring sovereign and the host sovereign sides into consideration. Dominique Strauss-Kahn, the managing director of the IMF, emphasized the imperative need for SWFs to function 'in ways that are consistent with global financial stability' (Das, D.K., 2008).

Existing IMF standards of governance and transparency

Before 2007, a range of fund guides produced by the IMF already existed for fiscal, monetary and financial transparency and for reserve management; these included IMF guidelines on fiscal transparency and reserve management.

- The fiscal transparency guidelines emphasize the legal composition of institutions and clarify their roles, objectives, responsibilities, information flow and assurances of integrity. Relevant standards include: The Code on Good Practices in Fiscal Transparency, Special Data Dissemination Standards, General Data Dissemination Systems, and the Code of Good Practice on Transparency in Monetary and Financial Policies. These are supported by the Guide on Resource Revenue Transparency and the Manual on Fiscal Transparency.
- The reserve management guidelines stress the significance of the roles, responsibilities and objectives of the financial agencies responsible for reserve management. They also strongly emphasize an open process for reserve management operations and the public availability of information on foreign exchange reserves, as well as accountability and assurances of integrity by reserve management agencies, achieved by a sound institutional and risk management framework. One of the relevant guides of this kind is the Guidelines for Foreign Exchange Reserve Management (IMF, 2009).

Santiago Principles

In April 2008, the IWG was established in Washington, at a meeting of twenty-three IMF member countries with SWFs; these were Australia, Azerbaijan, Bahrain, Botswana, Canada, Chile, China, Equatorial Guinea, Islamic Republic of Iran, Ireland, Korea, Kuwait, Libya, Mexico, New Zealand, Norway, Qatar, Russia, Singapore, Timor-Leste, Trinidad and Tobago, the UAE and the US. In addition to the member countries, the IWG has a number of permanent observers; Oman, Saudi Arabia, Vietnam, the OECD and the World Bank. The GAPP were created by the IMF according to the following guiding objectives for SWFs:

1　To assist maintenance of global financial stability and free flow of capital;
2　To observe all applicable regulatory and disclosure requirements in their host countries;
3　To have appropriate consideration of the economic and financial risk; and
4　To apply transparent and sound governance which provide adequate operational controls, risk management, and accountability.

(International Working Group of Sovereign Wealth Funds, 2008)

The IWG development after the creation of the GAPP

The IWG evolved into an informal coordinating and knowledge-sharing initiative and was renamed the International Forum of Sovereign Wealth Funds (IFSWF). The IFSWF held meetings in Kuwait City in April 2009 (International Working Group of Sovereign Wealth Funds, 2009a) (the IFSWF was established at this meeting), in October 2009 in Baku (International Forum of Sovereign Wealth Funds, 2009), in May 2010 in Sydney, and was scheduled to meet in April 2011 in Beijing (International Forum of Sovereign Wealth Funds, 2010). In the spirit of GAPP, a number of SWFs demonstrated their commitment to the Santiago Principles, having conducted self-assessments to ensure compliance with the principles. Some, including the ADIA and Mubadala, published their first annual public reports right after the introduction of GAPP. The creation of GAPP was a positive development in the international dialogue about SWFs. However, there has been little public assessment of the implementation of these principles by the twenty-six IWG signatories, and no third-party verification for the performance of GAPP by the SWF members of the IWG.

During the IFSWF meeting in Kuwait, subcommittees were established to work on such issues as: experiences in applying the Santiago Principles to date, investment and risk management practices, the international investment environment, and recipient country relationships (International Working Group of Sovereign Wealth Funds, 2009b). Overall, however, the process appears to be rather slow, and debate on the threat posed by SWFs seems to have peaked. But SWFs will remain active institutional investors for years to come, which will probably push the IFSWF into coming up with controlling measures that will increase SWF compliance with the GAPP.

The KIA's compliance with GAPP lagged behind that of the ADIA by 8 per cent in 2010 (see Figure 8.2), while the Peterson scoreboard showed 12 and 0.5 points respectively for the KIA and the ADIA on the initial index for the Gulf CSWFs. The KIA is reported to have been under substantial domestic pressure from parliament about its foreign investments, and has been pressed to play a more active role in stabilizing Kuwait's domestic economy (Behrendt, 2010). Furthermore, the volume of assets under the KIA's management is notably smaller than that of the ADIA. Thus, compared with the ADIA, small sizeof assets along with considerable pressure from the domestic policy makers have made the KIA less active in Western markets. This may make the KIA less motivated to improve its image as a transparent SWF.

Conclusion

The findings of this chapter show the key issue behind the transparency debate was to understand whether or not the SWFs were really a threat to the national security of the host countries. The debate over the SWFs' threat to the stability of host sovereign nations is a result of the issue of ownership in SWFs. In other words, sovereigns owning SWFs are capable of using the government's

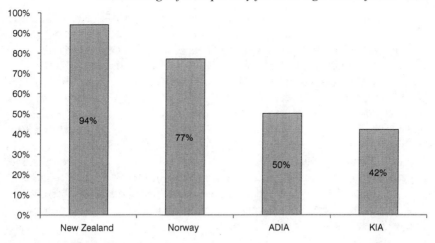

Figure 8.2 Selected funds' GAPP Compliance Index as of March 2010
Source: Sven Behrendt (2010)

financial resources to satisfy the interests of the government. This has become a source of mistrust in countries in which the SWFs invest, although the funds have taken no action and shown no intention of proving that such mistrust is rational. To undermine the notion of mistrust against the SWFs, a voluntary code of conduct for SWFs (GAPP) was created by the funds to promote transparency, accountability and good governance in these investment institutions, although the implementation of GAPP has been weak, and the process appears to have lost some of its earlier momentum. There are no formal authorities to enforce the GAPP.

To a great extent, the financial crisis that began in 2008 has changed perceptions of SWFs. Funds that were previously seen as threat to the national security of the USA became the providers of capital for struggling American financial institutions and even the strongest opposing US domestic politicians in the DPW case became the supporters of Arab SWFs' investments in Wall Street banks in the aftermath of the crisis. Therefore, the financial demand of the host economy is a key factor in forming the host sovereign nation's policies towards the SWFs. The world has undergone major changes since the financial crisis of 2008. Almost all the acquisitions by the SWFs have been approved and welcomed by Western host sovereign nations. The chang in attitude of the West resulted not from improved transparency in operation of these funds, but from a high demand for capital in the developed economies.

In the transparency debate, fears of the SWFs' non-commercial investment interests raised new concerns in the host economies about the risk of protectionism, now the greatest risk to the global economies. The possibility of the creation of unnecessary barriers to the free flow of capital into the global financial system has increased over the last few years. Competitive freedom and investment efficiency have been threatened by the growing risk of protectionist approaches among the host economies. It is unlikely that the Santiago initiative will help to minimize the threat.

It is hard to imagine the SWFs' compliance with the GAPP principles will prevent cases like CNOOC and the DPW. It is true that the US administration welcomed SWF investments in the US financial sector; nevertheless, the American government's perception of the country's strategic sectors is unlikely to have changed. The global financial crisis may have postponed such cases; however, with the increasing growth of SWF's assets it is expected that once the global economy recovers from the recent financial predicament there will be more similar cases. All in all, lack of trust in the SWFs and the debate over transparency has not ended with the introduction of GAPP. Even if compliance with the Santiago Principles becomes compulsory for all the SWFs, the US, and other Western governments in general, are unlikely to permit foreign governments to have ownership of their key industries.

9   Conclusion

CSWFs have grown drastically over the last few decades and it is anticipated that their assets will increase still more over the years to come, as a result of commodity price increases. The Gulf region is the origin of the some of the world's largest commodity-based funds, and they have gained a significant degree of financial power within the global economy that is expected to continue for the foreseeable future.

One of the core elements of the debate over the SWFs has been the issue of transparency. The Gulf SWFs have been ranked by various institutions as the least transparent SWFs in the world. Global initiatives for promoting transparency of operation and good governance of the SWFs have been taken rather well by some of the GCC funds, mainly by those from Abu Dhabi, and the sponsoring sovereigns of the Arab Gulf SWFs have broadly accepted that, in order to remain active in the financial markets of the developed world, they need to apply more transparent strategies. Hamad Al Hur Al-Suweidi, a key figure in the department of finance of the government of Abu Dhabi co-chaired the IWG of SWFs in 2008, and Bader Mohammad Al-Sa'd, managing director of the KIA, has co-chaired the IFSWF since the Forum was established by the IWG, and technically replaced it, in 2009. As a result of such close collaboration, the transparency index of the SWFs, sponsored by the government of Abu Dhabi and to a lesser degree by the KIA, has recorded improvement.

While some of the governments of the Gulf have taken active roles in leading the global initiative for transparency of the SWFs (i.e. Kuwait and Abu Dhabi), the government of Saudi Arabia has shown very little interest in contributing to this scheme. Saudi Arabia has remained a permanent observer of the IWG and did not become a member of IFSWF. The main reason why the Saudi government has applied such an approach comes from the fact that the SAMA has been the country's central bank and the government has remained somewhat reluctant to introduce the SAMA as an SWF. Though the agency has been a key organization in managing Saudi sovereign wealth, with the creation of the new government-owned investment institution, SES, the Saudi government may find it rather difficult to maintain the low profile of its sovereign wealth practices. If the SES becomes an active institutional investor in the global financial markets, the Saudi authorities may well need to comply with the GAPP.

Iran's SWF has been a member of the IWG and IFSWF. However, given that the investment strategy of the IFESA is focused mainly on the domestic economy, there has not been much pressure on the Iranian government to take a more transparent approach. Due to the prevailing economic sanctions, the IFESA has not been an active institutional investor globally; therefore, despite the domestic debt, there has been no pressure from the international financial system for the Iranian authorities to improve the governance and credibility of the IFESA. Nevertheless, the new initiative for the creation of the NDF shows that in the proposal that was submitted to the Majlis, the government has taken some of the principles of the GAPP into account. In particular, the principles that concern the independence of the fund's management from the political elite, and the principles related to having a clear savings policy, are evidently being taken into account. This shows that despite the significant lack of motivation for transparency and good governance because of Iran's economic isolation, the government has picked up some lessons both from participating in the global initiative for transparency of the SWFs, and from its poor performance in managing the country's sovereign wealth in previous years. Given the track record of the government in managing the oil income, there might be a gap between what has been proposed by the government regarding the NDF and what will be exercised in practice.

The transparency of the Norwegian government's sovereign wealth management strategy has enabled it to remain in the highest-ranked position amongst the world's CSWFs. The GPFG has set a great example for the transparency of sovereign wealth management in countries that possess rich natural resources. However, it would be very difficult to predict how long, if ever, it would take the Gulf's CSWFs to reach the same level of transparency that is practised by the Norwegian government.

The debate over the politically driven investment decisions of the SWFs has been a key element in the transparency debate. The strategy of the GCC funds has been focused on avoiding any investment whose gaol can be regarded as a non-commercial one. A good example of such a strategy is the KIA's investment in BP and its reducing of its share at the request of the British government. In contrast, the SAMA has managed a highly politicized portfolio. Over the past decades, it has heavily financed the US government's debt in order to maintain its links with the US government while the liquidity of the assets are maintained and the government is able to transfer those assets to the domestic economy rather quickly, should it be neeeded. One important factor in forming the investment strategy of the GCC funds over the decades of their operation, and particularly during their first twenty years, has been the role of the colonial powers. The KIA was initially created by the British government and the first governors and founders of the SAMA were American bankers from the US Treasury Department. The impact of such collaborations on shaping the investment strategy of the SAMA and the KIA are still visible today, and it is unlikely that the governments of Kuwait or Saudi Arabia will find it easy to diversify their financial strategies from their political alliance with the former colonial powers that assisted them in creating their sovereignty. After all, there would have been no SWF if there was not a sovereign. However, the political alliance would direct these funds towards strategies in support of the West, if at all, rather than to impose national security threats on Western host countries.

Iran's sovereign wealth management strategy is also one of the most politicized ones in the Gulf region. The recent experience of the TUSRC shows that the country's SWFs decision making is highly influenced by the government's political agenda. Although Iran's strategy for managing its sovereign wealth assets has not caused any particular global controversy, the government would have to make fundamental adjustments in the management strategy of the country's SWF, if it was to invest globally. Finally, Norway is an interesting case of a politicized investment strategy. The GPFG's investments can also be considered politicized because even if an investment is profitable commercially, the fund may still divest should the ethical guidelines suggest this course of action. Given that the ethical guidelines are based on the Norwegian government's democratic principles, the GPFG has, in some cases, chosen politics over profitability. Nevertheless, the politicization of the GPFG's investment strategy has never been a matter of concern for the host sovereign nations, which often share similar political principles with the Norwegian government.

Another important criticism of the Gulf funds in the transparency debate has been their reluctance to practise their ownership rights. Almost all the GCC CSWFs have been avoiding heavy involvement in the operation of companies in which they invest by not practising their ownership rights. In this respect, however, Mubadala is a relatively unique case. It is a cash-rich long-term investor that does not divest easily, and has been one of the very few companies in the region that has managed to keep hold of its investments, even during the peak of the financial crisis. Given that Mubadala has a social income generation strategy it is generally an active investor. In order to facilitate the transfer of technology to Abu Dhabi, most of Mubadala's managers have seats on the boards of different companies, and are actively involved in their decision making.

While most of the GCC funds have not taken an active role in the management of the companies in which they invest, Iranian and Norwegian CSWFs have adopted a different approach. The Norwegian GPFG has had clear guidelines for practising its ownership correctly. Indeed, as noted, such a strategy has played a key role in identifying the GPFG as the world's most transparent CSWF. Iran's IFESA is a different case from the SWFs of the GCC and Norway, since it mainly invests in state-owned businesses; hence the sponsor of the fund, the Iranian government, is also the major stakeholder in companies in which the IFESA invests. In most cases, therefore, the owner of the fund has full control over the management of the sponsored companies.

Another factor for which the transparency of the GCC funds has been ranked rather low amongst their peers in the global financial markets is their unclear risk management strategies. As a result of their poor investment risk management, the GCC CSWFs have been reported as being significantly affected by the financial crisis, and as a result of the collapse of the global financial markets, have lost a considerable share of their assets. However, there have been other factors leading to their loss of assets, namely the decline in crude prices, and the need for transferring their assets to their domestic economies. Nevertheless, their aggressive appetite for risk in most of their direct acquisitions has been a key factor contributing to their vulnerability during the crisis more than other CSWFs, particularly the GPFG. There has also been a certain element of nationalism involved in the decision-making processes of the Arab funds in order to make the region known and to establish their brand names in the global financial system. Good examples of such an investment strategy are the sovereign wealth management institutions of the UAE and, to a lesser extent, the KIA of Kuwait. The SAMA has, however, lagged behind the other GCC commodity-based funds in this respect. Investments in high profile and reputable assets have proved nevertheless to be often risky and have been significant factors for massive losses by the GCC funds in the aftermath of the crisis. The lessons of the crisis have indeed forced the funds to take a more careful approach in their investment strategies; however, they may go back to more reputable and somewhat flashy acquisitions in the future.

There is some speculation that the Iranian sovereign wealth management institution, the IFESA, has been also affected by the crisis, although Iran's case is not like those of the GCC countries, which have been heavily engaged in Western financial markets. The loss of the IFESA's assets has not been as a direct result of the collapse of the international markets, instead the Iranian government has been allocating a large share of the oil revenue to subsidize food and energy in the domestic markets. Therefore, because of the increases in food and energy prices, the government has been forced to spend a massive amount of the sovereign wealth assets on the subsidies. Although since January 2010, the government has started a subsidy cut plan through which the subsidies are paid directly to citizens in order to assist lower-income Iranians, the cash handouts have drained a sizeable share of the country's government revenue.

When it comes to risk management, the Iranian sovereign wealth management organization remains far behind all the case studies mentioned in this book. The IFESA has focused mainly on local investments, and the lending process for local investments is not based on clear risk management, since the country suffers from a high level of corruption, weak investment law and a strong lobbying system, particularly in the lending process when the profitability of each project is assessed. A combination of these factors often makes it difficult for certain businesses to benefit from the system, while the others have easy access to credit for investment projects that are not efficient at all.

The Gulf commodity-based funds have operated in the global economy for a number of decades, but the debate over the transparency of these funds has only intensified over the last few years. The findings of this study show that a large number of analysts from academia and the financial sector, both in the West and in the region, believe that the issue of transparency of SWFs has been exaggerated, and that cases like P&O and CNOOC are quite unlikely to happen again. The underlying assumption here is that, realistically speaking, the Western economies are not in a position to be able to decline investments from SWFs. This trend might change once the dust of the post-2008 crisis settles. Nevertheless in order to attract SWF investments, Western economies have to compete with emerging markets, hence more emphasis on transparency is going to scare the Gulf countries away from investing in the developed economies in West.

The main outcome of the global initiative for transparency of SWFs was the establishment of the IWG and the creation of the Santiago Principles. While the Santiago Principles were a significantly speedy action by the global community and made visible impact on some of the Gulf commodity-based funds, they will not end the controversial debate over the strategic investment of the funds. In other words, even if a SWF fully complies with the GAPP, when it initiates procedures to acquire strategic assets, such as an oil company or a border management company in the developed economies, the deal will most likely be blocked by the authorities because of national security concerns. Therefore, the SWFs' growing financial power is expected to be concentrated in specific sectors in the Western economies that do not impose national security threats on the host sovereign nations, and indeed they are likely to grow in the emerging markets.

The technical development of the GCC sovereign wealth management organizations has been materialized mainly as a result of engagement of foreign financial experts. Though, there has been a notion of mistrust amongst the local individuals towards the role of the foreign employees in these organizations. It is clear from the two financial scandals that have been reviewed in this study (the KIO in Spain and the BCCI) that when it comes to making wrong decisions, it is often the foreign partner who is to be blamed. In the case of the BCCI for example, while Agha Abedi was imprisoned and forced to leave the UAE, Al-Mazroui, who was heavily involved in the BCCI's activities from the beginning, was released shortly after he was initially arrested for investigation and was appointed as the head of the government's working group for investigating the scandal. Such mentality towards the expatriates still exists in the region's government investment institutions.

The Arab Gulf CSWFs have grown significantly in size and expertise. Each SWF of the case studies in this project has been following a mission heavily aligned with the government economic, social and political policies. The SAMA has been financing the US government's debt partly in exchange for the political and military security provided by the American administration. The KIA has been piling the country's surplus income outside Kuwait to provide a secured source of finance in the case of a potential crisis. Abu Dhabi SWFs have been actively working to materialize the government's ambitions for turning Abu Dhabi into an energy, technology and education hub in the Gulf. While the ADIA has been often investing in flashy assets to gain reputation in the global financial system and establish itself as the largest SWF of the world, Mubadala has been actively engaging in projects that can bring technology to Abu Dhabi in exchange for the Emirate's surplus petrodollars. Dubai government investment vehicles have been affected by the burst of the bubble in the Emirate; however, the important role of these institutions in establishing Dubai as an investment and financial centre, as well as a luxury tourist attraction, must not be ignored. Finally, Iran's SWF practice has provided the government with sufficient rent to distribute amongst the key political powers of the country. President Ahmadinejad's populist policies and distribution of cash amongst lower middle class Iranian citizens, both in the cities and rural areas, have assisted him in maintaining his popularity despite the controversies of the 2009 election. Moreover, the distribution of the country's oil revenue since 2005, which has supported the financial interests of the Revolutionary Guard, has created a strong shield for the regime's power domestically. Therefore, the SWFs of the Gulf that have been seeking to secure the interest of their sponsoring sovereign have all done a significant job in fulfilling their roles.

Appendix A

Generally Accepted Principles and Practices (GAPP) – Santiago Principles

- **GAPP 1. Principle**

The legal framework for the SWF should be sound and support its effective operation and the achievement of its stated objective(s).
  - *GAPP 1.1 Sub-principle* The legal framework for the SWF should ensure the legal soundness of the SWF and its transactions.
  - *GAPP 1.2 Sub-principle* The key features of the SWF's legal basis and structure, as well as the legal relationship between the SWF and the other state bodies, should be publicly disclosed.

- **GAPP 2. Principle**

The policy purpose of the SWF should be clearly defined and publicly disclosed.

- **GAPP 3. Principle**

Where the SWF's activities have significant direct domestic macroeconomic implications, those activities should be closely coordinated with the domestic fiscal and monetary authorities, so as to ensure consistency with the overall macroeconomic policies.

- **GAPP 4. Principle**

There should be clear and publicly disclosed policies, rules, procedures, or arrangements in relation to the SWF's general approach to funding, withdrawal, and spending operations.
  - *GAPP 4.1 Sub-principle* The source of SWF funding should be publicly disclosed.
  - *GAPP 4.2 Sub-principle* The general approach to withdrawals from the SWF and spending on behalf of the government should be publicly disclosed.

- **GAPP 5. Principle**

The relevant statistical data pertaining to the SWF should be reported on a timely basis to the owner, or as otherwise required, for inclusion where appropriate in macroeconomic data sets.

- **GAPP 6. Principle**

The governance framework for the SWF should be sound and establish a clear and effective division of roles and responsibilities in order to facilitate accountability and operational independence in the management of the SWF to pursue its objectives.

- **GAPP 7. Principle**

The owner should set the objectives of the SWF, appoint the members of its governing body(ies) in accordance with clearly defined procedures, and exercise oversight over the SWF's operations.

- **GAPP 8. Principle**

The governing body(ies) should act in the best interests of the SWF, and have a clear mandate and adequate authority and competency to carry out its functions.

- **GAPP 9. Principle**

The operational management of the SWF should implement the SWF's strategies in an independent manner and in accordance with clearly defined responsibilities.

- **GAPP 10. Principle**

The accountability framework for the SWF's operations should be clearly defined in the relevant legislation, charter, other constitutive documents, or management agreement.

- **GAPP 11. Principle**

An annual report and accompanying financial statements on the SWF's operations and performance should be prepared in a timely fashion and in accordance with recognized international or national accounting standards in a consistent manner.

- **GAPP 12. Principle**

The SWF's operations and financial statements should be audited annually in accordance with recognized international or national auditing standards in a consistent manner.

- **GAPP 13. Principle**

Professional and ethical standards should be clearly defined and made known to the members of the SWF's governing body(ies), management, and staff.

- **GAPP 14. Principle**

Dealing with third parties for the purpose of the SWF's operational management should be based on economic and financial grounds, and follow clear rules and procedures.

- **GAPP 15. Principle**

SWF operations and activities in host countries should be conducted in compliance with all applicable regulatory and disclosure requirements of the countries in which they operate.

- **GAPP 16. Principle**

The governance framework and objectives, as well as the manner in which the SWF's management is operationally independent from the owner, should be publicly disclosed.

- **GAPP 17. Principle**

Relevant financial information regarding the SWF should be publicly disclosed to demonstrate its economic and financial orientation, so as to contribute to stability in international financial markets and enhance trust in recipient countries.

- **GAPP 18. Principle**

The SWF's investment policy should be clear and consistent with its defined objectives, risk tolerance, and investment strategy, as set by the owner or the governing body(ies), and be based on sound portfolio management principles.
  - *GAPP 18.1 Sub-principle* The investment policy should guide the SWF's financial risk exposures and the possible use of leverage.
  - *GAPP 18.2 Sub-principle* The investment policy should address the extent to which internal and/or external investment managers are used, the range of their activities and authority, and the process by which they are selected and their performance monitored.
  - *GAPP 18.3 Sub-principle* A description of the investment policy of the SWF should be publicly disclosed.

- **GAPP 19. Principle**

The SWF's investment decisions should aim to maximize risk-adjusted financial returns in a manner consistent with its investment policy, and based on economic and financial grounds.
  - *GAPP 19.1 Sub-principle* If investment decisions are subject to other than economic and financial considerations, these should be clearly set out in the investment policy and be publicly disclosed.
  - *GAPP 19.2 Sub-principle* The management of an SWF's assets should be consistent with what is generally accepted as sound asset management principles.

- **GAPP 20. Principle**

The SWF should not seek or take advantage of privileged information or inappropriate influence by the broader government in competing with private entities.

- **GAPP 21. Principle**

SWFs view shareholder ownership rights as a fundamental element of their equity investments' value. If an SWF chooses to exercise its ownership rights, it should do so in a manner that is consistent with its investment policy and protects the financial value of its investments. The SWF should publicly disclose its general approach to voting securities of listed entities, including the key factors guiding its exercise of ownership rights.

- **GAPP 22. Principle**

The SWF should have a framework that identifies, assesses, and manages the risks of its operations.
  - *GAPP 22.1 Sub-principle* The risk management framework should include reliable information and timely reporting systems, which should enable the adequate monitoring and management of relevant risks within acceptable parameters and levels, control and incentive mechanisms, codes of conduct, business continuity planning, and an independent audit function.
  - *GAPP 22.2 Sub-principle* The general approach to the SWF's risk management framework should be publicly disclosed.

- **GAPP 23. Principle**

The assets and investment performance (absolute and relative to benchmarks, if any) of the SWF should be measured and reported to the owner according to clearly defined principles or standards.

- **GAPP 24. Principle**

A process of regular review of the implementation of the GAPP should be engaged in by or on behalf of the SWF.

(International Working Group of Sovereign Wealth Funds, 2008)

Bibliography

Abdelal, R. (2009) 'Sovereign Wealth in Abu Dhabi', *Geopolitics*, vol. 14, no. 2: 317–327.

Abu Dhabi Government. (2009) 'Abu Dhabi Economic Vision 2030.' Abu Dhabi: Abu Dhabi Council for Economic Development. Available http://www.abudhabi.ae/egovPoolPortal_WAR/appmanager/ADeGP/Citizen?_nfpb=true&_pageLabel=p_citizen_homepage_hidenav&did=131654&lang=en (accessed 2 August 2010).

Abu Dhabi Urban Planning Council. (2010) 'Abu Dhabi Real Estate Market Forecasts'. Available http://www.upc.gov.ae/template/upc/pdf/WEBVERSION.pdf (accessed 3 December 2011).

ADIA. (2009) 'Annual Review'. Available http://www.adia.ae/en/pr/Annual_Review_Website2.pdf (accessed 2 April 2010).

ADIA. (2010) '2010 Annual Review'. Available http://www.adia.ae/en/pr/Annual_Review_Website_2010.pdf (accessed 27 February 2012).

ADIA. (no date) 'Governance, Relationship with Government'. Available http://www.adia.ae/En/Governance/Abudhabi_Government.aspx (accessed 11 November 2010).

ADNOC. (no date) 'GASCO'. Available http://www.adnoc.ae/content.aspx?newid=34&mid=34 (accessed 27 October 2010).

Aftab News Agency. (2005) '*ikhtisas-i 30 darsad az mujudi-yi hisab zakhirah-yi arzi bi sanduq-i mihr-i riza*'. Available http://aftabnews.ir/vdciyuar.t1a5q2bcct.html (accessed 19 January 2012).

Ahmad, M. (2007) 'Mandelson Mulls EU Golden Share Against Takeovers', *Business Intelligence Middle East*. Available http://www.bi-me.com/main.php?id=11820&t=1&c=34&cg (accessed 18 February 2012).

Al-Dukheil, A. (2004) 'Impact of Dollar Depreciation on Saudi Economy' *Saudi Commerce and Economic Review*, vol. 118: 12–14.

Al-Ebraheem, Y. (1996) 'Kuwait's Economic Travails', *Middle East Quarterly*, 17–23.

Al-Otaiba, Mana Saeed. (1977) *Petroleum and the Economy of the United Arab Emirates*, London: Croom Helm.

Al Sa'ad, B. (2009) 'Overview on the Kuwait Investment Authority and Issues Related to Sovereign Wealth Funds, Keynote Speech at the First Luxembourg Foreign Trade Conference, 9 April 2009', *Kia*. Available http://www.kia.gov.kw/En/About_KIA/Overview_of_KIA/Pages/default.aspx (accessed 10 October 2010).

AME Info. (2009) 'H.E Hamad Al Sayari Assumes Chairmanship of the Council of the IFSB for 2009'. Available http://www.ameinfo.com/182763.html (accessed10 January 2011).

Arabian Business. (2011) 'UAE's Wealth Fund Eyes Shift in Investment Focus'. Available http://www.arabianbusiness.com/uae-s-wealth-fund-eyes-shift-in-investment-focus-400607.html (accessed 2 August 2011).

Arabian Business. (2010a) 'Expat Power 50'. Available http://www.arabianbusiness.com/expat-power-50-342475.html?view=profile&itemid=342550 (accessed 14 June 2010).

Arabian Business. (2010b) 'Gulf Wealth Funds May Cut Inv'ts in the West – Al Suwaidi'. Available http://www.arabianbusiness.com/gulf-wealth-funds-may-cut-inv-ts-in-west-al-suwaidi-271066.html (accessed 25 May 2010).

Arabian Times. (2011) 'Dubai World Shifts Ownership of Nakheel, Limitless To Govt'. Available http://www.arabtimesonline.com/NewsDetails/tabid/96/smid/414/ArticleID/171194/reftab/69/t/Dubai-World-shifts-ownership-of-Nakheel-Limitless-to-govt/Default.aspx (accessed 25 March 2011).

Askari, H. (1990) *Saudi Arabia's Economy: Oil and Search for Economic Development (Contemporary Studies in Economic and Financial Analysis)*, New York: JAI Press.

Bahgat, G. (2008) 'Sovereign Wealth Funds: Dangers and Opportunities', *International Affairs*, vol. 84, no. 4: 1189–1204.

Bank of England. (1961) 'Kuwait Investment Policy', Bank of England note enclosed in J.M. Stevens' letter to Sir Denis Rickett, 28 March, T 236/6315.

Bansal, P. (2008) 'Mideast Sovereign Funds Seek Reciprocal Investment', *Reuters*. Available http://www.reuters.com/article/2008/09/08/swf-mideast-idUSN0841486220080908 (accessed 8 September 2008).

Barbary, V. and Chin E. (2009) 'Testing Time: Sovereign Wealth Funds in the Middle East and North Africa and the Global Financial Crisis', *Monitor Group Research*. Available http://www.monitor.com/Portals/0/MonitorContent/imported/MonitorUnitedStates/Articles/PDFs/Monitor_Testing_Time_SWF_MENA_May_2009.pdf (accessed 2 June 2009).

Barboza, D. and Sorkin A.R. (2005) 'Chinese Oil Giant in Takeover Bid for U.S. Corporation', *New York Times*. Available http://www.nytimes.com/2005/06/23/business/worldbusiness/23unocal.html (accessed 21 November 2011).

Barkley, T. (2008) 'IMF Report: SWF Growth Could Hurt Dollar', *Wall Street Journal Blog*. Available http://blogs.wsj.com/economics/2008/10/02/imf-report-swf-growth-could-hurt-dollar/ (accessed 2 January 2009).

Barysch, K., Tilford S. and White, P. (2008) 'State, Money and Rules: An EU Policy for Sovereign Investments', *Centre for European Reform*. Available http://www.cer.org.uk/publications/archive/essay/2008/state-money-and-rules-eu-policy-sovereign-investments (accessed 18 February 2012).

BBC. (2006) 'Rival Bows out of P&O Bid Battle'. Available http://news.bbc.co.uk/1/hi/business/4700144.stm (accessed 21 November 2011).

BBC. (1991) '1991: International Bank Closed in Fraud'. Available http://news.bbc.co.uk/onthisday/hi/dates/stories/july/5/newsid_2495000/2495017.stm (accessed 3 December 2010).

BBC Persian. (2008) '*vakunish-ha bi inhilal-i hay'at umana-yi hisab zakhirah-yi arzi*'. Available http://www.bbc.co.uk/persian/business/story/2008/05/080512_he-ka-currency-fund.shtml (accessed 19 January 2012).

BBC Persian. (2007) '*sazman-i barnamahrizi va mudiriyat munhal shud*'. Available http://www.bbc.co.uk/persian/iran/story/2007/07/070710_ka-mpo.shtml (accessed 17 January 2012).

Beck, R. and Fidora, M. (2008) 'The Impact of Sovereign Wealth Funds on Global Financial Markets', *European Central Bank Occasional Paper Series*, no. 91. Available http://papers.ssrn.com/sol3/papers.cfm?abstract_id=1144482 (accessed 26 November 2009).

Behrendt, S. (2010) 'Sovereign Wealth Funds and the Santiago Principles, Where do they Stand?', *Carnegie Papers*, no. 22. Available http://carnegieendowment.org/files/santiago_principles.pdf (accessed 18 February 2012).

Behrendt, S. (2008) 'When Money Talks Arab Sovereign Wealth Funds in the Global Public Discourse', *Carnegie Papers*. Available http://www.carnegieendowment.org/files/arab_sovereign_wealth_funds.pdf (accessed 13 January 2009).

Birger, V. (2008) 'Norges Bank Experiences with the Organization of Global Pension Fund-Global', *Commodities, Energy and Finance, The European Money and Finance Forum*. Available http://www.suerf.org/download/studies/study20082.pdf (accessed 7 March 2012).

Birks, J.S. and Sinclair, C.A. (1982) 'The Domestic Political Economy of Development in Saudi Arabia', in T. Niblock (ed.) *State, Society and Economy in Saudi Arabia*, London: Croom Helm.

Bladd, J. (2011) 'Nakheel Plans to Split from Dubai World by June', *Arabian Business*. Available http://www.arabianbusiness.com/nakheel-plans-split-from-dubai-world-by-june-400679.html (accessed 25 March 2011).

Bloom, D., Canning, D., Mansfield, R. and Moore, M. (2006) 'Demographic Change, Social Security Systems and Savings', *National Bureau of Economic Research*, Working Paper 12621. Available http://www.nber.org/papers/w12621 (accessed 23 November 2009).

Central Bank of the UAE Statistical Bulletin (1978) Available from the Arab World Documentation Unit, University of Exeter.

Central Bank of the UAE Statistical Bulletin (1985) Available from the Arab World Documentation Unit, University of Exeter.

Clark, A. (2009) 'Abu Dhabi Takes Action against Citigroup over $5.7bn Investment', *The Guardian*. Available http://www.guardian.co.uk/business/2009/dec/16/citigroup-clashes-with-abu-dhabi-wealth-fund (accessed 18 January 2009).

CNN. (2010) 'Saudi Arabia's Economy'. Available http://edition.cnn.com/video/?/video/international/2010/01/29/mme.b.saudi.arabia.monetary.cnn (accessed 28 April 2010).

Cohen, B. (2009) 'Sovereign Wealth Funds and National Security: The Great Trade-off', *International Affairs*, vol. 85, no. 4: 713–731.

Cohen, R. (1993) 'Missing Millions – Kuwait's Bad Bet – A Special Report; Big Wallets and Little Supervision', *The New York Times*. Available http://www.nytimes.com/1993/09/28/business/missing-millions-kuwait-s-bad-bet-special-report-big-wallets-little-supervision.html?pagewanted=all&src=pm (accessed 12 March 2010).

Critchlow, A. (2009) 'Adia's Wounded Pride Over Citi', *The Wall Street Journal*. Available http://online.wsj.com/article/SB10001424052748704541004574599782018215974.html (accessed 18 December 2009).

Crystal, J. (1992) *Kuwait: The Transformation of an Oil State*, Oxford: Westview Press.

Das, A. (2008) 'Investing the Wealth of Nations-Sovereign Wealth Fund: A Trillion here, a Trillion There, and Pretty Soon we're Talking "Real Money"', Dresdner Kleinwort Markets Research and Strategy. Available http://www.econ.puc-rio.br/mgarcia/Seminario/textos_preliminares/Investing%20the%20Wealth%20of%20Nations.pdf (accessed 3 March 2010).

Das, D.K. (2008) 'Sovereign-wealth Funds: A New Role for the Emerging Market Economies in the World of Global Finance', *International Journal of Development Issues*, vol.7, no. 2: 80–96.

Davidson, C. (2005) *The United Arab Emirates: A Study in Survival*, Boulder, CO: Lynne Rienner Press.

Dehghan, Saeed Kamali. (2011) 'Iran's former president Rafsanjani steps down from assembly role', *The Guardian*, Available http://www.guardian.co.uk/world/2011/mar/08/ iran-president-rafsanjani-assembly (accessed 21 January 2012).

Deutsche Welle Persian. (2011) '*tusi'ah-yi mitru: bi 'itinayi-i davlat va israr-i majlis*'. Available http://www.dw.de/dw/article/0,,6448461,00.html (accessed 21 January 2012).

Diwan, C. Smith. (2009) 'Sovereign Dilemmas: Saudi Arabia and Sovereign Wealth Funds', *Geopolitics*, vol. 14, no. 2: 345–359.

The Economist. (2008) 'The Rise of State Capitalism'. Available http://www.economist. com/node/12080735 (accessed 14 June 2010).

Economist Intelligence Unit. (2012) '*Iran Country Report*'. Available http://viewswire.eiu. com/index.asp?layout=oneclick&pubtype_id=1086275908&country_id=1120000312 (accessed 6 March 2012).

Economist Intelligence Unit. (2011) 'Norway: Country Fact Sheet'. Available http:// viewswire.eiu.com/index.asp?layout=oneclick&pubtype_id=1086275908&country_ id=1410000141 (accessed 7 March 2012).

Economist Intelligence Unit. (2010) 'Kuwait: Country Factsheet'. Available http://viewswire. eiu.com/index.asp?layout=VWArticleVW3&article_id=408424825&region_ id=&country_id=290000029&channel_id=190004019&category_ id=240004024&refm=vwCat&page_title=Article (accessed 2 October 2010).

Economist Intelligence Unit. (2004) 'Saudi Arabia Country Factsheet'. Available http:// viewswire.eiu.com/index.asp?layout=VWArticleVW3&article_id=1457426945&region_ id=&country_id=470000047&channel_id=190004019&category_ id=240004024&refm=vwCat&page_title=Article (accessed 14 June 2010).

Economist Intelligence Unit. (2001) 'Kuwait in the 1990s, a Society Under Siege', EIU special report no. 20 35.

Economist Intelligence Unit. (1998) 'Kuwait: Country Profile', London: Economist Intelligence Unit.

El-Erian, M. (1997) 'Accumulation for Future Generations: Kuwait's Economic Challenges', Kuwait from Reconstruction to Accumulation for Future Generations, IMF Occasional Paper, 150: 2–7.

England, A. (2008a) 'Interview Transcript: Mansour Al-Maiman', *Financial Times*. Available http://www.ft.com/cms/s/0/1eb10c3e-155b-11dd-996c-0000779fd2ac. html#axzz1pCMuDPwd (accessed 9 January 2010).

England, A. (2008b) 'Saudis to Launch $5.3 Billion Sovereign Fund', *Financial Times*. Available http://www.ft.com/cms/s/0/b6a50b1e-1563-11dd-996c-0000779fd2ac. html#axzz1pCMuDPwd (accessed 29 April 2008).

England, A. and Khalaf, R. (2007) 'Saudi Public Investment Fund Eyes Broader Role', *Financial Times*. Available http://www.ft.com/cms/s/0/de0378c2-9254-11dc-8981-0000779fd2ac.html#axzz1pCMuDPwd (accessed 1 December 2009).

Eriksen, T. (2006) 'Norwegian Petroleum Sector and the Government Pension Fund-Global', *Regjeringen*. Available http://www.regjeringen.no/upload/FIN/Statens%20pensjonsfond/ The_Norwegian_Petroleum_Sector_te.pdf (accessed 7 March 2012).

Ettelaat. (2011) '*agar dawlat i'itibar-i mitru ra ta'min nakunad, vaziran-i marbuta istizah mishavand*'. Available http://www.ettelaat.net/10-juli/news.asp?id=49172 (accessed 21 January 2012).

European Commission. (no date) 'Provisions of the Treaty on the Functioning of the European Union'. Available http://ec.europa.eu/internal_market/capital/framework/ treaty_en.htm (accessed 18 February 2012).

Fars News Agency. (2009a) '*haddiaqall 100 miliyard dular zakhirah-yi arzi va 10 sal zakhirah-yi tala*'. Available http://www.farsnews.com/newstext.php?nn=8907300153 (accessed 19 January 2012).

Fars News Agency. (2009b) '*mikanizm-i qanuni ra'ayat mishud hisab-i zakhirah-yi arzi 100 miliyard dular mujudi dasht*'. Available http://www.farsnews.com/newstext.php?nn=8806240490 (accessed 19 January 2012).

Fasano, U. (2000) 'Review of the Experience with Oil Stabilization and Saving Funds in Selected Countries', *IMF Working Paper*, WP/00/12. Available http://www.imf.org/external/pubs/cat/longres.aspx?sk=3648.0 (accessed 25 April 2010).

Fennell, S. (1997) 'Budget Structure and Implications of Fiscal Policy', *Kuwait from Reconstruction to Accumulation for Future Generations, IMF Occasional Paper*, vol. 150: 8–15.

Field, M. (1976) 'The Oil Surplus', *Financial Times Survey*.

Fletcher, R. (2007) 'China Buys Stake in Barclays in ABN Twist', *The Telegraph*. Available http://www.telegraph.co.uk/finance/markets/2812645/China-buys-stake-in-Barclays-in-ABN-twist.html (accessed 18 February 2012).

Fletcher Research. (2010) 'Abu Dhabi Investment Authority'. Available http://fletcher.tufts.edu/SWFI/SWFI-Research-and-Activities (accessed 20 December 2010).

Foley, S. (2010) *The Arab Gulf States, Beyond Oil and Islam*, London: Lynne Rienner.

Folketrygdfondet. (no date) 'The Government Pension Fund Norway'. Available http://www.ftf.no/en/c-305-The-Government-Pension-Fund-Norway.aspx (accessed 9 March 2012).

Ford, J.A. (1959) 'Persian Gulf States and the Sterling Area', Draft paper, T236/5181.

Foreign Office. (1961) 'Kuwait Investment Policy', 28 March, FO 371/156864.

Franco, J. (2008) 'Dubai Group to Invest $1bn in US Equities', *Khaleej Times*. Available http://www.khaleejtimes.com/DisplayArticle.asp?xfile=data/business/2008/September/business_September629.xml&section=business&col= (accessed 27 March 2011).

Gai, P. and Shin, H.S. (2003) 'Transparency and Financial Stability', *Bank of England Financial Stability Review*. Available http://www.bankofengland.co.uk/publications/Documents/fsr/2003/fsr15art5.pdf (accessed 20 November 2011).

Ghanem, S.M.A. (1992) *Industrialization in the United Arab Emirates*, Aldershot: Avebury.

Government Accounting Office (GAO). (1979) 'Are OPEC Financial Holdings a Danger to the US Banker or the Economy?', GAO, ID 79-45. Available http://archive.gao.gov/f0302/109900.pdf (accessed 12 October 2011).

Government of Norway. (2011) 'The Management of the Government Pension Fund in 2010', Report No. 15 (2010–2011) to the Storting. Available http://www.regjeringen.no/pages/16516288/PDFS/STM201020110015000EN_PDFS.pdf (accessed 7 March 2012)

Government Pension Fund – Global. (2010a) 'Annual Report'. Available http://www.nbim.no/Global/Reports/2010/ENGLISH%20Annual%20Report%202010%2024%20March%20(printed).pdf (accessed 7 March 2012).

Government Pension Fund – Global. (2010b) 'GPFG Responsible Investment'. Available http://www.regjeringen.no/upload/FIN/brosjyre/2010/spu/english_2010/SPU_hefte_eng_ebook.pdf (accessed 7 March 2012).

Griffith-Jones, S. and Ocampo, J.A. (2010) 'Sovereign Wealth Funds a Developing Country Perspective'. *Policy Dialogue*. Available http://policydialogue.org/files/events/Griffith-JonesSovereign_Wealth_Funds.pdf (accessed 16 March 2012).

Haider, H. (2006) 'ADIA to be Replaced by ADIC', *Khaleej Times*. Available http://www. khaleejtimes.com/DisplayArticleNew.asp?xfile=data/business/2006/October/business_ October678.xml&section=business (accessed 23 October 2006).

Hall, C. (2011) 'Saudi Arabia: $500 Billion and Counting', *Financial Times*. Available http://blogs.ft.com/beyond-brics/2011/08/30/saudi-arabia-500bn-and-counting/#axzz1pCQLGoUo (accessed 30 August 2011).

Hamshahri. (2011) '*i'ilam-i juz'iyat-i afzayish-i tashilat-i banki*'. Available http:// hamshahrionline.ir/print-131417.aspx (accessed 19 January 2012).

Hamshahri. (2008a) '*ashna-yi ba hisab-i zakhirah-yi arzi*'. Available http:// hamshahrionline.ir/news.aspx?id=65483 (accessed 17 January 2012).

Hamshahri. (2008b) '*tajrubah-yi hisab-i zakhirah-yi arzi*'. Available http:// hamshahrionline.ir/news-60434.aspx (accessed 19 January 2012).

Hauser, C. (1994) 'BCCI Men Jailed and Ordered to Pay Dollars 9bn by Abu Dhabi Court: Former Chief Executive and Founder of Collapsed Bank Sentenced in Their Absence', *The Independent*. Available http://www.independent.co.uk/news/business/bcci-men-jailed-and-ordered-to-pay-dollars-9bn-by-abu-dhabi-court-former-chief-executive-and-founder-of-collapsed-bank-sentenced-in-their-absence-1422790.html (accessed 10 February 2010).

Heard, D. (1999) 'Development of Oil in the Gulf: The UAE in Focus', in R. Hollis (ed.) *Oil and Regional Developments in the Gulf*, London: Royal Institute of International Affairs.

Hertog, S. (2010) *Princes, Brokers, and Bureaucrats, Oil and the State n Saudi Arabia*, Ithaca, NY: Cornell University Press.

Hua, T. (2007) 'World's Largest Pension Funds: $10 Trillion Strong', *Pensions & Investments*. Available http://www.pionline.com/apps/pbcs.dll/article?AID=/20070903/ PRINTSUB/70830018/1010 (accessed 23 November 2009).

Hussein, T. (1995) *Kuwaiti Oil Fires: Regional Environmental Perspectives*. Oxford: BPC Wheatons.

Ibrahim, Y.M. (1993) 'Financial Scandal is Shaking Kuwait', *New York Times*. Available http://www.nytimes.com/1993/01/10/world/financial-scandal-is-shaking-kuwait.html (accessed 12 March 2010).

IMF. (2011a) 'IMF Country Report', no. 11/241. Available http://www.imf.org/external/ pubs/ft/scr/2011/cr11241.pdf (accessed 21 January 2012).

IMF. (2011b) 'IMF Executive Board Concludes 2011 Article IV Consultation with Saudi Arabia'. Available http://www.imf.org/external/np/sec/pn/2011/pn11114.htm (accessed 2 May 2011).

IMF. (2009) 'Sovereign Wealth Funds – A Work Agenda'. Available http://www.imf.org/ external/np/pp/eng/2008/022908.pdf (accessed 18 November 2011).

Independent, The. (1999) 'Kuwaiti Sheikh to Fight Ruling'. Available http://www. independent.co.uk/news/business/kuwaiti-sheikh-to-fight-ruling-1102628.html (accessed 20 March 2010).

Independent, The. (1992) 'The Strange Abu Dhabi Connection: BCCI Affair'. Available http://www.independent.co.uk/news/business/the-strange-abu-dhabi-connection-bcci-affair-1559507.html (accessed 20 January 2008).

International Forum of Sovereign Wealth Funds. (2010) 'Sydney Statement'. Available http://www.ifswf.org/pr/pr4.htm (accessed 18 February 2012).

International Forum of Sovereign Wealth Funds. (2009) 'Sovereign Wealth Funds Issue "Baku Statement" Reaffirming the Need for Maintaining Open Investment Environment'. Available http://www.ifswf.org/pr/pr2.htm (accessed 18 February 2012).

International Institute for Strategic Studies. (2011) 'The Military Balance 2011'. Available http://www.economist.com/blogs/dailychart/2011/03/defence_budgets (accessed 2 February 2012).

International Working Group of Sovereign Wealth Funds. (2009a) '"Kuwait Declaration": Establishment of the International Forum of Sovereign Wealth Funds'. Available http://www.iwg-swf.org/mis/kuwaitdec.htm (accessed 18 February 2012).

International Working Group of Sovereign Wealth Funds. (2009b) 'Working Group Announces Creation of International Forum of Sovereign Wealth Funds'. Available http://www.iwg-swf.org/pr/swfpr0901.htm (accessed 18 February 2012).

International Working Group of Sovereign Wealth Funds. (2008) 'Sovereign Wealth Funds Generally Accepted Principles and Practices "Santiago Principles"'. Available http://www.iwg-swf.org/pubs/eng/santiagoprinciples.pdf (accessed 2 April 2010).

Invest AD. (2010a) 'Emerging Africa Fund Fact Sheet'. Available http://www.investad.ae/Files/Libraries/220fccc3-f172-46a3-8ce3-d6a0bf6d3793.pd (accessed 12 January 2012).

Invest AD. (2010b) 'GCC Focused Fund Prospectus'. Available http://www.investad.ae/Files/Libraries/1382a126-8e9c-41bd-a512-4c3c2d3cef48.pdf (accessed 12 January 2012).

Invest AD. (2010c) 'Iraq Opportunity Fund Fact Sheet'. Available http://www.investad.ae/Files/Libraries/7533b3e6-1439-4a44-861f-fb1e7f452844.pdf (accessed 12 January 2012).

Invest AD. (2010d) 'UAE Total Return Fund Fact Sheet'. Available http://www.investad.ae/Files/Libraries/a46eab5a-3630-4794-b188-a588e25106f5.pdf (accessed 12 January 2012).

Invest AD. (no date) 'Nazem Fawwaz Al Kudsi CEO, Invest AD'. Available http://www.investad.ae/Files/Libraries/7f616d08-4b88-441e-9cc8-f99a843a7453.pdf (accessed 12 January 2012).

Iran newspaper. (2001) '*Khatami az buhran-hayi pinhan-i kishvar sukhan guft*'. Available http://www.iran-newspaper.com/1380/800603/html/iranews.htm#s43074 (accessed 2 April 2011).

Jen, S. (2007) 'How Big Could Sovereign Wealth Funds Be by 2011?', *Morgan Stanley Global Economic Forum*. Available http://www.morganstanley.com/views/gef/archive/2007/20070504-Fri.html (accessed 20 November 2009).

Jen, S. and Miles, D. (2007) 'Sovereign Wealth Funds and Bond and Equity Prices', *Morgan Stanley Global Economic Forum*. Available http://www.petersoninstitute.org/publications/pb/pb08-3.pdf (accessed 2 May 2008).

Jin, H.H., Mitchell, O.S. and Piggott, J. (2005) 'Socially Responsible Investment in Japanese Pension', *National Bureau of Economic Research*, Working Paper, 11747. Available http://www.nber.org/papers/w11747 (accessed 10 June 2009).

Johnson-Calari, J. and Rietveld, M. (2008) *Sovereign Wealth Management*, London: Central Banking Publication.

KCIC. (no date) 'Formation of KCIC'. Available http://www.kuwaitchina.com/ (accessed 10 October 2010).

Kern, S. (2010) 'The Role of SWFs – Towards a New Equilibrium', Presentation at *Edinburg SWF Dialogue*. Available http://sovereignwealthfocus.com/Resources/S_Kern.pdf (accessed 20 August 2010).

Kern, S. (2009) 'Sovereign Wealth Funds – State Investments during the Financial crisis', *Deutsche Bank Research*. Available http://www.dbresearch.com/PROD/DBR_INTERNET_EN-PROD/PROD0000000000244283.pdf (accessed 2 January 2010).

Kern, S. (2008) 'Control Mechanisms for Sovereign Wealth Funds in Selected Countries', *CESifo DICE*, Report 4/2008. Available http://www.cesifo-group.de/portal/pls/portal/docs/1/1193062.PDF (accessed 2 January 2010).

Kerr, S. (2009) 'Dubai Asks Rothschild to Advise on State Fund', *Financial Times*. Available http://www.ft.com/cms/s/0/142166da-1fbc-11de-a1df-00144feabdc0.html#axzz1nUqn WTtg (accessed 27 March 2011).

Kerr, S. and Khalaf, R. (2009) 'Dubai Overhaul Business Empire to Cut Costs', *Financial Times*. Available http://www.ft.com/cms/s/0/10969fd8-1f1e-11de-a748-00144feabdc0. html#axzz1nUqnWTtg, (accessed 27 December 2011).

Kerr, S. and Khalaf, R. (2008) 'Abu Dhabi Fund Hires Media Experts', *Financial Times*. Available http://www.ft.com/cms/s/0/bb85a726-c633-11dc-8378-0000779fd2ac.html (accessed 18 February 2012).

Kerr, S., England, A. and Wigglesworth, R. (2010) 'Emirate's carefully molded plan welcomed', *Financial Times*. Available http://www.ft.com/cms/s/0/fd5a525c-3849-11df-8420-00144feabdc0.html#axzz1nUqnWTtg, (accessed 27 March 2011).

Khabar Bazar. (2012) '*payan-i hakimiyat 30 salah-yi shirkat-i naft*'. Available http://www. bazarkhabar.ir/News.aspx?ID=16467 (accessed 20 June 2012).

Khalaf, R. (2008) 'Sovereign Wealth Funds Do Not Have All the Answers', *Financial Times*. Available http://www.ft.com/cms/s/0/aa9e7d9e-8e37-11dd-8089-0000779fd18c. html#axzz1pIlvcWGD (accessed 12 March 2010).

Khouja, M.W. and Sadler, P.G. (1979) *The Economy of Kuwait, Development and Role in International Finance*, London: McMillan Press.

KIA. (no date a) 'Governance at KIA'. Available http://www.kia.gov.kw/En/About_KIA/ Governance/Pages/default.aspx (accessed 12 May 2009).

KIA. (no date b) 'GRF and FGF'. Available http://www.kia.gov.kw/En/About_KIA/ Overview_of_Funds/Pages/default.aspx (accessed 12 October 2010).

KIA. (no date c) 'Mission and Principles'. Available http://www.kia.gov.kw/En/About_ KIA/Mission_Principles/Pages/default.aspx (accessed 20 November 2011).

KIA. (no date d) 'Law No. 47 of 1982'. Available http://www.kia.gov.kw/En/About_KIA/ Tansparency/Pages/default.aspx (accessed 18 November 2011).

Kimmit, R. (2008) 'Public Footprints in Private Markets, Sovereign Wealth Funds and the World Economy' *Foreign Affairs*, 87(1), 119–130.

Krimly, R. (1999) 'The Political Economy of Adjusted Priorities: Declining Oil Revenues and Saudi Fiscal Policies', *Middle East Journal*, vol. 53, no. 2: 254–267.

Kuwaiti Constitution (no date) Available at http://www.swfinstitute.org/swfs/kuwait-investment-authority/

Laessing, U. (2009) 'Kuwait Boosts Investments in Local Bourse', *Arabian Business*. Available http://www.arabianbusiness.com/kuwait-boosts-investment-in-local-bourse-85525.html (accessed 20 March 2010).

Landler, M. and Maynard, M. (2007) 'Chrysler Group to Be Sold for $7.4 Billion', *New York Times*. Available http://www.nytimes.com/2007/05/14/automobiles/14cnd-chrysler.html?pagewanted=all (accessed 22 March 2010).

Long, D.E. and Maisel, S. (2010) *The Kingdom of Saudi Arabia*, Gainsville, FL: University Press of Florida.

Lowe, Z. (2009) 'Searmen & Sterling, Skadden, Frshfields on Daimler-Abu Dhabi Stock Deal', *AM Law Daily*. Available http://amlawdaily.typepad.com/amlawdaily/2009/03/ shearman.html (accessed 24 March 2009).

Luciani, G. (2010) 'The Way Forward for Reserve Currencies', Presentation at Jeddah Economic Forum. Paper prepared for the workshop on Sovereign Wealth Funds organized by the Andean Development Corporation, London, 18 February 2008.

Macalister, T. (2010) 'Kuwait Investment Office in Talks to Raise BP Stake', *The Guardian*. Available http://www.guardian.co.uk/business/2010/jul/04/bp-kuwait-investment-office-oil-spill (accessed 5 July 2010).

MacDonald, C. (2011) 'New name, same focus', *Global investor ISF*. December/January 2011.

McGeehan, P. (2006) 'Despite Fears, a Dubai Company Will Help Run Ports in New York', *New York Times*. Available http://www.nytimes.com/2006/02/17/nyregion/17ports. html (accessed 21 November 2011).

McLachlan, K.S. and Ghorban, N. (1978) *Economic Development of the Middle East Oil Exporting States: A Review of Economic Changes in and Future Prospects for Saudi Arabia, Iran, Kuwait, Iraq, The United Arab Emirates, Bahrain And Qatar*, London: Economist Intelligence Unit.

Majlis Research Centre. (2005a) *'arzyabi-yi guzarish-i 'amalkard-i hisab-i zakhirah-yi arzi'*, Report no. 8126. Available http://rc.majlis.ir/fa/report/show/733848 (accessed 19 January 2012).

Majlis Research Centre. (2005b) *'barrisi-yi layihah-yi barnamah-yi tusi'ah-yi panjum'*, Report no. 10260. Available http://rc.majlis.ir/fa/report/show/772872 (accessed 21 January 2012).

Majlis Research Centre. (2005c) *'nukati darbarah-yi hisab-i zakhirah-yi arzi'*, Report no. 7607. Available http://rc.majlis.ir/fa/report/show/727978 (accessed 19 January 2012).

Majlis Research Centre. (2006) *'izhar-i nazar-i karshinasi darbarah-yi tarh: ijad sanduq-i zakhirah-yi riyali'*, Report no. 7114. Available http://rc.majlis.ir/fa/report/show/733502 (accessed 17 January 2012).

Majlis Research Centre. (2007) *'ba namayandigan-i mardum dar majlis-i hashtum, hisab-i zakhirah-yi arzi'*, Report no. 8861. Available http://rc.majlis.ir/fa/report/show/730078 (accessed 17 January 2012).

Majlis Research Centre. (2009a) *'sanduq-i tusi'ah-yi milli'*, Report no. 9913. Available http://rc.majlis.ir/fa/report/show/739011 (accessed 19 January 2012).

Majlis Research Centre. (2009b) *'sanduq-i tusi'ah-yi milli'*, Report No. 9894. Available http://rc.majlis.ir/fa/report/show/739011 (accessed 17 January 2012).

Majlis Research Centre. (2009c) *'vaz'iyat-i hisab-i zakhirah-yi arzi dar sal-i 1378'*, Report No. 9543. Available http://rc.majlis.ir/fa/report/show/780789 (accessed 19 January 2012).

Mann, C. (1964) *Abu Dhabi: Birth of an Oil Sheikhdom*, Beirut: Khayats.

Marcom, J. (1991) 'The New Face of Spain', *Forbes*, 147(5), 11–13.

Mardomsalari. (2008) *'bardasht 34 miliyard dular az sanduq-i zakhirah-yi arzi'*. Available http://www.mardomsalari.com/template1/News.aspx?NID=28039 (accessed 19 January 2012).

Mitchell, A., Sikka, P., Arnold, P., Cooper, C. and Willmott, H. (2001) *The BCCI Cover-up*, Basildon: Association for Accountancy and Business Affairs. Avaialble hhtp;//visar.csustan.edu/aaba/BCCICOVERUP.pdf

Mitchell, O.S. and Hsin, P.L. (1994) 'Public Pension Governance and Performance', *National Bureau of Economic Research*, Working Paper No. 4632. Available http://www.nber.org/papers/w4632 (accessed 23 November 2009).

Mitchell, O.S., Piggot, J. and Kumru, C. (2008) 'Managing Public Investment Funds: Best Practice and New Challenges', *National Bureau of Economic Research*, Working Paper 14078. Available http://www.nber.org/papers/w14078 (accessed 10 June 2009).

Moini, A. and Haji Mirzaee, S.M.A. (2005) *The Financial Regimes in Oil Industry*, Tehran: The Institute for International Energy Studies (in Farsi).

Momani, B. (2008) 'Gulf Cooperation Council Oil Exports and the Future of the Dollar', *New Political Economy*, vol. 13, no. 3: 293–314.

Monk, A. (2010) 'Insider Trading at KIA? Just Ask KIA', *Oxford SWF Project Blog*. Available http://oxfordswfproject.com/2010/09/23/insider-trading-at-kia-just-ask-kia/ (accessed 9 January 2011).

Monk, A. (2009a) 'Recasting the Sovereign Wealth Fund Debate: Trust, Legitimacy, and Governance', *New Political Economy*, vol. 14, no. 4: 452–468

Monk, A. (2009b) '*Sanabil al-Saudi*', Oxford SWF Project Blog. Available http://oxfordswfproject.com/2009/04/28/sanabil-al-saudia/ (accessed 13 January 2011).

MSNBC. (2005) 'China's CNOOC Drops Bid for Unocal'. Available http://www.msnbc.msn.com/id/8795682/ns/business-oil_and_energy/ (accessed 21 November 2011).

Mubadala. (2012) 'Board of Directors'. Available http://www.mubadala.ae/about/board_of_directors/ (accessed 20 June 2012).

Mubadala. (2010) 'Annual Report 2010'. Available http://mubadala.ae/images/uploads/Mubadala_AR10_English.pdf (accessed 10 November 2011).

Mubadala. (2009) 'Annual Report 2009'. Available http://mubadala.ae/images/uploads/Annual_Report_2009_-_English.pdf (accessed 2 February 2011).

Mubadala. (2008) 'Annual Report 2008'. Available http://mubadala.ae/images/uploads/Annual_Report_2008.pdf (accessed 2 February 2011).

Murphy, K. (1993) '$5-bn Loss Riles Even Oil-rich Kuwaitis. Scandal: Parliament's Probe of Public Funds Poses the Most Serious Challenge Ever to the Ruling Family's Power', *Los Angeles Times*. Available http://articles.latimes.com/1993-02-10/news/mn-1352_1_public-funds (accessed 20 March 2010).

Nanakorn, P. (2009) 'The Offset Programme as a Development Tool in the UAE', unpublished thesis, University of Exeter.

NDF. (2011) '*sanad-i chishmandaz-i bist salah va siyasat-hayi kulli-yi nizam*'. Available http://www.ndf.ir/programsdetail.aspx?id=16 (accessed 21 January 2012).

New York Daily News. (2012) 'Ahmadinejad Summoned Before Iran Parliament'. Available http://articles.nydailynews.com/2012-02-07/news/31035770_1_esfandiar-rahim-mashaei-president-mahmoud-ahmadinejad-iran-parliament (accessed 21 January 2012).

New York Times. (2010) 'Sheikh Ahmed bin Zayed al-Nahyan, Abu Dhabi Investment Authority's Chief, Dies at 41'. Available http://www.nytimes.com/2010/04/01/world/middleeast/01ahmed.html (accessed 31 March 2010).

Niblock, T. (1982) 'Social Structure and the Development of the Saudi Arabian Political System', in T. Niblock (ed.) *State, Society and Economy in Saudi Arabia*, London: Croom Helm.

Norges Bank Investment Management. (no date a) 'NBIM Investor Expectations on Children's Rights'. Available http://www.nbim.no/Global/Brochures/ChildrensRights.pdf (accessed 9 March 2012). UPDATE?

Norges Bank Investment Management. (no date b) 'Government Pension Fund Global'. Available http://www.nbim.no/en/About-us/Government-Pension-Fund-Global/ (accessed 9 March 2012).

Norges Bank Investment Management. (no date c) 'Market Value'. Available http://www.nbim.no/en/Investments/Market-Value/ (accessed 9 March 2012).

Norwegian Ministry of Finance. (2012) 'The Management of the Government Pension Fund in 2011', Meld. St. 17 (2011–2012) Report to the Storting (white paper). Available http://www.regjeringen.no/en/dep/fin/Documents-and-publications/propositions-and-reports/Reports-to-the-Storting/2011-2012/meld-st-17-20112012-2.html?id=680515 (accessed 9 March 2012).

Norwegian Ministry of Finance. (2011a) 'The Norwegian Government Pension Fund Global's adherence with the Santiago principles'. Available http://www.regjeringen.no/Upload/FIN/brosjyre/2011/GapSurvey_Global.pdf (accessed 9 March 2012).

Norwegian Ministry of Finance. (2011b) 'Provisions on the Management of the Government Pension Fund as of 1 January 2011'. Available http://www.regjeringen.no/en/dep/fin/Selected-topics/the-government-pension-fund/the-guidelines-for-the-management-of-the.html?id=434605 (accessed 9 March 2012).

Norwegian Ministry of Finance. (2010) 'Press Release No. 48/2010'. Available http://www.regjeringen.no/en/dep/fin/press-center/press-releases/2010/three-companies-excluded-from-the-govern.html?id=612790 (accessed 9 March 2012).

Norwegian Ministry of Finance. (2009) 'Report No. 20 (2008–2009) to the Storting'. Available http://www.regjeringen.no/pages/2185603/PDFS/STM200820090020000EN_PDFS.pdf (accessed 7 March 2012).

Norwegian Ministry of Finance. (2008a) 'Press Release No. 67/2008'. Available http://www.regjeringen.no/en/dep/fin/press-center/press-releases/2008/norway-endorses-the-santiago-principles.html?id=532131 (accessed 9 March 2012).

Norwegian Ministry of Finance. (2008b) 'Report No. 16 (2007–2008) to the Storting'. Available http://www.regjeringen.no/pages/2064594/PDFS/STM200720080016000EN_PDFS.pdf (accessed 7 March 2012).

Norwegian Ministry of Finance. (2007) 'Report No. 24 (2006–2007) to the Storting'. Available http://www.regjeringen.no/pages/1966215/PDFS/STM200620070024000EN_PDFS.pdf (accessed 7 March 2012).

Norwegian Ministry of Finance. (no date) 'Responsible Investments'. Available http://www.regjeringen.no/en/dep/fin/Selected-topics/the-government-pension-fund/responsible-investments.html?id=446948 (accessed 7 March 2012).

OECD. (2008a) 'Codes of Liberalisation of Capital Movements and of Current Invisible Operations'. Available http://www.oecd.org/document/63/0,3343,en_2649_34887_1826559_1_1_1_1,00.html (accessed 18 February 2012).

OECD. (2008b) 'Freedom of Investment, National Security and "Strategic" Industries: An Interim Report'. Available http://www.oecd.org/dataoecd/1/24/40476055.pdf (accessed 18 February 2012).

OECD. (2005) 'Guidelines on the Corporate Governance of State-Owned Enterprises'. Available http://www.oecd.org/document/33/0,3746,en_2649_34847_34046561_1_1_1_1,00.html (accessed 18 February 2012).

OECD. (2000) 'Declaration and Decisions on International Investment and Multinational Enterprises'. Available http://www.oecd.org/document/24/0,3746,en_2649_34887_1875736_1_1_1_1,00.html (accessed 18 February 2012).

Pollak, J. (1993) 'Unfinished Business in Madrid: Spain's Economy Falters as It Struggles to Meet Strict Maastricht Requirements', *Los Angeles Times*. Available http://articles.latimes.com/1993-02-21/business/fi-798_1_strict-requirements (accessed 20 March 2010).

Porteus, L. (2006) 'Dubai Co. to Give up Stake in US Ports Deal', *Fox News*. Available http://www.foxnews.com/story/0,2933,187307,00.html (accessed 21 November 2011).

Radio Goftogoo. (2010) '*tarh-i istifadah az zakhayir-i arzi barayi mitru*'. Available http://www.radiogoftogoo.ir/Left_News/news_leftview.php?ID=1251 (accessed 21 January 2012).

Radio Zamaneh. (2011) '*ist'ifa-yi farzand-i Hashimi-yi Rafsanjani az mudiriyat-i mitru-yi tihran*'. Available http://www.radiozamaneh.com/news/iran/2011/03/04/2254 (accessed 21 January 2012).

Rauh, J. (2007) 'Risk Shifting Versus Risk Management: Investment Policy in Corporate Pension Plans', National *Bureau Of Economic Research*, Working Paper 13240. Available http://www.nber.org/papers/w13240 (accessed 10 June 2009).

Reuters. (2011a) 'Saudi Central Bank Governor – Fahad Al Mubarak'. Available http://www.reuters.com/article/2011/12/28/saudiarabia-cenbank-idUSCENBANKSA20111228 (accessed 12 March 2012).

Reuters. (2011b) 'Saudi Slashes Oil Output, Says Market Oversupplied'. Available http://www.reuters.com/article/2011/04/17/us-saudi-oil-idUSTRE73G14020110417 (accessed 2 September 2011).

Reuters. (2008a) 'German Hapag-Lloyd Workers March Against NOL Takeover'. Available http://www.reuters.com/article/2008/08/19/germany-hapaglloyd-idUSLJ5253072 0080819 (accessed 18 February 2012).

Reuters. (2008b) 'Kuwait's KIA Withdraws $3.7 Bln from Abroad – Paper'. Available http://uk.reuters.com/article/2008/11/24/idUKLO62312520081124 (accessed 2 March 2010).

Reuters. (2008c) 'Kuwait's KIA Assets up 14.4 pct at $264.4 bn'. Available http://in.reuters.com/article/2008/06/20/kuwait-assets-idINL2037679320080620 (accessed 20 June 2008).

Reuters. (2008d) 'Kuwait's KIA Withdraws 3.7 bln from Abroad-Paper'. Available http://uk.reuters.com/article/2008/11/24/idUKLO62312520081124 (accessed 2 March 2010)

Reuters. (2008e) 'Kuwait Signed $27 bn of Deals in Asian Tour – Paper'. Available http://uk.reuters.com/article/2008/08/17/kuwait-asia-idUKLH49515120080817 (accessed 12 March 2012).

Richards, A. (1999) 'The Banking System of the UAE in a Time of World Financial Turmoil', *Middle East Policy*, vol. 6, no. 4: 1–33.

Richmond (1960) Letter to Walmsley, No. 1117/60, 26 April T 236/6314.

Roberts, L. (2008) 'Saudi Details First Sovereign Wealth Fund', ArabianBusiness.com. Available http://www.arabianbusiness.com/509041-saudi-plans-first-sovereign-wealth-fund-?ln=en (accessed 12 January 2011).

Roubini Global Economics. (2011) 'The Kuwait Investment Authority (KIA) Turns Inward?'. Available http://www.roubini.com/critical-issues/14263.php (accessed 15 February 2012).

Roubini Global Economics. (2012) *Updated Estimates of Sovereign Wealth Under Management*. London: Roubini Global Economics.

Roxburgh, C. Lund, S., Lippert, M., White, O.L. and Zhao, Y. (2009) 'The New Power Brokers: How Oil, Asia, Hedge Funds, and Private Equity are Faring in the Financial Crisis', *McKinsey Global Institute*. Available http://www.mckinsey.com/Insights/MGI/Research/Financial_Markets/How_the_new_power_brokers_are_faring_in_financial_crisis (accessed 2 January 2010).

Royal Courts of Justice. (2000) 'Court of Appeal Report'. Available http://www.ucc.ie/law/restitution/archive/englcases/al-sabah.htm (accessed 20 March 2010).

Rozanov, A. (2009) 'Investing Russia's Oil Wealth: Sharing the GCC Experience', in M. Terterov (ed.) *Russian and CIS Relations with the Gulf Region, Current Trend in Political and Economic Dynamics*, Dubai: Gulf Research Centre.

Rozanov, A. (2005) 'Who Holds the Wealth of Nations?', *Central Banking Journal*, vol. 14, no. 4: 52–57.

Salama, V. (2010) 'Abu Dhabi Fund Names Sheikh Hamed Al Nahyan as Chief', *Bloomberg Business Week*. Available http://www.bloomberg.com/apps/news?pid=20602011&sid=a_JLbXCXXwzc (accessed 14 June 2010).

SAMA Annual Report (1982) Available from the Arab World Documentation Unit, University of Exeter.

Saudi Arabia Ministry of Finance. (2011) 'Recent Economic Developments and Highlights of Fiscal Years 1432/1433 (2011) and 1433/1434 (2012)'. Available http://www.mof. gov.sa/English/DownloadsCenter/Budget/Statement%20by%20the%20Ministry%20 of%20Finance%202012%20Final.pdf (accessed12 February 2012).

Setser, B. and Ziemba, R. (2008) 'GCC Sovereign Funds Reversal of Fortune', *Council on Foreign Relations Center for Geoeconomic Studies*. Available http://www.cfr.org/ CGS_WorkingPaper_5.pdf (accessed 2 February 2010).

Seznec, J.F. (2008) 'The Gulf Sovereign Wealth Funds: Myths and Reality', *Middle East Policy*, vol. 15, no. 2: 97–110.

Shaheen, K. and Hassan, H. (2010) 'FNC Calls for Fairer Federal Finances', *The National*. Available http://www.thenational.ae/news/uae-news/fnc-calls-for-fairer-federal-finances (accessed 16 June 2010).

Shamma, S. (1959) 'The Oil of Kuwait Present and Future', *Middle East Oil Monographs*, no.1, Beirut: Middle East Research and Publishing Centre.

Shea, T.W. (1969) 'The Riyal: A Miracle in Money', *Saudi Aramco World*, vol. 20, no. 1. Available http://www.saudiaramcoworld.com/issue/196901/the.riyal-a.miracle.in.money. htm (accessed 25 February 2011).

Sidel, R. (2007) 'Abu Dhabi to Bolster Citigroup with $7.5 Billion Capital Infusion: Government Investment Arm to Become a Top Holder, With Up to a 4.9% Stake', *Wall Street Journal* (via NOW Truth). Available http://nwotruth.com/abu-dhabi-to-bolster-citigroup-with-75-billion-capital-infusion/ (accessed 18 February 2012).

Skancke, M. (2008) 'Statement in the US Congress on the Goverment Pension Fund — Global' Ministry of Finance, Norway. Available http://www.regjeringen.no/en/dep/ fin/News/news/2008/statement-in-the-us-congress-on-the-gove.html?id=502622 (accessed 15 August 2012).

Sleima, M. (2007) 'UAE Sets Up Authority to Invest Nation's Oil Wealth', *Market Watch*. Available http://www.marketwatch.com/story/uae-sets-up-authority-to-invest-nations-oil-wealth (accessed 2 March 2011).

Spiro, D.E. (1999) *The Hidden Hand of American Hegemony: Petrodollar Recycling and International Markets*, Ithaca, NY: Cornell University Press.

SWF Institute. (2012) 'Sovereign Wealth Fund Rankings'. Available http://www. swfinstitute.org/fund-rankings/ (accessed 12 March 2012).

SWF Institute. (no date a) 'Kuwait Investment Authority'. Available http://www. swfinstitute.org/swfs/kuwait-investment-authority/ (accessed18 December 2011).

SWF Institute. (no date b) 'Linaburg-Maduell Transparency Index'. Available http://www. swfinstitute.org/statistics-research/linaburg-maduell-transparency-index/ (accessed 18 February 2012).

Tabnak. (2010) '*zakhirah-yi arzi i'ilam mishavad, tuti'ah mikunand*'. Available http:// www.tabnak.ir/fa/news/106364 (accessed 19 January 2012).

Tehran Times. (2011) 'Mohsen Hashemi Resigns as Tehran Metro CEO'. Available http:// www.tehrantimes.com/index_View.asp?code=236796 (accessed 21 January 2012).

TheCityUK. (2011) 'Sovereign Wealth Funds', Financial Markets Series'. Available http://www. thecityuk.com/assets/Uploads/Sovereign-Wealth-Funds-2011.pdf (accessed 2 March 2011).

The Telegraph. (2010) 'Gulf sheikh Ahmed bin Zayed al-Nahyan Found Dead in Morocco'. Available http://www.telegraph.co.uk/finance/newsbysector/banksandfinance/7539274/ Gulf-sheikh-Ahmed-bin-Zayed-al-Nahyan-found-dead-in-Morocco.html (accessed 1 April 2010).

The White House. (2006) 'Fact Sheet: The CFIUS Process And The DP World Transaction'. Available http://georgewbush-whitehouse.archives.gov/news/releases/2006/02/20060222-11.html (accessed 21 November 2011).

Thomas, L. (2008) 'Cash-rich, Publicly Shy, Abu Dhabi Fund Draws Scrutiny', *New York Times*. Available http://www.nytimes.com/2008/02/28/business/worldbusiness/28fund.html?pagewanted=all (accessed 28 February 2008).

Timmons, H. (2005) 'China Oil Giant Expected to Vote Wednesday on Unocal Bid', *New York Times*. Available http://www.nytimes.com/2005/06/22/business/worldbusiness/22unocal.html (accessed 20 November 2011).

Timmons, H. and Werdigier, J. (2007) 'For Abu Dhabi and Citi, Credit Crisis Drove Deal', *New York Times*. Available http://www.nytimes.com/2007/11/28/business/worldbusiness/28invest.html?pagewanted=all (accessed 18 February 2012).

Torchia, A. (2012) 'Iran Economy Could Limp Along Under Sanctions', *Reuters*. Available http://www.reuters.com/article/2012/02/06/uk-iran-sanctions-idUSTRE8150ME201 20206 (accessed 21 January 2012).

Trend. (2011) '*Husayni: 100 miliyard dular zakhirah-yi arzi darim*'. Available http://pda.trend.az/fa/1875601.html (accessed 19 January 2012).

Truman, E. (2010) 'Sovereign Wealth Funds: Threat or Salvation?', Peterson Institute for International Economics. Available http://bookstore.piie.com/book-store/4983.html (accessed 18 February 2012).

Truman, E. (2008a) 'A Blueprint for Sovereign Wealth Fund Best Practices', Peterson Institute for International Economics Policy, Brief Number PB08-3:1-21. Available http://www.iie.com/publications/interstitial.cfm?ResearchID=902 (accessed 18 February 2012).

Truman, E. (2008b) 'The Rise of Sovereign Wealth Funds: Impacts on US Foreign Policy and Economic Interests, Testimony before the Committee on Foreign Affairs', US House of Representatives. Available http://www.iie.com/publications/testimony/truman0508.pdf (accessed 18 November 2011).

Truman, E. (2007) 'A Scoreboard for Sovereign Wealth Funds', paper at the Conference on China's Exchange Rate Policy', Peterson Institute for International Economics, Washington, DC. Available http://www.iie.com/publications/papers/truman1007swf.pdf (accessed 20 November 2011).

UAE Cabinet. (2012) 'The Supreme Council'. Available http://www.uaecabinet.ae/English/UAEGovernment/Pages/TheSupremeCouncil.aspx (accessed 6 June 2012).

UNCTAD. (2010) 'World Investment Report'. Available http://www.unctad.org/en/docs/wir2010_en.pdf (accessed 20 March 2011).

US Treasury Department. (2005) 'Semiannual Report on International Economic and Exchange Rate Policies'. Available http://www.treasury.gov/resource-center/international/exchange-rate-policies/Pages/index.aspx (accessed 20 November 2009).

Veron, N. (2011) 'Europe Needs Consistency in Welcoming Foreign Investors'. *VOX*. Available http://www.voxeu.org/index.php?q=node/6029 (accessed 18 February 2012).

Wayne, A. (2008) 'Wealth Funds Draw Profits and Attention', *The National*. Available http://www.thenational.ae/business/banking/wealth-funds-draw-profits-and-attention (accessed 18 February 2012).

Wayne, L. and Barboza, D. (2005) 'Unocal Deal: A Lot More Than Money is at Issue', *New York Times*. Available://www.nytimes.com/2005/06/24/business/worldbusiness/24china.html?pagewanted=all (accessed 21 November 2011).

Webster, J. (1993) 'Kio's Spanish Inquisition: The Growing Scandal of Kuwait's Massive Losses in Spain is Exposing the Dirty Linen of One of the World's Most Secretive Investment Agencies and Ringing Government Alarm Bells', *The Independent*.

Available http://www.independent.co.uk/news/business/kios-spanish-inquisition-the-growing-scandal-of-kuwaits-massive-losses-in-spain-is-exposing-the-dirty-linen-of-one-of-the-worlds-most-secretive-investment-agencies-and-ringing-government-alarm-bells-as-the-feud-spills-into-the-courts-justin-webster-looks-at-what-lies-behind-the-grupo-torras-disaster-1477729.html (accessed 20 March 2010).

Wells, D.A. (1974) *Saudi Arabian Revenues and Expenditures, the Potential for Foreign Exchange Savings*, Baltimore, MD: Johns Hopkins University Press.

Winfield Bean, B. (2010) 'Attack of the Sovereign Wealth Funds: Defending the Republic from the Threat of Sovereign Wealth Funds?', Legal Studies Research Paper Series of Michigan State University College of Law, Research Paper No. 08-01, vol. 18, no. 1: 1–50. Available http://papers.ssrn.com/sol3/papers.cfm?abstract_id=1537323## (accessed 21 November 2011).

Woertz, E. (2011) *GCC Financial Markets*, Dubai: GRC.

Woertz, E. (2010) 'Challenges of Financial Sector Regulation after the Global Financial Crisis', Presentation at Jeddah Economic Forum.

Yahoo. (2009) 'Saudi Arabia SWF'. Available http://en.news.maktoob.com/20090000002005/Saudi_to_launch_$5_33_bln_SWF_next_week/Article.htm (accessed 12 January 2011).

Young, A.N. (1983) *Saudi Arabia: The Making of a Financial Giant*, New York: New York University Press.

Zawya. (2007) 'Khalifa Reshuffles ADIA's BoD'. Available http://www.zawya.com/marketing.cfm?zp&p=/story.cfm/sid2007010316394600001/Khalifa%20reshuffles%20ADIA's%20BoD%20(CORRECTED (accessed 3 April 2010).

Zawya. (no date) 'Invest AD – Libya Opportunity Fund'. Available http://www.zawya.com/funds/mutual_funds.cfm/mid093413012011 (accessed 12 January 2012).

Ziemba, R. (2008) 'Petrodollars: How to Spend it', *Roubini Global Economic Monitor*.

Ziemba, R. (2012) 'Updated Estimates of Sovereign Wealth Under Management.' Unpublished report by Roubini Global Economics, March.

Websites

ADIA. http://www.adia.ae/En/Governance/Abudhabi_Government.aspx (accessed 18 November 2011).

ADGAS. http://www.adgas.com (accessed 2 November 2010).

ADNOC. http://www.adnoc.ae (accessed 27 February 2010).

Drydocks World. http://www.drydocks.gov.ae/en/default.aspx (accessed 20 March 2011).

Dubai Group, Overview. http://www.dubaigroup.com/aboutus/default_en_gb.aspx (accessed 25 March 2011).

Dubai Maritime City. http://www.dubaimaritimecity.com/ (accessed 20 March 2011).

Dubai Port World. http://webapps.dpworld.com/portal/page/portal/DP_WORLD_WEBSITE (accessed 20 March 2011).

Dubai Properties Group. http://dubaipropertiesgroup.ae/ (accessed 5 June 2012)

Dubai World, Board of Directors. http://www.dubaiworld.ae/board-of-directors/ (accessed 25 March 2011).

Economic Zones World. http://www.ezw.ae/ (accessed 20 March 2011).

Emirate Investment Authority. http://www.eia.gov.ae/index.htm (accessed 2 March 2010).

Folketrygdfondet. http://www.ftf.no/en/home.aspx (accessed 9 March 2012).

GASCO. http://www.gasco.ae (accessed 2 November 2010).

International Energy Agency. http://www.iea.org (accessed 2 November 2010).

Istithmar World. http://www.istithmarworld.com/ (accessed 20 March 2011).

Jumeirah.   http://www.jumeirah.com/en/Jumeirah-Group/About-Jumeirah-Group/Portfolio/ (accessed 25 March 2011).

Limitless. http://www.limitless.com/en-GB/home.aspx (accessed 25 March 2011).

MRC. http://www.majlis.ir/mhtml/index.php?newlang=english (accessed 14 April 2011).

Nakheel. http://www.nakheel.com/en (accessed 20 March 2011).

National Development Fund. http://www.ndf.ir (accessed 21 January 2012).

Norges Bank. http://www.norges-bank.no (accessed 9 March 2012).

Norges Bank Investment Management. http://www.nbim.no (accessed 9 March 2012).

Saudi Arabian Monetary Agency. http://www.sama.gov.sa (accessed 2 November 2010).

SWF Institute. http://www.swfinstitute.org/fund/gic.php (accessed 18 February 2012).

TECOM Investments. http://www.tecom.ae (accessed 20 June 2012).

Index